The
John Whitmer
Historical Association
JOURNAL

The John Whitmer Historical Association JOURNAL

Edited by William D. Morain

Spring/Summer 2020
Volume 40, Number 1

About This Journal

The *John Whitmer Historical Association Journal* is published semi-annually by the John Whitmer Historical Association. The association's purposes are to create and encourage interest in Latter Day Saint history, especially the history of Community of Christ, to promote communication, research, and publication in the field of Latter Day Saint history, and to provide vehicles for the dissemination of scholarly research to persons interested in Latter Day Saint history. For more information, visit the association website: *www.jwha.info*.

Papers for consideration will be reviewed by the editorial committee and should be submitted in a digital file (preferably Microsoft *Word*) using the most current *Chicago Manual of Style* format. Send all submissions and queries to the editor via email: *anplsurg@grm.net*.

© 2020 by the John Whitmer Historical Association
Printed in the United States of America
ISSN 0739-7852

Copyright for articles and book reviews published in this issue of the *John Whitmer Historical Association Journal* is held jointly between the author and the association. The association reserves the right to publish an electronic version of the journal. Copies of articles in this journal may be made for teaching and research purposes free of charge and without securing permission, as permitted by sections 107 and 108 of the United States Copyright Law. For all other purposes, permission must be obtained from the author.

Cover design and typesetting by John C. Hamer.

The John Whitmer Historical Association Journal

Spring/Summer 2020, Vol. 40, No. 1

COURTESY OF COMMUNITY OF CHRIST ARCHIVES

John Whitmer (ca. 1870)

EDITORIAL STAFF
William D. Morain, *Editor*
Ryan C. Tittle, *Copy Editor*
Christin Mackay, *Book Review Editor*
John C. Hamer, *Production Director*

EDITORIAL BOARD
Gary Bergera
Clyde Forsberg
Craig Foster
Matt Harris
Katherine Hill
David Howlett
Melvin Johnson
Tom Kimball
Michael Marquardt
Brent Metcalfe
Russell Osmond
William Russell
William Shepard
Steven Shields
Chrystal Vanel

OFFICERS OF THE ASSOCIATION
Jill Brim, *President 2019–2021*
Christin Mackay, *President-Elect 2020–2022*
Rachel Killebrew, *Immediate Past President 2018–2019*
Jerry J. Mogg, *Treasurer 2019–2021*
Cheryle Grinter, *Executive Director*

BOARD OF DIRECTORS OF THE ASSOCIATION
Seth Bryant
Scott Esplin
Joe Geisner
Katherine Hill
Dan Kelty
Daniel Stone
Dan Whittemore

Table of Contents

The John Whitmer Historical Association Journal

Editor's Note: Burned-over with Bob Flanders
   William D. Morain 1
The editor channels a former professor to characterize the Journal's spring issue.

Articles

Heroines of Restoration History: Two Extraordinarily Resourceful Women
   Rachel Killebrew 3
In her Presidential Address, Rachel Killebrew chronicles the lives of Edna Easter, who pioneered the success of programs for girls in Community of Christ; and Martha Maria Hughes Cannon, Latter-day Saint physician, suffragette, Utah state senator, polygamous wife, and public health advocate.

Discerning Supernatural Presences: Experiential Claims and Restorationist Movements in the Burned-Over District
   Ann Taves 20
For her Richard Howard lecture, Ann Taves contrasts the dissimilar descriptions of the founding Mormon visions related by Joseph Smith Jr. vs. those by his mother. When weighing the two against the documented historical record, she concludes that 1824 – not 1820 – was the valid founding episode and chronicles Smith's progressive elevation of his self-image thereafter.

The Palmyra Revival of 1824-25, From Methodist, Presbyterian and Baptist Records: Its Impact on the Restoration Movement
H. Michael Marquardt 39

Mike Marquardt reviews the detailed Palmyra denominational records from 1824-25 to understand clues to understanding later retrospective accounts of founding Mormon events. He concludes that Joseph Smith's 1838-39 description of an 1820 vision does not fit the historical evidence but was likely fashioned instead for theological purposes.

How the Erie Canal Corridor Became the Burned-over District: Rochester and the Advent of Mormonism
Bruce W. Worthen 48

Bruce Worthen describes the extraordinary socioeconomic upheaval that ensued from construction of the Erie Canal, especially in the region surrounding Rochester, New York. He demonstrates how Mormonism arose as a working-class movement vis-à-vis rival spiritual paradigms in this disorderly milieu.

Layered Grief in the Burned-over District: Religious Ecstasy as a Healing Balm
Russell L. Osmond 65

Russ Osmond argues that the common denominator of the Burned-over District was not religious revival but rather the constant chaos of extreme social disorder occasioned upon the headlong construction of the Erie Canal. This, in turn, set the stage for the tension-releasing ecstasy that Mormonism's charismatic founder could engender among the displaced.

The Family That Built Canals
Vickie Cleverley Speek 70

As a result of an accidental discovery, Vickie Speek chronicles a notable Mormon-connected family who played a major role in the construction of the Erie Canal as well as numerous other American landmarks.

Thomas A. Lyne, the Latter-day Saints, and the American Theatre: Confluences and Influences, 1844-1904
Lee Krähenbühl 88

Lee Krähenbühl presents a convincing argument that Thomas A. Lyne was the dramatic coach behind the Nauvoo Temple ceremony and that he went on to inspire many LDS stage performers whose careers intersected with momentous events in American theatre history.

Why Did the RLDS Youth Programs Disappear After a Half-Century of Success?
Sherry Mesle-Morain 104

Sherry Mesle-Morain chronicles the expansion of Community of Christ (RLDS) youth programs from their inception in 1910 to their rich success in the 1960s, followed by their piecemeal decline through the turn of the century.

Forerunner or Revisionist? The Puzzle of Solomon Chamberlin
Johnny Stephenson 119

Johnny Stephenson uses recently disclosed documents to dispute the claim of Solomon Chamberlin to have received prophetic foreknowledge of Joseph Smith's movement.

The Temple Lot in Jackson County, Missouri, and How Early Church Members Worshipped
H. Michael Marquardt 136

Mike Marquardt reviews the history of the 1831 declaration of the site for a Latter Day Saint temple in Independence, Missouri, and cites research findings regarding the nature of worship activities during the period.

Book Reviews

Scott Esplin. *Return to the City of Joseph: Modern Mormonism's Contest for the Soul of Nauvoo*
    Reviewed by David J. Howlett 145

Scott Esplin. *Return to the City of Joseph: Modern Mormonism's Contest for the Soul of Nauvoo*
    Reviewed by Christin Mackay 148

Will Bagley. *River Fever: Adventures on the Mississippi, 1969-1972*
    Reviewed by Michael Allen 151

Ron Romig. *Behind the Scenes Tour of the Kirtland Temple: From Basement to Bell Tower.*
    Reviewed by Christin Mackay 154

Jana Riess. *The Next Mormons: How Millennials Are Changing the LDS Church.*
    Reviewed by Katherine R. Pollock 156

EDITOR'S NOTE

Burned-Over with Bob Flanders

Bill Morain

When I was a sophomore at Graceland College in the early 1960s, I remember my young professor Robert Flanders musing about a project he thought he might research one day. "What did people really do in Nauvoo?" he wondered. "How did they even make a living? We have focused so much on those religious things that we have overlooked the economic and so many other factors that we really ought to know." Of course it was his landmark *Kingdom on the Mississippi* that flowed from those musings to help jumpstart the New Mormon History.

That memory came back as I sorted through the manuscripts that flowed into our office after last fall's Rochester, New York, JWHA Annual Meeting, whose theme was "Back to the Burned-Over District 200 Years Later, 1819-2019: Impact of the Second Great Awakening on the Restoration Movements."

In my mind, this issue of the John Whitmer Historical Association Journal channels Bob's original template by presenting five disparate viewpoints on the economic and social milieu of the Burned-Over District. One wonders if Bob might have titled this issue *Chaos on the Canal*.

Bruce Worthen portrays how the Erie Canal's construction changed the market economy of the Rochester region and how this altered the social needs of the working class. Behaviorist Russ Osmond describes how the disordered chaos of the canal builders' lives appears to have led to their desperate escape into the ecstatic expression of the era. Richard Howard lecturer Ann Taves focuses on the documentary history of the Restoration's founding moment, favoring Lucy's version of events over Joseph's. Mike Marquardt follows with details of three Palmyra-area Protestant church records, coincidentally in support of Taves' thesis. And Vickie Speek reviews the story of a Mormon-connected family whose members were instrumental in building the canal itself.

But readers will more than feel the Burn [ed-Over] from this issue. Rachel Killebrew's Presidential Address features profiles of two women, one each from Community of Christ and the Church of Jesus Christ of Latter-day Saints, whose remarkable careers contributed enormously to their respective communities.

Lee Krähehenbühl contributes a lyrical chronicle of a Mormon thespian who not only seems to have stage-directed the Nauvoo Temple ceremonies but whose protégés went on to play roles in an infamous 1865 event at Washington's Ford's Theater.

Sherry Mesle-Morain describes the booming rise and distressing dissolution of the Community of Christ youth programs from 1910 to the turn of the century. Johnny Stephenson disputes the legend of Solomon Chamberlin prophetically foretelling Joseph Smith's movement. And Mike Marquardt reviews the 1831 siting of the Temple Lot in Independence. (And five book reviews.)

One would hope that nonagenarian Professor Flanders might yet be able to appreciate in this issue of the *John Whitmer Historical Association Journal* how his legacy continues to cast a lingering shadow across his many appreciative journeymen and women. The rest of us certainly do.

Heroines of Restoration History: Two Extraordinarily Resourceful Women

Rachel Killebrew

2019 JWHA Presidential Address

When I discovered I'd be giving this presentation, I culled my list of topics by turning to our JWHA "after-conference" surveys. They told us that our presentations should be inclusive of all Restoration movements and eras. With respect to your guidance, I have endeavored to structure my Presidential Address to reflect your wishes.

This project was fun because I truly enjoy pursuing history. It is what sets my heart on fire—research, learning, and discovery. I love embracing my inner Alice and falling down the proverbial rabbit hole—not for the topic, but for the adventure. That being said, I don't feel I would be doing my job as a librarian-archivist if I didn't channel the White Rabbit as a spur for your own historical investigations. I hope you walk away with questions that will send you down your own rabbit holes in a search for the past.

In lieu of the Cheshire Cat or Queen of Hearts, I have chosen instead to feature two remarkable Restoration women: Edna Easter of the Reorganized Church of Jesus Christ of Latter Day Saints and Martha Hughes Cannon of the Church of Jesus Christ of Latter-day Saints.

If you will remember last year, our beloved Immediate Past-President, Sherry Mesle-Morain, wrote about her father Carl Mesle, pastor extraordinaire and boyscout leader. In like manner, I'd like to focus on his counterpart, Edna Easter, who played the same role with the girls. Many of you may remember Edna. One of the wondrous parts of my research for this event was to see the beaming smiles on the faces of my fellow Community of Christ members and coworkers whenever I mentioned her name. Edna worked for the church for over thirty years and left a legacy that echoed far beyond for both the church and the community roundabout.

Edna Easter was born on a farm in Cameron, Missouri, on February 6, 1910.[1] She was the second oldest of ten children, seven of whom were boys.[2] She attended the RLDS church as a young child, but the family's move to the country when she was ten left her without a nearby congregation to attend.

After graduation, Edna returned to Independence, Missouri, where she resumed her RLDS attendance but still did not join. While feeling the need for baptism, she harbored doubts "as to the authenticity of the church."[3] She chose to study a variety of books of both the RLDS persuasion and that of other denominations in her quest to find the right church for her. In 1936 she wrote:

> [s]earching for and wondering just what is the church of God, I was reminded that when crossing a dangerous stream or muddy bog, we do not always use the perfect stepping stones, we use the best available. I believe it would be well for me to join the church I now attend, as being, in my mind, the most perfect; then, as I grow spiritually, I will be able to ascertain positively whether or not it is the true church.[4]

Her decision made, she was baptized into the RLDS church at the age of twenty-seven on Easter Sunday, March 28, 1937. This was a fitting day due to the pre-existing annual jest from her fellow church goers, "[i]t's Easter, it must be your birthday!" She embraced the humor and made it her "rebirthday."[5]

After her baptism, her involvement in church activities grew. In 1939, she became involved as a volunteer in girls' work and camping, assisting Lenoir Woodstock in the organization of Camp Oececa, the first Oriole girls' camp.[6] This camp became so popular that it required two weeklong sessions every year to accommodate all the girls who wanted to attend. The program included activities such as nature study, swimming, story hour, and evening campfire.[7]

Camp Oececa was the third youth camp organized by the church and the first RLDS camp to be held at Lake Gardner in Excelsior Springs, Missouri. It drew such positive attention for the church and for its girls' group that, when the owners of Lake Gardner chose to sell the property, the RLDS church had first option on its purchase.[8] That campground, known today as Lake Doniphan, has been under church ownership since 1944.[9]

---

1. "Edna I. Easter," *Independence Examiner*. December 9, 1997.
2. "We'd Like You to Know," *The Saints' Herald*, June 25, 1951.
3. "My Year in the Church," *The Saints' Herald*, April 2, 1938.
4. Ibid.
5. Deceased Member Files, Community of Christ Library Archives.
6. Easter, Edna, Box 2, RG 13-1, f 64, Public Relations Biographical, Community of Christ Library Archives.
7. "History of Girls' Work in Independence, MO," Box 12, RG22, f170, Community of Christ Library Archives.
8. "Oriole Pageant," Box 12, RG 22, f 167, Girls' Work: Historical, Community of Christ Library Archives.
9. "Purchase of Gardner Lake Property," *The Saints' Herald*, October 14, 1944.

Edna was well suited for volunteer work in this field, having cherished a lifelong love of cross-country camping with her family. Her obvious passion resulted in a job offer to her on August 14, 1942 by RLDS President Frederick M. Smith upon a recommendation from Christian Education Director Floyd McDowell.[10] She declined, preferring to remain in volunteer capacity as General Church Director of Girl's Work. But, in 1945, she did accept an offer to become a paid employee in the position and was confirmed that year at General Conference.

While it was an excellent opportunity to embrace what she loved, her appointment meant leaving behind her thirteen years as Executive Secretary of the International Printing Ink Division of the Interchemical Corporation. In a letter to L. F. P. Curry on April 27, 1948, she shared her three-year struggle over the decision, writing, "[f]rom the standards of the world, there was no reason why I should make the change…It cost me more than any of them will ever know…Yet, I believe I was led Divinely into this work."[11]

In her new role, she readily recognized where change was needed and made moves to ensure it happened. One major innovation within the children's program was the creation of the Light of Life Award for the girls. Edna had noticed that the boys could earn the God and Country award, but girls had no parallel achievement for their own hard work. Now the Light of Life award provided a new balance.[12] The name stemmed from John 8:12: "I am the light of the world; he that followeth me shall not walk in darkness, but shall have the light of life."[13]

The badge, created in 1946, could be earned by Orioles as well as by Girl Scouts, Camp Fire Girls, 4-H groups, and other national organizations. The badge itself was designed to reflect church beliefs, emblazoned as it was with purple and gold colors and with a haloed image of the three books and the church seal.

The requirements for the award were a year of study that included membership in the program, regular church attendance (including Sunday school, daily devotions, and the stewardship program), over 100 hours of community service, and a life consistent with church ideals.[14] The goal was to give the girls leadership opportunities and to enhance their quality of life. RLDS girls were also required to study the

---

10. Frederick M. Smith to Edna Easter, August 14, 1942. Correspondence, Unprocessed Edna Easter Collection Acc#7716, Community of Christ Library Archives.

11. Edna Easter to L. F. P. Curry, April 27, 1948. Correspondence, Unprocessed Edna Easter collection, Acc #7716, Community of Christ Library Archives.

12. Easter, Edna, transcript of an oral history conducted in 1975 by Ronald VanFleet, Oral History Interview Collection, Community of Christ Library Archives.

13. "With Our Girls," Box 12, RG22, f169. Community of Christ Library Archives.

14. *The Oriole Leader's Handbook* (Independence: Herald Publishing House, 1960).

Inspired Version of the Bible (JST), the Book of Mormon, and the Doctrine and Covenants.[15]

Another change occurred in 1950 when Edna realized that "Blue Birds," the name of the younger girls' group, was shared with a similar organization within the Camp Fire Girls. In order to prevent confusion and encourage growth amongst the church's group, Edna encouraged the girls to vote for a new name. They chose to rename their age group the Skylarks as a complement to the Orioles, the older girls' group.[16]

Edna's passion for girls' work was not limited to church activities. As a certification-standards visitor for the American Camping Association, she used her talents to help develop camping programs for many organizations.[17] She served as a member of numerous professional groups, including the Association for Childhood Education International, the Editors' and Children's sections of the National Council of Churches, the Professional Teacher's Association, and the Communication Arts Association of the RLDS church.[18]

She became known for her kindness and humility. One retiree remembered her fondly, stating:

> When I was a new tour guide in 1969, I got lost while taking a group on my very first tour. Edna was walking to her office and quickly realized what had happened. She quietly joined the tour and took us to all sorts of special places, places I didn't know existed, and she did it like a friend. The tour group had a fun time without ever realizing their tour wasn't the status quo. Edna never told our coworkers what happened.[19]

When the church needed someone to recognize a longtime girls' work employee, Edna was asked to celebrate her. In her paper, "The Five Lives of Ruth Holman," Edna made a point to discuss Ruth's childhood, her musical gifts and education, her family life, her writings of articles and books, and her girls' work activities. Edna ensured everyone knew Ruth was gifted in many realms, not just the one they saw on a daily basis.[20]

She was a natural at advancing people's full potential and in fostering friendships. The Community of Christ Archives' Edna Easter collection features hundreds of letters she wrote to retired employee friends and those she met at camp. Despite her ever-busy schedule, she always made sure to keep former staff friends specifically

---

15. "With Our Girls," ibid.
16. Easter, Edna, transcript of oral history, ibid.
17. "Edna I. Easter," ibid.
18. Easter, Edna, Public Relations Biographical, ibid.
19. Julie A. Meisinger in discussion with the author, May 2019.
20. "The Five Lives of Ruth Holman," Box 12, RG22, f170. Girls' Work: History, Independence, Missouri. Community of Christ Library Archives.

apprised as to their old colleague's whereabouts, the status of the office, and other current events.

Her letters were never superficial, always deep with raw honesty. Letter after letter depicted massive turnover and restructuring within the Christian Education Department, reflecting her deep frustration with the ever-changing events. In 1961 she wrote:

> It seems the turn-over of employees at the Auditorium is continuous—at least it is in our Department; and we are constantly playing "Fruit Basket upset" with offices. I have just made my eleventh move since working for the department.[21]

The frequent moves and restructurings continued to add to her plate. In 1964, she indicated that her load included the vacation church school and reunion materials, the *Stepping Stones* and *Zion's Hopes* publications, authorship of seven books with coworker Bob Seeley, and her continuing fieldwork in aquatic and other camps.[22] That same year, she wrote her friend Edie saying:

> I thought I had been working to capacity for many years. Now, besides the two papers to edit—all the way from asking writers, editing, and making layout—I still have the regular editing of materials—particularly all the children's materials, and several of our authors did not get all their materials in, so I had…to write the rest…[23]

Between 1961 and 1967, she did not take a single day of vacation from work—and did all of this while taking night classes.[24]

Her thirst for learning was never quenched. Studying sometimes required her to stay up all night and she had a difficult time finding support at work. In 1961, she wrote her friend and colleague Joanne out of frustration, "I had to quit night school because there just wasn't any time to go nor to study. Then about a week later…Cliff asked the presidency for permission for Hazel to get off work and go to school days! I was surprised and hurt." She explained in further detail that her hours were so complicated because so much was overdue coming into the office "from the men."[25]

This setback lasted only a short while. The next year, she found another way to participate in school in the form of a distance education model provided by KCMO-

---

21. Edna Easter to Gladys Tyree, August 28, 1962. Correspondence, Unprocessed Edna Easter collection, Acc#7716, Community of Christ Library Archives.

22. Edna Easter to Bill, Lois, and family, May 12, 1964. Correspondence, Unprocessed Edna Easter collection, Acc#7716, Community of Christ Library Archives.

23. Edna Easter to Edie Ballew, December 14, 1964. Correspondence, Unprocessed Edna Easter collection, Acc#7716, Community of Christ Library Archives.

24. Inter-Office Memo to Don from Edna re Summer activities. Religious Education Correspondence: Edna Easter 1965-1967. Box 12, RG 22 f43. Community of Christ Library Archives.

25. Edna Easter to Joanne and Larry, June 1, 1961. Correspondence, Unprocessed Edna Easter collection, Acc#7716, Community of Christ Library Archives.

TV. The "College of the Air" courses were offered between 7:00 and 7:30 a. m. Monday through Friday. Each student was provided a study guide and two textbooks. Every other week students met at the university for a discussion group. Edna "attended" this class by going to her Aunt's house in the morning to watch it on the television.[26] Her stubborn tenacity paid off and, by 1969, Edna had earned a Master of Education from the University of Missouri. Not one to consider her education complete, she then took courses towards a Master of Religious Education at St. Paul School of Theology. Regardless of what classes she took, she always made sure they would help with her work at the church.[27]

As a part of the Religious Education Department, Edna served as acting World Church Camping Director for two years prior to Carl Mesle taking the role.[28] From the start, she realized that most of the girls' work effort would not be formally supported for lack of institutional interest and funding. She said, "F. M. Smith, as President of the Church…in several public meetings mentioned the worth of the girls' programs. However, the general pattern seemed to be…growth came from the grass roots up, rather than the administration down."[29]

In 1960, Edna's position changed to Executive Secretary of the Christian Education Department. Her director had requested the change because of her ever-expanding range of abilities. Regardless of her official position, she always felt a special dedication to girls' work and was often sought out for assistance in the planning of major events. She repeatedly put herself on the line to protect the girls' programs. She wrote her friend saying:

> Girls' work is now a part of the children's division and has a man over it, that helps, plus an appointee man. I am sure the watchdogging I did with the junior high committee did have results as far as making the committee was aware there was a girls' program…I do not know what the future will bring, but we have a better chance of saving girls' work than it seemed we had for some time.[30]

In the 1975 oral history that she completed upon her retirement, she recommended that if the church wanted to succeed with girls' work, they would first need to know the girls and only then to build a program to accommodate them. Her vision

---

26. Edna Easter to G. L. DeLapp, September 28, 1962. Correspondence, Unprocessed Edna Easter collection, Acc#7716, Community of Christ Library Archives

27. Religious Education Correspondence: Edna Easter, Box 12, RG 22 f43, Community of Christ Library Archives

28. Sampling of Department Activities, Chronologically. Religious Education Correspondence Edna Easter. Box 12, RG 22 f 43. Community of Christ Library Archives.

29. Easter, Edna, transcript of oral history, ibid.

30. Edna Easter to Joanne and Larry, ibid.

saw a program that would evolve over time in various ways but would always result in relevance to "today's girls."

As an editor, she followed an all-encompassing approach in her guidance to fellow writers, beginning any rejection letters with constructive criticism. But, after stating the negatives, she would typically offer specific instructions as to how the piece could be improved, would make an effort to compliment the writer, and would add a contact for someone who might further assist.[31]

Her lifelong dedication to youth and camping resulted in many contributions to both the church and society at large. She worked at over eighty youth camps and organized eleven girls' camps. In her fieldwork she often served as a waterfront instructor, teaching swimming, boating, and canoeing. As a certified swim instructor for the Midwestern Area American Red Cross, she issued over a thousand swim certifications. She also taught outdoor education skills ranging from primitive camping to astronomy.

Throughout her career, Edna was aware that females of all ages needed greater representation and she fought for it when necessary. In May 1967, Christian Education Director Lee Hart expressed surprise that women had written camp material. Edna responded the next day with a list of twelve female writers, noting that others had not been credited and she made sure to carbon copy three others in the office.[32]

Her transcribed oral history paints a vivid picture of the gender relations of her time. At one point, she specifically mentioned to her interviewer how her retirement celebration had been an embarrassment because, while she was formally recognized in the *Herald*, two other women retiring from the same department around the time were not. When asked to comment on a list of church leaders she had worked with over the years, her interviewer did not name a single woman in her published history despite her years of work with well-known women in the Christian Education department.[33]

An article dedicated to her retirement in *Insight Magazine* shared her sage advice for women:

> Over the years, Edna has developed a constructive sensitivity towards contributions that women can make in the life of the church. Her advice for such persons would be to make careful educational and personal preparation to set high professional goals and to work hard to achieve them.[34]

---

31. Religious Education Correspondence: Edna Easter, ibid.
32. Edna Easter to Lee Hart, May 3, 1967. Box 12 RG 22 f43, Community of Christ Library Archives.
33. Easter, Edna, transcript of oral history, ibid.
34. "Edna Easter: Thirty Years of Resources," *Insight*, February 1975.

She found determination in the most difficult of situations, using them as a source of inspiration. After one particularly trying time, she wrote:

> I believe fully that God is with us (if we will let Him be). I don't know why the trials. Maybe if we accept them in the right spirit...the trials are only for our strengthening for future tasks ahead...I think we might as well face up to the fact that our calling is to lead (thanks to God, rather than any special worth on our own part.) This means we shall always find disappointments and discouragements...I think we will find better days ahead. When we do our best, God will bless.[35]

Edna dedicated over thirty years of employment to the RLDS church, for which she was recognized at the 1978 World Conference. Two months later, she was gifted a photo of the event to which was unsurprisingly attached a note from camping coordinator Fred Bozarth, requesting that she contact him regarding upcoming Missouri Valley activities.[36]

Edna's collection in the Community of Christ Archives gives insight into the personal and professional lives of the women and men who shaped the church, thereby fulfilling her wish that other women in the church be similarly recognized. She died in 1997, leaving a legacy that will be fondly remembered by all that knew her.

To introduce the second distinguished woman of my presentation, I would note that we are meeting tonight near Seneca Falls, New York, where Elizabeth Cady Stanton, Lucretia Mott, and others held the first Women's Rights Convention. In homage to the 100-year anniversary of the passage of the 19th amendment and the works of a remarkable woman, I will now recognize the first female State Senator elected in the United States of America, Martha Hughes Cannon of the Church of Jesus Christ of Latter-day Saints.

Martha Maria Hughes Cannon, affectionately known as Mattie by those who knew her, was born July 1, 1857 in Llandudno, Caernarvon, North Wales, to Peter and Elizabeth Hughes. In 1860, the family, along with 624 of their fellow Latter-day Saints, began their journey to the United States. They were assisted by the Perpetual Emigration Fund, a Latter-day Saint company created to assist newly converted members on their way to Utah by providing loans to be repaid when the recipients were financially stable enough to do so.

Martha's group was sent by Asa Calkin across the ocean on the ship Underwriter. The group left Liverpool on March 30, 1860 and disembarked in New York on May 1.[37] Once there, the family spent time working and resting so that Peter could regain his strength after the long sea trip. When ready, they once again acquired assistance

---

35. Edna Easter to Joanne and Larry, ibid.
36. Fred Bozarth to Edna Easter, June 26, 1978. Photo collection. D4488, Community of Christ Library Archives.
37. Perpetual Emigrating Fund Company ship passenger lists, 1852-1864; 1874; List of passengers shipped by Asa Calkin, Liverpool, per ship Underwriter to New York, 1860 March 30; Church History Library, https://catalog.

from the Perpetual Emigrating Fund.[38] They traveled by rail and steamer to Florence, Nebraska, where they joined with the 228-member Joseph Horne Company. The party's train of sixty-two wagons departed for Utah between July 1 and 4, 1861.[39]

Along the way, on September 3, Martha lost her little sister Annie, who was buried in a tin box along the trail.[40] Her father died three days after arriving in Utah. These awful events of the trek left a mark on young Martha, influencing the course of the rest of her life.

As a devout Latter-day Saint, she was aware that President Brigham Young was not fully in favor of modern medicine. But, in his January-February 1868 general epistle, he had a change of heart that altered her destiny. He wrote:

> …we wish the sisters…to learn bookkeeping, telegraphy, reporting, typesetting…we hope an early opportunity will be given for instruction in anatomy, surgery, chemistry… physiology, the practice of midwifery by the sisters, the preservation of health and the properties of medicinal plants…[41]

This now opened the way for Martha to consider a variety of occupations, including medicine.

At the fragile age of fourteen, Martha began work as a schoolteacher.[42] She also developed a skill for typesetting and began to work for the *Deseret Evening News* and the *Woman's Exponent*,[43] where her five years of earnings provided needed money for her school.[44] When she graduated from the University of Deseret with a degree in

---

churchofjesuschrist.org/assets?id=f514dee2-1f69-4946-bc9a-dad7e60ceff3&crate=0&index=9 (accessed: June 15, 2019)

38. Richard E. Turley, and Brittany Chapman Nash, *Women of Faith in the Latter Days*, vol. 3 1846-1847 (Salt Lake City: Deseret Book Company, 2014).

39. The Church Historian's Press, "Joseph Horne Company (1861) Pioneer Overland Travels" Accessed April 20, 2019. https//history.churchofjesuschrist.org/overlandtravel/companies/158/joseph-horne-company-1861.

40. The Church Historian's Press, "Annie Lloyd Hughes-Pioneer Overland Travel." Accessed April 20, 2019. https://history.churchofjesuschrist.org/overlandtravel/pioneers/42155/annie-lloyd-hughes.

41. Brigham Young office files, 1832-1878 (bulk 1844-1877); General Epistles, 1841-1868; General epistle, circa 1868 January-February; Church History Library, https://catalog.churchofjesuschrist.org/assets?id=2702726e-8c8a-4932-944d-e9294d6d0376&crate=0&index=65 (accessed: July 24, 2019)

42. Thomas G. Alexander and Davis Bitton, *Historical Dictionary of the Latter Day Saints*. Salt Lake City: Rowman & Littlefield, 2019).

43. Constance L. Lieber, and John R. Sillito, *Letters from Exile: The Correspondence of Martha Hughes Cannon and Angus M. Cannon, 1886-1888* (Salt Lake City: Signature Books, in association with Smith Research Associates, 1989).

44. Elizabeth Cannon Porter McCrimmon, "About My Mother, Martha," accessed July 25, 2019, https://www.sendmartha.com/about-my- mother-martha.

chemistry, John Taylor and George Q. Cannon met with her in the historian's office to give her a blessing and "commissioned her to labor among the sick."[45]

Mattie went to the University of Michigan to work on her medical degree and discovered a new opportunity. When her fellow medical students kept inquiring about Mormonism and polygamy, she wrote to President John Taylor for permission to prepare a formal lecture declaring the virtues of the religion. Seeking no fame for herself, her heart was set on changing hearts, removing prejudice, and earning money "to pour gold into the coffers of Zion." Instead of disseminating her knowledge for free, she chose to charge for attendance and sent half of it back to church headquarters, keeping the other half to do her own work for the church as she saw fit.[46]

It was in anticipation of these lectures that Martha elected to enter oratorical school. She located several such institutions on the East Coast near friends and reputable hospitals where she could continue her work in medical training while pursuing her oratorical degree. Confident that her topic would draw in large groups, she hoped that proper credentials would assure that her lectures would be taken seriously.[47]

At the end of her formal training, Mattie had earned a Bachelor of Chemistry from the University of Deseret, a Medical Doctorate from the University of Michigan, and a Bachelor of Science in pharmacy from the Auxiliary School of Medicine of the University of Pennsylvania. The last of these was earned concurrently with a degree from the National School of Elocution and Oratory. In 1882, she returned to Utah and began work as house physician at Deseret Hospital.[48]

It was here that she met Angus Munn Cannon, the president of the hospital board.[49] Despite the Edmunds Act of 1882 that prohibited polygamous marriage and cohabitation, the two took more than casual interest in one another. On October 6, 1884, Martha and Angus were married. She was Angus Cannon's fourth wife.

The Edmunds Act made their relationship difficult by declaring polygamy a felony and cohabitation a misdemeanor, punishable by "a fine of not more than five hundred dollars and by imprisonment for a term of more than five years…."[50] This

---

45. First Presidency (John Taylor) correspondence, 1877-1887; Letters, 1879; Martha Hughes letters, 1879; Martha Hughes letter, Ann Arbor, Michigan, to John Taylor; Church History Library, https://catalog.churchofjesuschrist.org/assets?id=6d918d6c-ead1-4608-a4de-634f5ef8498c&crate=0&index=4 (accessed: September 13, 2019)

46. First Presidency (John Taylor) correspondence, 1877-1887; ibid.

47. First Presidency (John Taylor) correspondence, 1877-1887, ibid.

48. Turley and Nash, ibid.

49. McCrimmon, ibid.

50. Full text of "The Edmunds act: reports of the Commission, rules, regulations and decisions, and population, registration and election tables, &c. For the information of registration and election officers in Utah". Bancroft Library, 2007. http://www.archive.org/stream/edmundsactreportoounitrich/edmundsactreportoounitrich_djvu.txt.

forced them to keep their marriage secret to keep Angus out of jail because he already shared a home with three wives, each in her own "apartment," with meals taken on a wifely rotation. Angus and Martha did not live together nor did they mention their relationship, even to their closest friends.

On March 21, 1885, she wrote to her college friend Barbara:

> It has been widely rumored that I am the third wife of one of the leaders of the Mormon church. Have actually been arraigned before the "grand jury" on the charge of polygamy…but after having given my testimony…came to the conclusion that if the Mormon Chieftan had married a lady doctor they had got ahold of the wrong one![51]

Martha's marriage was not the only legal hurdle or reason for secrecy—she wanted to protect her patients. Her occupation as a doctor put her in the unique position to have inside knowledge regarding families, specifically of their paternity. This meant she also had inside knowledge regarding polygamous relationships and could thus be called to testify to her knowledge of family structures in court.[52]

Martha was held on $200 bond to testify against Samuel B. Smith. She again wrote to her friend Barbara, "…[t]o me it is a serious matter to be the cause of sending to jail a father upon whom a lot of little children are dependent, whether those children were begotten by the same or different mothers, the fact remains they all have little mouths to feed."[53]

Unfortunately for Angus and his family, he was one of the first convicted under the Edmunds Act for unlawful cohabitation. He began his six-month jail sentence on May 9, 1885 and paid a fine of $300. His lawyers extended his prison stay by two months while attempting to redefine the term "cohabitation" in appellate court. Letters depict his time in prison as tolerable, passing the time reading, playing croquet, and receiving regular family visits, especially from his wife Amanda.[54]

As for Martha, after some time evading authorities, she took an eastbound train, boarded the SS Wyoming of the Guion line, and sailed off to visit relatives in England.[55] This was a brave adventure, given that she did not know the relatives personally and that they knew nothing of her arrival. On May 4, 1886, Martha wrote, "I am thankful to meet my relatives, and my poor dear Uncle is quite overcome in meeting me, it is all so unexpected to them." In the same letter, she described informing

---

51. Martha H. Cannon collection, 1883-1912; Letters from Martha H. Cannon to Barbara Replogle, 1883-1893; Church History Library, https://catalog.churchofjesuschrist.org/record?id=7da9d9aa-8d5d-4d62-8ca8-d324598f2051&view=browse&subView=arrangement (accessed: July 24, 2019)

52. Martha H. Cannon collection, 1883-1912, ibid.

53. Martha H. Cannon collection, 1883-1912, ibid.

54. Donald Q. Cannon and David J. Whittaker, *Supporting Saints: Life Stories of Nineteenth-Century Mormons* (Salt Lake City: Deseret, 2012).

55. Lieber and Sillito, ibid.

her relatives that she had "married a widower" to avoid admitting her polygamous marriage to her family, who would certainly disapprove.⁵⁶ She soon relocated to the countryside for health reasons, though it is possible she was endeavoring to protect Elizabeth from her drunkard aunt and vicious cousins who had been instructed to rough up the "spoiled" little girl.

In her exile, she found little opportunity to practice medicine because her patients could afford neither her services nor her medicines.⁵⁷ She focused instead on gathering European books to use as training materials for her return to Utah as her sights were clearly set on the days following her exile.⁵⁸ During this time she wrote, "I feel that the spark of ambition is not yet dead within, but smolders ready to burst into flame when legitimate opportunity presents itself."⁵⁹

In another attempt to help those left behind in Utah, she once again turned to her oratorical skills: "If I am ever blessed with strength and talent sufficient I will give a series of lectures to aid those which this crusade has plunged in distress. Husbands are ruthlessly plunged into prison, others are exiles while their business goes to wreck and families in consequence suffer."⁶⁰

Mattie was no stranger to physical suffering as both she and Elizabeth anguished from various health issues. Mattie was afflicted with a repeated illness of "the womb," which she chose to view as a blessing. She described her difficulties as a gift from a loving God, meant to curb her "rebellious spirit" and force her to walk with God.⁶¹

Her illnesses were a constant source of frustration on multiple fronts. Whenever seeking treatment, she was aware that her doctor lacked sufficient knowledge of her treatment needs. Yet, because she felt she could not disclose her own medical background, she sought a second opinion at St. Thomas Hospital in London. But, much to her chagrin, she discovered that they allowed "inexperienced boy students" to learn by practicing on patients, whereupon she left untreated even though it was difficult to take care of young Elizabeth in her condition."⁶²

Elizabeth was also almost constantly sick, mostly of natural illness, but at least once from her own mischief. One time, when Martha had turned away for a moment, little Elizabeth drank a bottle of strong ammonia from Mattie's suitcase, resulting in

---

56. Lieber and Sillito, ibid.

57. Lieber and Sillito. *Letters from Exile*, ibid.

58. Martha H. Cannon collection, 1883-1912; Letters from Martha H. Cannon to Barbara Replogle, 1883-1893; Church History Library, https://catalog.churchofjesuschrist.org/record?id=7da9d9aa-8d5d-4d62-8ca8-d324598f2051&view=browse&subView=arrangement (accessed: July 24, 2019).

59. Martha H. Cannon collection, 1883-1912; Letters from Martha H. Cannon to Barbara Replogle, 1883-1893, ibid.

60. Martha H. Cannon collection, 1883-1912; Letters from Martha H. Cannon to Barbara Replogle, ibid.

61. Martha H. Cannon collection, 1883-1912, ibid.

62. Martha H. Cannon collection, 1883-1912, ibid.

"the most extreme agony her mother had ever witnessed in a mortal human being." Mattie forced Elizabeth to drink consecrated oil and called the elders to administer to her. The next day, when Elizabeth showed signs of improvement, one of the elders declared that the Word of Wisdom had saved Elizabeth by protecting the two of them from harm.[63]

Angus questioned Martha's recurring illnesses, but she was not one to mince words. In one instance she wrote, "[d]id you come to the conclusion that my case was not an urgent one, that I showed symptoms little indicating uterine trouble?...The situation is this, loved one, I need the treatment referred to."[64] On this occasion, she refused to return to Utah until Elizabeth's illness and her own bladder infection had been properly treated. Martha always put her family's health first.

Despite her distance from Angus, her love did not diminish for some time. During the early years of their marriage, she often wrote to Angus as well as her friend Barbara, declaring her love for him. But, over the years, her letters oscillated between states of love and bitterness. For most of their marriage, they remained apart with Mattie in and out of exile, first in Europe and later in California for health issues.

Polygamy proved to be a difficult path for Martha. While she felt it was right, she also struggled to find peace with it. Martha wrote:

> were it not for daily petitions to God for strength, the adversary would make me feel and believe it really a condition of degradation instead of one of honorable wifehood. If only you knew the subterfuges one has to resort to in order to make any movement appear reasonable to sensible people with whom I meet…

Over time, her letters came to suggest that the idealistic view of her youth had faded over the years as a result of personal experience.

Part of her difficulty stemmed from jealousy, but she was not alone in this. Angus himself was jealous of Martha's past lovers, while Martha remained jealous of Angus' growing household of wives, one of which, Maria Bennion, he had married just days before Martha left on her self-imposed exile. This had a lasting effect on her, for not only was she jealous as the man she loved kept taking more wives, but it also affected her self-esteem. She wrote Angus:

> I don't think you will find me lashing myself into jealous rages if you see fit to take additional young wives for eternity, and to propagate the species, as I have come to the conclusion that I am totally unfit for the work and must see others do it.[65]

---

63. Lieber and Sillito, ibid.
64. Lieber and Sillito, ibid.
65. Lieber and Sillito, ibid.

On return from exile, Martha resumed her strong activity within the community. She ran a private practice until giving birth to her son. Thereafter she moved to California for two years before returning to Salt Lake and jumping into politics.

Mattie had grown up in Utah which, as a territory, had given women the right to vote in 1870. However, the 1887 Tucker Amendment to the Edmunds Act included a stipulation that cost women that right. But this loss only encouraged women to fight back and Martha joined the ranks. Her experience as a learned doctor gave credence to her voice. In 1893, she spoke alongside Emmeline B. Wells, Susan B. Anthony, and others on the topic of suffrage at Chicago's Columbian Exposition.[66]

At the time, men and women espoused different views regarding the inclusion of women voters in Utah's new constitution. Latter-day Saint men felt that women's right to vote would show others that polygamous wives were not oppressed after all. Anti-Mormon politicians, on the other hand, hoped that women voters would use their power to end polygamous marriages altogether.[67]

Latter-day Saint women wanted to show the world through their voting privilege that they had a voice and were not held captive by polygamy. However, non-Latter-day Saint women felt that polygamy just gave a polygamous man more votes since his wives would vote in agreement with him. Accordingly, the non-Mormon women created a petition and were able to acquire 15,366 signatures against the women's right to vote. But Latter-day Saint women outmatched that petition with their own, featuring 24,801 signatures.[68]

In January 1896, Utah officially became a state where women could vote and, in November, they were ready to help select the second state legislature. There were five seats open with ten candidates running. Five were Democrats, one of whom was Martha, along with five Republicans, one of whom was Angus. Martha earned 10,288 votes to Angus' 8,054, giving Martha the fifth-most votes and Angus the seventh.[69] This was enough to secure Martha a seat, making her the first woman state senator in the nation's history. It should be noted that Martha was not the only heroine in the election. At the same time, Utah elected Sarah Elizabeth Anderson and Eurithe LaBarthe to its House of Representatives.[70]

---

66. Emmeline B. Wells, "Utah Women in Chicago," *Deseret Weekly*, July 1, 1893.

67. "Utah and the 19th Amendment (U.S. National Park Service)." National Parks Service. U.S. Department of the Interior, n.d. https://www.nps.gov/articles/utah-women-s-history.htm.

68. Jill Mulvay Derr, Janath Russell Cannon, and Maureen Ursenback Beecher, *Women of Covenant: The Story of Relief Society* (Salt Lake City: Deseret Book Co., 2000).

69. "Salt Lake Tribune Newspaper Archives, Nov 5, 1896, p. 3." NewspaperArchive.com. Salt Lake Tribune, November 5, 1896. https://newspaperarchive.com/salt-lake-tribune-nov-05-1896-p-3/.

70. Elizabeth M. Cox, *Women State and Territorial Legislators, 1895-1995* (Jefferson, NC: McFarland & Company Inc., 1996).

With her new platform Martha was able to make a major difference in the lives of Utah citizens. She helped start the state Board of Health. She worked to help establish some of the first pure food laws in the nation. She fought against those trying to eliminate the State Board of Public Examiners that certified doctors and midwives. She also introduced a successful bill that forbade teachers with tuberculosis to work in the classroom.[71]

Martha campaigned for vaccinations, not wanting to send children to school while capable of spreading disease. Despite the fact that the state provided the vaccinations, many church members were unwilling to receive them because of misinformation about alleged dangers reported by Brigham Young Jr. and the Deseret News. When the vaccinations thus slowed from this resistance, Martha countered in her own way. When the area was hit by a smallpox epidemic in 1898-1899, she worked with the Board of Health to eliminate shared drinking cups attached to water fountains.[72]

In her role as state Senator, Martha fought for the inclusion of women in politics. On February 15, 1898, she eloquently testified before the United States House of Representatives regarding the state of suffrage in Utah. She said:

> [n]one of the unpleasant results which were predicted have occurred. The contentions in families, the tarnishment [sic] of woman's charms, the destruction of fake ideals, have all been found to be but ghosts of unfounded prejudices. The divinity which doth hedge woman about the subtle perfume has not been displaced. Women have quietly assumed the added power which was always was theirs by right, and with the grace and ready adaptation to circumstances peculiar to the women of America, they have so conducted themselves that they have gained admiration and respect while losing none of their old-time prestige. Before women were granted suffrage, they had ideas upon public questions. Suffrage gave them opportunity to give practical expression to their views. They gave more attention to political affairs. They studied political economy more earnestly.[73]

Despite her determination and that of so many others, it would be another twenty-one years before women were given the right to vote nationwide.

As Senator, Martha helped found a nursing school as well as schools for the deaf and blind. Governor Heber Wells appointed her to both the Board of Health and the Board of Directors for the School of the Deaf and the Dumb. She was re-elected

---

71. Mari Graña. *Dr. Martha: The Life of a Pioneer Physician, Politician, and Polygamist* (Guilford, CT: TwoDot, 2015).

72. Graña, ibid.

73. "Hearing on House Joint Resolution 68: Providing as Follows, 'Section I. The Right of Citizens of the United States to Vote Shall Not Be Denied or Abridged by the United States or Any State on Account of Sex.' 'Section 2. The Congress Shall Have Power, by Appropriate Legislation, to Enforce the Provisions of This Article." The Library of Congress. United States Congress, n.d. https://www.loc.gov/item/07039904/.

for a second term, even while keeping her private practice doors open and struggling with her finances. During this time, she often wrote to Angus, begging for money to clothe the children, pay the rent, and feed the family. Despite her husband's financial success in his mining business, he often forgot this portion of his family in financial support.

Martha did not run for a third term as state Senator because of her pregnancy with her third child Gwendolyn; however, she did continue her Board of Health duties until 1903. Her fight against tuberculosis continued as she became a member of the Medico-Legal Society of New York, a group that focused on a variety of health issues, but especially on tuberculosis.[74] In 1920, she became Vice-President of the group.

Through all her successes, family remained at the forefront of her mind and Martha and daughter Lizzie shared an exceptionally close bond. After moving away from her mother, Lizzie wrote of Martha to her papa at one difficult moment:

> I have sent word to James that he is to telegraph me the minute she is worse and unless she is properly cared for…I shall leave for Pacific Grove immediately. I suppose it shall damage my reputation as a teacher and I've been making a good record here, but everything else in the world matters nothing to me should anything happen to mama.[75]

In return, shortly after Lizzie left, Martha shared a reciprocal letter with Angus, writing, "[t]elegraph me at once if Elizabeth should get sick. No one on earth has ever nursed her in case of illness but her mother. It would break my heart to have her sick and me so far away."[76]

Martha not only recovered from her illness on this occasion, but continued to live a successful and productive life. During her golden years, she divided her time between her son James' home in Los Angeles and Elizabeth's husband's ranch in Utah. Her final five years were spent in her own home in Los Angeles working for the Graves Clinic. She outlived Angus by seventeen years and her youngest child, Gwendolyn, by four.

In 2020, in honor of her service, a statue of Martha Hughes Cannon will be permanently installed in statuary hall in the United States Capitol to accompany that of Brigham Young. It will replace the statue of Philo T. Farnsworth, a Utah inventor who held over 300 patents for telecommunications work and for the Farnsworth-

---

74. Graña, ibid.

75. Martha H. Cannon collection, 1883-1912; Letters from Elizabeth Cannon to Angus M. Cannon, 1904-1912; Church History Library, https://catalog.churchofjesuschrist.org/record?id=7da9d9aa-8d5d-4d62-8ca8-d324598f2051&view=browse&subView=arrangement (accessed: July 25, 2019)

76. Martha H. Cannon collection, 1883-1912; Letters from Martha H. Cannon to Angus M. Cannon, ibid.

Hirsch fusor.[77] At the same time, Llandudno, Wales, is planning to erect a statue in honor of Martha on their Great Orme.[78]

This has been a story of two very different women from different backgrounds with different interests. Both exercised great influence on their worlds: Edna, a talented editor and outdoorswoman; and Martha, a doctor and Senator. Both excelled in eras where men had traditionally held such roles, and both left legacies that molded future generations.

I hope this paper has sparked a fire within you to venture forth into the rabbit holes of Restoration history in order to discover the uninvestigated stories of women that are waiting to be told. Only by recounting their tales may we gain a more complete picture of the past that molds our world today and the future to come.

RACHEL KILLEBREW is the World Church Librarian-Archivist and Records Manager for Community of Christ, as well as a member of the Church History and Sacred Story team. She has served in a variety of roles for the John Whitmer Historical Association, including its presidency.

---

77. Alexander and Bitton, ibid.

78. Neil Prior, "Llandudno Statue Plan for US Senate Pioneer Martha Hughes Cannon," BBC News. BBC, July 28, 2019. https://www.bbc.com/news/uk-wales-49129567.

Discerning Supernatural Presences: Experiential Claims and Restorationist Movements in the Burned-Over District

Ann Taves

2019 HOWARD LECTURE

Introduction

I WAS DELIGHTED to accept this invitation for a number of reasons. The burned-over district was a hot topic when I was in graduate school in the early 80s and I was interested to revisit the literature and see what had been done since. I knew that the burned-over district was the context in which Joseph Smith's visionary experiences took place, but in my most recent book, I focused on the context in which he wrote his histories—the 1830s—rather than the context in which the events depicted in the histories ostensibly took place. Recently, however, the Special Collections Department of the University of California at Santa Barbara (UCLB) Library acquired the diaries of Benajah Williams, a Methodist preacher who was assigned to the Bloomfield circuit in 1820, which was adjacent to, but did not include, Palmyra where the Smiths were living. The Williams diaries not only promised to illuminate the revival context but included a reference to Rev. George Lane, the minister to whom some historians have speculated Joseph Smith recounted his First Vision.[1] I was excited to figure out what this source, which I thought was little known, could tell us. On top of that, my family had lived just off the Pittsford-Palmyra Road when I was in school, and I recognized all the towns and villages mentioned in Williams' diary. So, after an initial round of research, I said yes and wrote my abstract.

---

1. Benajah Williams diaries, American Religions Collection (ARC MSS 85), Special Collections, University of California at Santa Barbara.

As the time came to actually write this presentation, I dug more deeply into the literature, and the more I dug, two things became clear. First, the burned-over district has been burned over by historians. There are very few secrets left, few stones left unturned. Not only that, but the Benajah Williams diaries are not news. When I told LDS historian Steve Harper I had a new source, he immediately guessed what it was and I learned that scholars apparently have had access to the diaries for some time. Rereading Mark Staker's book on Smith's Ohio revelations, I realized that he had quoted extensively from them in 2009, and that Harper had cited the Williams diaries in 2012 as well.² Second, I didn't have an argument. As I worked my way back into the primary sources starting with the Williams diary and the most recent secondary literature, I'd have an idea, but then, like Joseph Smith's treasures, it would slip away in a tide of conflicting evidence. It was not until I finally read Wesley Walters' article on the first vision that an argument started to emerge.³ But it was only when I went back and re-read Whitney Cross, that I realized that I was wrestling with a version of Cross' question.

Whitney Cross's *The Burned-over District*, published in 1950, was a pioneering effort to explain "ultra-isms" in light of the interplay between intellectual and social factors.⁴ As critics of his book have noted, however, it wasn't clear which factors

---

2. Mark L. Staker, *Hearken, O Ye People: The Historical Setting of Joseph Smith's Ohio Revelations* (Salt Lake City: Greg Kofford Books, 2009), xviii, 128-129, 136. Steven C. Harper, *Joseph Smith's First Vision: A Guide to the Historical Accounts* (Salt Lake City: Deseret Books, 2012). Staker gets some of the details confused, however. He offers a lengthy description of a camp meeting (pp. 128-129) that he claims took place "in a village somewhere near Palmyra, while Williams was stationed on the nearby 'Richmond Circuit.'" In fact, Williams was describing a "prayer meeting" that took place in Truxton, which was on the Cortland Circuit in the Chenango District in Central New York, south of Syracuse, almost 80 miles from Palmyra. Williams, who was from the area, was just getting started that year (1817-1818) as a "local preacher" (George Peck, *Early Methodism within the bounds of the Old Genesee Conference, from 1788 to 1828* [NY: Carlton & Porter, 1860], 400; on the Cortland Circuit, see pp. 399-403). Williams attended his first Annual Conference in Lansing (near Ithaca in Cayuga County) in July 1818, where he was admitted to the Genesee Conference as an itinerant preacher "on trial" and assigned to the Bloomfield Circuit (not Ridgeway) in the Genesee District, which at that time included most of Western New York from Palmyra to Buffalo. Palmyra was located on the Ontario Circuit, just to the east of the Bloomfield Circuit. At the next Annual Conference, which was held in Vienna, NY, in July 1819, Williams was again assigned to the Bloomfield Circuit (*Minutes of the Annual Conferences of the Methodist Episcopal Church for the years 1773-1828*, vol. 1 [hereafter *MEC Minutes*; NY: Methodist Episcopal Church, 1840], 302-303, 318). Staker (p. 136) indicates that, when "Benajah Williams was preaching on the Ridgeway Circuit near Rochester...[he] 'found Br. Lane a Presiding Elder from Susquehanna District with five more preachers' working up a congregation.'" At the time (July 1820), Williams was still assigned to the Bloomfield Circuit; the meeting in question took place in Richmond, a village on the Bloomfield Circuit near Honeoye Lake, about 30 miles from Palmyra. The visitors, including Lane, were *en route* to the 1820 Annual Conference in Niagara in Lower Canada (*MEC Minutes*, 337). Much to his dismay, Williams was assigned to the remote Ridgeway Circuit, which was located halfway between Rochester and Buffalo, in 1820 (*MEC Minutes*, 352).

3. Wesley P. Walters, "New Light on Mormon Origins from the Palmyra Revival," *Dialogue: A Journal of Mormon Thought* 4/1 (1969): 60-81.

4. Whitney R. Cross, *The Burned-Over District: The Social and Intellectual History of Enthusiastic Religion in Western New York, 1800-1850* (Ithaca: Cornell University Press, 1950), 173, quote p. 198.

were most important nor how they interacted to produce "ultraism."⁵ The problem, I think, is that Cross didn't explore the "ultraist state of mind"—as he called it—deeply enough from the "ultraists" point of view. "Ultraism" was not a term that people used to describe themselves. Orthodox Protestants of the time used it to describe those who were—in their view—going to extremes and on the verge of heterodoxy. Cross hints at the "ultraist" perspective when he indicates that "the ultraist state of mind rose from an implicit, even occasionally an explicit, reliance upon the direct guidance of the Holy Ghost" fostered by the orthodox tendency to "attribut[e] revival conversions to this supernatural agency."⁶

As a movement that arose in response to visionary experiences, the orthodox definitely viewed Mormonism as "ultraist," and Cross discusses it as such. Although—like Cross—I am interested in how and why new religious movements emerged, I don't think it is enough simply to look—as he did—at the interaction of social and intellectual factors as if "factors" simply interact to produce things. We need to consider what knits these factors together to create something. The missing element is the human process of meaning-making, whereby people decide what is happening. People make sense of events in the present and reinterpret what happened in the past in light of new developments. Meaning-making not only entails figuring out what happened but also why it happened and what it means that it happened for them and for those around them.

To reconstruct this meaning-making process, however, we can't start with how insiders (or outsiders) later interpreted events—that is—with their retrospective views of what took place. As historians, we have to do our best to reconstruct how people—future insiders and outsiders—interpreted events as they unfolded in their own—often uncertain and conflictual—terms. To do this, we have to analyze the sources carefully to distinguish between those that most closely reflect what people were thinking at the time and those that offer later reflections on the event. Because a careful historical reconstruction has to begin with the best real-time sources, it does not necessarily begin where insiders—or outsiders—would begin their account of what happened. But it does allow us to better understand how these later accounts emerged.

This is the way that I approached the emergence of Mormonism in *Revelatory Events*.⁷ I didn't begin with Smith's histories, which were written in the 1830s, but

---

5. Judith Wellman, "Review: Crossing Over Cross: Whitney Cross's Burned-Over District as Social History Reviewed Work(s): *The Burned-Over District: The Social and Intellectual History of Enthusiastic Religion in Western New York, 1800-1850* by Whitney Cross," *Reviews in American History* 17/1 (1989): 159-174. For a more recent review of the literature, see Judith Wellman, *Grass Roots Reform in the Burned-Over District of Upstate New York* (New York: Garland, 2000), vii-xxviii.

6. Cross, *The Burned-Over District*, 198.

7. Ann Taves, *Revelatory Events: Three Case Studies of the Emergence of New Spiritual Movements* (Princeton: Princeton University Press, 2016), 17-22.

with the best real-time sources, which were the early revelations, the first of which was recorded in July 1828 in the midst of translating the plates. Participants in the translation process were privy to these revelations as they were proclaimed and to the Book of Mormon narrative as it was dictated and transcribed. Then, with the publication of the Book of Mormon in March 1830 and the founding of the Church of Christ in April (1830), Smith and his followers had to negotiate two major transitions. First, they had to shift from producing new scripture to evangelizing based on it and second, they had to shift from the revelation-guided production of scripture to recounting the history of the church. With the founding of the church, Smith and his followers had to explain not only how this new scripture and new restored church had come into being, but why it was needed. The church's history had to offer reasons for insiders and outsiders to accept the new book as revelation, the new church as authentically restored, and Smith's role and function as seer, prophet, revelator, and first elder of the newly founded church.[8]

This is the context in which I analyzed Smith's histories. For me, the striking thing was that up until 1830, the story began with the appearance of an angel who announced the presence of an ancient record preserved on golden plates. This is how Joseph Smith recounted the story in his letter to his father's family in 1828; how his mother, Lucy Mack Smith, recounted it in her letter to her siblings, Solomon and Lydia, in 1831; and, generally, how it was understood by insiders in the early 1830s.[9] In the draft version of her history, which she recounted in 1844-45, Lucy Smith still began the story of the church's restoration with the revelation of the plates.[10]

---

8. Taves, *Revelatory Events*, 72.

9. In a letter from Jesse Smith (Joseph Smith Jr.'s uncle) to Hyrum Smith in 1829, Jesse refers to a (now missing) 1828 letter that Joseph Smith Jr. wrote to Asahel Smith. In Jesse's recounting of the earlier letter, the story begins with the discovery of the plates (see Dan Vogel, *Early Mormon Documents*, vol. 1 [hereafter *EMD* 1]; Salt Lake City: Signature Books, 1996, 551-554). In January 1831 Lucy Mack Smith also begins the story with the recovery of the plates in her letter to her brother, Solomon Mack, and sister, Lydia Mack Bill (*EMD* 1:216). According to the editors, "the history of the church, as it was then generally understood [in the early 1830s], began with the gold plates" (Joseph Smith, *Joseph Smith Histories, 1832-1844*, ed. Karen Lynn Davidson et al., The Joseph Smith Papers [hereafter cited as *JSP, H1*; Salt Lake City: The Church Historian's Press, 2012, 6. Sentence appears in Taves, p. 73.

10. For source notes and an introduction to Lucy's history, see *EMD* 1:227-230 and *The Joseph Smith Papers* "Sources Notes" and "Historical Introduction" (see links below). According to the latter, Lucy Mack Smith dictated a rough draft version of her history to Martha Jane Knowlton Coray (with some additional scribal help from Martha's husband, Howard) beginning in 1844 and concluding in 1845. In 1845, the Corays used the rough draft and other notes and sources to create two revised, or "fair," copies. The sole extant fair copy is titled "The History of Lucy Smith Mother of the Prophet." The other fair copy (no longer extant) was printed in England under the title, *Biographical Sketches of Joseph Smith, the Prophet, and His Progenitors for Many Generations*, by Lucy Smith, Mother of the Prophet (Liverpool: S. W. Richards, 1853). The draft version–Lucy Mack Smith, History, 1844–1845; handwriting of Martha Jane Knowlton Coray and Howard Coray; 240 pages–is held in the Church History Archives in Salt Lake City. The draft version is printed in parallel with the published version in EMD 1:227-450. The draft version and the extant fair copy are available online at Lucy Mack Smith, History, 1844–1845,

The brief history of the church that appeared in the Articles and Covenants (c. April 1830 [LDS D&C 20]) did offer a bit more of a preamble, telling us that after Smith "had received remission of his sins, he was entangled again in the vanities of the world, but after truly repenting, God visited him by an holy angel..."[11] Smith started offering more detailed accounts of an experience in which his "sins were remitted" in the context of proselytizing because, as he later elaborates, this was the context in which he said he first started to wrestle with the question of which church was right. Elaborating on this experience, I argued, thus helped him to explain to ever-wider audiences how he and his followers knew that all the extant churches were wrong and why the Bible, which they already had, was insufficient.[12]

In working with the histories, I saw no reason to doubt that Smith struggled with the question of which church was correct as a young teenager and I thought his description of the denominational competition for converts in the context of revivals rang true.[13] But since I was viewing Smith's histories in relation to the challenges he and his followers faced in the 1830s, I didn't try to determine how accurately they had reflected developments in the 1820s. I was interested in how new religious movements emerged, not with the degree of historical accuracy of Smith's accounts. As a result, I largely sidestepped the debates that attempted to locate Smith's histories in relation to events of the 1820s.

Preparing this talk plunged me into those debates, which centered to a great extent on whether the revival that Smith associated with his first vision took place in 1820, as his 1838 account suggests, or in 1824, as Lucy Smith's history would suggest. Rather than rehash the evidence in detail, I want to ask what difference it would make for our understanding of the emergence of Mormonism if the revival that Smith was remembering in his 1838 account took place in 1824 instead of 1820. Or, to put it another way, I'd like to engage in a thought experiment that explores what difference it would make if we adopt Lucy Smith's chronology, which places the revival after the revelation of the plates, rather than Joseph's, which places it before.

I'm going to argue that the change in order has significant consequences: it maintains 1823 as the beginning of the Mormon story, grounds the story in a visionary treasure-seeking milieu populated with supernatural presences, and brings the prob-

---

https://www.josephsmithpapers.org/paper-summary/lucy-mack-smith-history-1844-1845 and Lucy Mack Smith, History, 1845 at https://www.josephsmithpapers.org/paper-summary/lucy-mack-smith-history-1845/1.

11. Joseph Smith, *Documents*, vol. 1, ed. Dean C. Jesse et al., *The Joseph Smith Papers* (hereafter cited as *JSP, D1*; Salt Lake City: The Church Historian's Press, 2013), 121, as quoted in Taves, *Revelatory Events*, 73. When Peter Bauder interviewed him in October 1830, some six months later, Smith apparently did not mention this experience. Indeed, Bauder reported: "he [Smith] could give me no Christian experience, but told me that an angel told him he must go to a certain place in the town of Manchester, Ontario Country, where was a secret treasure concealed, which he must reveal to the human family" (*EMD* 1:16-18).

12. Taves, *Revelatory Events*, 74.

13. Ibid.

lem of discerning who is present into the revival context. In terms of supernatural presences, Joseph's history is framed in terms of an encounter with deities (the Father and the Son); Lucy's draft history is a story of encounters with an intermediary—messenger who is also an angel, a spirit, and an ancient Nephite. Historically speaking, I think Lucy's history is closer to the story that insiders—and outsiders—heard as the events unfolded, whether they embraced Smith's claims or not. Joseph's history, I would argue, reflects an understanding of divine presence that likely emerged in the context of translating the plates and then was used to re-interpret what happened earlier.

I'll explore this alternative approach to Mormon origins in three steps. First, I'll review the first vision controversy to highlight the central role that Lucy Smith's chronology played in the debate. Second, I'll discuss the supernatural appearances in Lucy's history to indicate what Mormon origins looked like from her point of view. Finally, I'll consider competing interpretations of the intermediaries Lucy described and indicate the point at which I think Smith began to claim he was communicating with deities rather than intermediaries.

Part I: The First Vision Controversy—A Recap

HERE IS THE DESCRIPTION of the revival that Joseph Smith associated with his first vision in his 1838 account and published in *Times and Seasons* in 1842:

> Some time in the second year [1821] after our removal to Manchester, there was in the place where we lived an unusual excitement on the subject of religion. It commenced with the Methodists, but soon became general among all the sects in that region of country, indeed the whole district of Country seemed affected by it, and great multitudes united themselves to the different religious parties, which created no small stir and division amongst the people, Some Crying, "Lo, here," and some Lo, there. Some were contending for the Methodist faith, Some for the Presbyterian, and some for the Baptist…I was at this time in my fifteenth year. My Fathers [sic] family was proselyted to the Presbyterian faith and four of them joined that Church, Namely, My Mother Lucy, My Brothers Hyrum, Samuel Harrison, and my Sister Sophronia.[14]

Mormons traditionally assumed this revival took place in 1820 since Smith said he was 15 at the time. This dating of the revival—and the associated visionary expe-

---

14. *JSP*, H1:208; reprinted in "Smith's History," *Times and Seasons* 3/10 (15 Mar. 1842), pp. 719–734. The *JSP* note on the "excitement… [that] commenced with the Methodists" indicates that "Methodists held camp meetings at Palmyra in June 1818 and at Oaks Corners, near Vienna and within six miles of Palmyra, in July 1819" (*JSP*, H1:209). The note on Smith's family joining the church reads: "Lucy Mack Smith and three of her children, Hyrum, Sophronia, and Samuel, attended the Western Presbyterian Church in Palmyra. Lucy wrote that their affiliation began following the death of her son Alvin in November 1823, or near the end of JS's eighteenth year" (ibid.). No attempt is made to reconcile the differences in Smith's age (and thus the date) in relation to the two presumably connected events (the "excitement" and his family joining the church).

rience—allow us to distinguish between a "first" vision in which, according to some of his accounts, Smith is visited by the Father and Son and a "second" vision in September 1823, in which Smith is visited by a "personage" who reveals the existence of the golden plates.

Fawn Brodie called this dating into question with the publication of *No Man Knows My History* in 1945, and Wesley Walters, a Presbyterian minister, marshaled considerable evidence to suggest that the revival in question actually took place in 1824-25.[15] Walters submitted his article to *Dialogue* in 1967, but it did not appear there until LDS historians were prepared to respond to it, some two years later. In his recent book on the first vision, Steven Harper provides a detailed account of Walters' efforts, the consternation it aroused among LDS intellectuals, and the immediate efforts made to mobilize LDS scholars to investigate the early history of the church in upstate New York.[16] The results of their research were published in a special issue of *Brigham Young University Studies Quarterly* in 1969.[17] Shortly thereafter, Walters' article was published in *Dialogue* with a response by Richard Bushman and a follow-up reply by Walters.[18]

Bushman incorporated the research of the late sixties in *Joseph Smith and Early Mormonism*, published in 1984.[19] In it, he offered a more historically nuanced account of Mormon origins, while preserving the traditional chronology. In doing so, he made two important moves. First, he reconciled the difference between Smith's 1832 and 1838 histories by taking a developmental approach, arguing that, by 1838, "aspects [of his first vision experience] took on an importance they did not possess at first."[20] Second, he maintained the conventional dating of the first vision by associating the revival with the meeting of the Genesee Conference of the Methodist Episcopal Church in Vienna (later Phelps) near Palmyra in July 1819 and by indicating that Lucy joined the Presbyterian Church in Palmyra "at some unspecified date," probably "before 1823."[21] He did not mention the evidence for the 1824 revival in Palmyra nor

---

15. Fawn Brodie, *No Man Know My History: The Life of Joseph Smith, the Mormon Prophet* (New York: A. A. Knopf, 1945). Wesley P. Walters, "New Light on Mormon Origins from Palmyra (N.Y.) Revival," *Bulletin of the Evangelical Theological Society* 10, no. 4 (Fall 1967): 241.

16. Steven C. Harper, *First Vision: Memory and Mormon Origins* (New York: Oxford University Press, 2019), 219-228.

17. The special issue, edited by Truman G. Madson, contained articles by James B. Allen and Leonard Arrington, Dean C. Jessee, Milton V. Backman, Jr., Larry C. Porter, T. Edgar Lyon, and Marvin S. Hill (see "Full Issue," *BYU Studies Quarterly* 9/3 [1969]. Available at: https://scholarsarchive.byu.edu/byusq/vol9/iss3/13).

18. Wesley P. Walters and Richard L. Bushman, "Roundtable: The Question of the Palmyra Revival," *Dialogue: A Journal of Mormon Thought* 4/1 (Spring 1969): 59-100.

19. Richard L. Bushman, *Joseph Smith and the Beginnings of Mormonism* (Urbana: University of Illinois Press, 1984).

20. Bushman, *Joseph Smith and the Beginnings of Mormonism*, 57.

21. Bushman, 53.

Lucy's statement that she joined the church in the context of a revival that took place there after her son Alvin's death in 1823.

Ten years later, Michael Marquardt and Wesley Walters published *Inventing Mormonism*, which summarized the results of their intensive research into Mormon origins.[22] Although Bushman generally applauded their research efforts and their "generous, fair-minded tone" in his review of their book, he highlighted a key instance in which he thought their efforts to separate fact from interpretation fell short.[23] In their timeline, he wrote:

> The authors list under 1825 the admission of Lucy and three of the Smith children into the Palmyra Presbyterian church as if this were a well-attested fact. But the authors have no direct evidence that this highly contested event occurred in 1825.[24]

In contrast to Bushman, LDS historian Marvin Hill found Lucy Smith's chronology compelling. As he writes:

> [Lucy] said she attended the revival with hope of gaining solace for Alvin's loss. That kind of detail is just the sort that gives validity to Lucy's chronology. She would not have been likely to make up such a reaction for herself or the family nor mistake the time when it happened. I am persuaded that it was 1824 when Lucy joined the Presbyterians.[25]

Ten years later, Dan Vogel was also convinced. In *Joseph Smith: The Making of a Prophet*, Vogel followed Lucy's chronology, arguing that, while Smith may have concluded at an early age that all the churches were corrupt, this would have "conformed to the religious views of both parents." It was in response to his mother's decision to join the Presbyterians in the context of the 1824 revival, Vogel contends, that the "subject of which church was true became extremely important." Vogel thus concludes that "Joseph twice lifted the revival out of its historical context, pushing it back to 1823 [in revising Cowdery's history], then to 1820 [in his 1838 history]."[26] Vogel also observed that Smith's statement that a Methodist preacher treated his vision with contempt makes more sense in 1824-25 than in 1820, especially if we consider the possibility that "Smith actually related his 1823 and 1824 encounters with the

---

22. H. Michael Marquardt and Wesley P. Waters, *Inventing Morminism: Tradition and the Historical Record* ([San Francisco]: Salt Lake City: Smith Research Associates; Distributed by Signature Books, 1994).

23. Richard L. Bushman, "Just the Facts Please," *Review of Books on the Book of Mormon 1989–2011* 6/2 (1994), Article 9, p. 133. Available at: https://scholarsarchive.byu.edu/msr/vol6/iss2/9.

24. Bushman, "Just the Facts Please," 131.

25. Marvin Hill, "The First Vision Controversy: A Critique and Reconciliation," *Dialogue* 15/2 (Summer 1982), 31-46, quote p. 39. Hill adds: "Indicating that the angel had told Joseph of the plates prior to the revival, Lucy added that for a long time after Alvin's death the family could not bear any talk about the golden plates, for the subject had been one of great interest to him and any reference to the plates stirred sorrowful memories."

26. Dan Vogel, *Joseph Smith: The Making of a Prophet* (Salt Lake City: Signature Books, 2004), 60.

heavenly messenger," i.e., the revelation of the plates, to the minister rather than the Lord's forgiveness of his sins.[27]

Vogel's account precipitated a lengthy response from D. Michael Quinn in defense of the 1820 date of the revival, which Vogel found unconvincing.[28] In *Rough Stone Rolling*, Bushman incorporates Smith's 1835 history without significantly altering the account of Mormon origins he proposed in his earlier work. He also acknowledges the 1824 revival and debates over the first vision in the notes, but doesn't discuss them in the text.[29]

Here is a brief summary of the evidence for each date. In 1820, Presbyterians, Baptists, and Methodists were present in the Palmyra area. The 1819 Methodist Annual Conference was held in nearby Vienna. Rev. George Lane, who is mentioned in Cowdery's account and was then the Presiding Elder for the Susquehanna District, was present at the 1819 Annual Conference. As Marquardt and Walters note, "[t]here is no record that he [Lane] preached or that a camp meeting was held in connection with this conference [in Vienna in 1819]." While annual conferences brought all the preachers together to receive their new assignments, quarterly conferences, which brought together everyone on the circuit, were more often associated with revivals.[30]

---

27. Vogel, *Joseph Smith: The Making of a Prophet*, 64.

28. D. Michael Quinn, "Joseph Smith's Experience of a Methodist 'Camp-Meeting' in 1820," *Dialogue Paperless*, E-Paper #3, December 20, 2006, http://www.dialoguejournal.com, accessed April 2008. For Vogel's response, see Dan Vogel, "What is a Revival?" *Dialogue: A Journal of Mormon Thought* 41/4, viii-x.

29. See Richard L. Bushman, *Joseph Smith: Rough Stone Rolling* (New York: Alfred A. Knopf, 2005), 35-41). For his acknowledgement of the debates, see p. 570, notes 27 and 30.

30. Marquardt and Walters, *Inventing Mormonism*, 29. They add: "In 1826, when a camp meeting was actually held, the conference minutes contain reference to the ministers who were put in charge of the arrangements for the meeting. No indication of any such arrangement appears in the 1819 minutes." Peck provides a summary of proceedings of the annual meetings of the Genesee Conference which involved the passage of resolutions on church matters and, above all, the review and reassignment of the itinerant preachers who were members of the conference (*Early Methodism*, 496-512). With the establishment of geographically defined annual conferences in 1796, they became closed meetings largely limited to the itinerant preachers. This limited the potential for associated revivals. (Russell Richey, *The Methodist Conference in America: A History* (Nashville: Kingswood Books), 52-61. After 1800, revivals of religion were typically associated with quarterly meetings, which were held four times per year on every circuit. They brought together all the members of the Society, including the local preachers, exhorters, and class leaders (none of whom were members of the annual conference), along with the presiding elder for the district and the itinerants assigned to the circuit. Itinerants from neighboring circuits might attend as well. Some business was conducted, but most of the two-day meeting was devoted to preaching and worship, typically including communion and a love feast. Nonmembers, who were welcome at all but the business meeting and the love feast, often participated in large numbers. In suggesting that the revival Smith described could have taken place in conjunction with the 1819 Annual Conference in Vienna, Staker (*O Hearken*, 130) conflates annual and quarterly conferences, noting that "one devout woman regularly traveled forty or fifty miles to attend *these conferences* every chance she could." The source (Peck, *Early Methodism*, 317) actually states: "She [Mrs. Lee] was present at all *the quarterly meetings* within her reach, often going forty and fifty miles, and driving her own carriage, or riding on horseback" (emphasis added). It is possible, as Bushman (1969, p. 89) indicates, "that either during the conference or as it broke up these ministers preached in nearby towns." For a discussion of quarterly meetings, see Lester Ruth, *A Little Heaven Below: Worship at Early Methodist Quarterly Meetings* (Nashville:

Lane also participated in a meeting in Richmond on the Bloomfield Circuit (about thirty miles from Palmyra) on his way to the 1820 Annual Conference in Lower Canada (Williams diary).[31] The Methodists did hold camp meetings on the Vienna Road just outside of Palmyra and, as Bushman notes, "Orasmus Turner, a newspaperman in Palmyra who knew the Smiths personally, recalls that Joseph caught 'a spark of Methodism in the camp meeting' somewhere along the road to Vienna."[32] In his response to Bushman, Walters agreed that Turner likely made these observations prior to 1822 and suggests that a camp meeting experience "may have provided the one core of truth around which [Smith] later wove his various vision stories."[33] We also know that claims to have experienced the presence of God were not all that rare at the time, since Benajah Williams regularly referred to God or the Lord being present at Methodist meetings in his diary. Finally, Lucy Smith indicates that she changed her course, presumably in relation to joining a church, when her oldest son Alvin "attained his 22nd year," which would have been in 1820, but she does not offer any details.[34]

The 1824-25 revival in Palmyra—by way of contrast—is attested by Presbyterian, Baptist, and Methodist membership records.[35] Rev. Lane, who was appointed as

---

Kingswood Books, 2000) and Russell Richey, "From Quarterly to Camp Meeting," *Early American Methodism* (Bloomington, IN: Indiana University Press, 1991), 21-32.

31. Though Williams does not mention a communion service or business meeting, this two-day meeting, which included preaching, exhorting, a prayer meeting, and a love feast, had the general form of a quarterly meeting.

32. Orasmus Turner, quoted in Richard L. Bushman, "The First Vision Story Revived," *Dialogue: A Journal of Mormon Thought* 4/1 (1969): 89. Bushman adds: "Since Turner left Palmyra in 1822, we can presume that the camp meeting and Joseph's awakening occurred before that date. All told, there can be little doubt that the Methodists were up to something in 1819 and 1820." The full quote, as cited in Maquardt and Walters (p. 29) reads: "after catching a spark of Methodism in the camp meeting, away down in the woods, on the Vienna road, he [Smith] was a very passable exhorter in evening meetings."

33. Wesley P. Waters, "A Reply to Dr. Bushman," *Dialogue: A Journal of Mormon Thought* 4/1 (1969): 99.

34. In her draft history, Lucy Mack Smith indicates that, while they were still living in Vermont, she "covenanted with God [in the context of a serious illness] if he would let me live I would endeavor to get that religion that would enable me to serve him right whether it was in the Bible or where ever it might be found even if it was to be obtained from heaven by prayer and Faith" (*EMD* 1: 240). After much searching, she concluded, "there is not on Earth the religion which I seek." As a result, she decided, "I will hear all that can be said read all that is writen [sic] but particularly the word of God shall be my guide to life and salvation which I will endeavor to obtain if it is to <be> had by diligence in prayer[.] This course I pursued for many years till at last I concluded that my mind would be easier if I were baptized and I found a minister who was willing to baptize me and leave me free from any membership in any church after which I pursued the same course [i.e., she "continued to read the Bible as formerly" (1853 ed.)] untill [sic] the a my oldest attained his 22nd year" (*EMD* 1: 242). She does not indicate what she did after this time.

35. For an extended discussion of the evidence, see Marquardt and Walters, 15-27.

Presiding Elder of the Ontario District (that included Palmyra) in 1824, published a lengthy account of the revival the following year.[36] In it, Lane indicates:[37]

> the work [of revival on the Ontario Circuit] commenced in the spring [in Palmyra], and progressed moderately until the time of the quarterly meeting, which was held on the 25th and 26th of September [1824]. About this time it appeared to break out afresh.

In December, he learned "that the work, which had for some time been going on in Palmyra, had broken out from the village like a mighty flame, and was spreading in every direction."[38] Not only does Lucy place the revival and her decision to join the church in the wake of Alvin's death in 1823,[39] but Joseph's brother William said Joseph got the idea of asking God what church he should join from a sermon preached by Rev. Lane in the context of "a joint revival in the neighborhood between the Baptists, Methodists, and Presbyterians … [in which] the question arose which church should have the converts"[40] According to William, the Presbyterian minister, Rev. Stockton, said "they ought to join the Presbyterians," but the next night, Rev. Lane "preached a sermon on 'what church shall I join?' And the burden of his discourse was to ask God, using as a text [James 1:5]."[41] Denominational sources for 1824 confirm that Stockton was the minister of the Western Presbyterian Church in Palmyra. Neither Stockton nor Lane had appointments anywhere near Palmyra prior to 1824.

Two things surprised me when I dug into these sources. Above all, I was surprised at how much evidence there was for a revival in 1824 of the sort Smith described in his 1838 account, especially given how little I had heard about it, and how sketchy the evidence was for 1820. Beyond that, I was surprised at how long it took me to realize that I didn't have to privilege Joseph's histories over Lucy's or seek to reconcile them. I could use her account to help me think through alternatives to the official origin story.

---

36. George Lane, "Revival of Religion on Ontario District" [Letter from the Rev. George Lane, dated Wilkesbarre, January 25, 1925], *The Methodist Magazine* 8 (April 1825), pp. 158-161.

37. Lane, "Revival of Religion on Ontario District," 159.

38. George Lane, "Revival of Religion on Ontario District," pp. 160.

39. *EMD* 1:306-7.

40. *EMD* 1:513.

41. According to Alexander Neibaur (24 May 1844), Smith—at times anyway—linked his first vision with the revival meeting in which his mother and siblings "got religion," but he did not and, instead, thinking of James 1:5, went to the woods to pray: "Br Joseph tolt [sic] us the first call he had a Revival Meeting his <u>Mother</u> & <u>Br</u> & <u>Sister</u> got Religion, he wanted to get Religion too wanted to feel & shout like the Rest but could feel nothing, opened his Bible the first Passage that struck him was if any man lack Wisdom let him ask of God who giveth to all Men liberallity [sic] & upbraidet [sic] not went into the Wood to pray…" Alexander Neibaur, Journal, 24 May 1844, extract," p. [23], *The Joseph Smith Papers*, accessed December 21, 2019, https://www.josephsmithpapers.org/paper-summary/alexander-neibaur-journal-24-may-1844-extract/1.

Part II: Mormon Origins—Lucy's Version

IF WE COMPARE Joseph and Lucy Smith's histories, both depict Joseph as wrestling with a similar problem, that is, determining which church was right, and in both cases, one or more supernatural beings appear and one way or another Joseph learns that all the churches are wrong. They differ, however, with respect to the context in which the issue arose, the supernatural being(s) that appeared, why they appear, and what they tell him. Most notably, in Joseph's history, these things take place in two events—one in 1820 and one in 1823; in Lucy's history there is only one event in 1823.

Joseph Smith's three versions of his history, although differing in specifics, all distinguish between a "first vision" in which deities appear and a subsequent event in which an "angel of the Lord" informs him of the existence of the ancient records. All the accounts of the first vision indicate that Smith was distressed in the context of contention between the churches, albeit for different reasons. In the earliest account, he was distressed because he was "convicted of [his] sins" and uncertain where to turn for forgiveness because all the churches had apostatized. In his 1835 and 1838 accounts, he was "wrought up…respecting the subject of religion," because he didn't know "who was right and who was wrong" (1835). In 1838, this uncertainty arose in the context of the revival we have been discussing. In the earliest account he searched the scriptures for an answer; in the latter two accounts, he had "a realizing sense" that he should "ask of God" (1835). When he asked, "two personages" appeared. In 1838, the personages, who are explicitly identified as the Father and the Son, tell him that he must not join any church "for they are all wrong." In the first account, he figures out that all the churches are wrong based on his own reading of scripture; in the later accounts, he acquires this information on much higher authority—the deity weighs in to proclaim that all the churches are wrong.[42]

In Lucy's draft history, there is no first vision, and the question of which church was right was a topic of discussion within the family, which in her history is a topic that had long interested both her and her husband. As she tells the story:

> One evening [in September 1823] we were sitting till quite late conversing upon the subject of the diversity of churches that had risen up in the world and the many thousand opinions in existence as to the truths contained in scripture…After we ceased conversation he [Joseph] went to bed <and was pondering in his mind which of the churches were the true one.> an but he had not laid there long till <he saw> a

---

42. For a comparison and discussion of the versions, see Ann Taves and Steven C. Harper, "Joseph Smith's First Vision: New Methods for the Analysis of Experience-Related Texts," *Mormon Studies Review* 3 (January 1, 2016): 53–84, https://doi.org/10.18809/msr.2016.0107. An annotated list of many of the primary accounts of Smith's "first vision" is available on the Joseph Smith Papers website, see: https://www.josephsmithpapers.org/site/accounts-of-the-first-vision?p=1&highlight=first%20vision.

bright <light> entered the room where he lay[.] he looked up and saw an angel of the Lord stood <standing> by him[.][43]

As she tells it, Joseph did not search scripture or ask of God. The "angel of the Lord" simply appeared and said to him:

> I perceive that you are enquiring in your mind which is the true church[.] there is not a true church on Earth[.] No not one [Nor <and> has not been since Peter took the Keys <of the Melchesidec priesthood after the order of God> into the Kingdom of Heaven[.] the churches that are now upon the Earth are all man made [sic] churches.[44]

In Lucy's draft account, "the angel of the Lord" appears because Joseph is "enquiring in his mind" and informs him not only that there is no true church on earth, but also that there is a record that he must recover buried in a nearby hillside that is "to bring forth that light and intelligence that has long been lost in the Earth." In the final (1853) version of Lucy's history, the editors inserted the *Times and Seasons* account of the Joseph's vision of the Father and Son, which gives the impression that she described two visions and two Palmyra revivals, one in 1820 and another after Alvin's death in November 1823.[45] The 1853 edition, moreover, substitutes Joseph's account of his 1823 vision for Lucy's, eliminating her description of the family's discussion and simply stating that "he retired to his bed in a quite a serious and contemplative state of mind," whereupon he "betook himself to prayer and supplication to Almighty God."[46]

If, at the time of the 1824 revival, Joseph's encounters with this messenger were foremost in his mind, Vogel's suggestion that Smith might have related this visionary encounter to Rev. Lane seems worth considering. If Smith told a Methodist minister that an angel of the Lord had informed him that there was no true church on earth and that he had been instructed to recover an ancient record that would restore the true church, the minister would most likely have told him. "Sorry, the Methodists have things right, the canon of scripture is closed, and no new revelation is needed."

If we now turn to the supernatural appearances in Lucy's book, we find that an "angel of the Lord" is the primary supernatural being that appears and speaks to Joseph in Lucy's account. There are references to God and the Lord, but they do not appear or speak directly. At most, they speak through an angel, which she sometimes

---

43. "Lucy Mack Smith, History, 1844–1845, Page [1], bk. 3," p. [10], bk. 3, *The Joseph Smith Papers*, accessed September 21, 2019, https://www.josephsmithpapers.org/paper-summary/lucy-mack-smith-history-1844-1845/40.
44. Ibid.
45. See *EMD* 1:288n87.
46. *EMD* 1:289.

refers to as a "personage"[47] or a "divine messenger."[48] There are also good and evil Spirits, which the angel teaches Joseph how to distinguish.[49]

The first set of references to the angel appear in Lucy's discussion of the revelation of the buried record in 1823[50] The angel appears again in 1827 to chastise Joseph for his negligence in recovering the buried record.[51] The angel then appears in conjunction with the actual recovery of the record,[52] at which point the angel directs him to keep it safe from "wicked men." The next set of references occurs after Joseph and Martin Harris began translating the record in Harmony, Pennsylvania, and Joseph allows Harris to take the translated portion of the manuscript home to Palmyra. While Harris was away, Emma Smith gave birth to their first child, who died the same day. But Emma, worried about the lack of news from Harris, encouraged Joseph nonetheless to go to Palmyra to find out what had happened. At the dining table in the Smith's home in Manchester, Harris confessed that the manuscript had disappeared and Lucy provided a graphic eyewitness account of Joseph's anguished realization that he had disobeyed the angel's instructions.[53]

Two months later in September 1828, Lucy and Joseph Sr. visited Harmony to find out what had happened after Joseph returned. According to Lucy, Joseph recounted:

> After I arrived here I commenced humbling myself in mighty prayer before the Lord and <as> I poured out my soul in supplication to him that if possible I might obtain mercy at [his] hands and be forgiven of all that I had done which was contrary to his will—As I was doing this an Angel stood before me and answered me saying that I had sinned in [delivering]…the manuscript into the hands of a wicked man.[54]

Lucy then adds, "soon after this he received a following revelation from the Lord," whereupon the text of the July 1828 revelation published as D&C 3 (1844 edition) is inserted into both the draft and edited versions of Lucy's history.[55]

---

47. *EMD* 1:29. She also reports (*EMD* 1:347-348) that "a personage" appeared to Lucy Harris in a dream and showed her the plates, such that she "then described the record minutely," after which she offered Joseph "28 dollars that her mother gave her just before she died when she was on her death bed."

48. *EMD* 1:297.

49. *EMD* 1:292.

50. *EMD* 1: 289-298.

51. *EMD* 1:325.

52. *EMD* 1:338.

53. *EMD* 1:356-365.

54. *EMD* 1:370.

55. *EMD* 1:370n179.

An angel continued to play a critical role in Lucy's history, laying the plates before the three witnesses,[56] transporting the plates from one place to another, and generally withdrawing and returning them as needed.[57]

Part III: Distinguishing Presences in a Folk Christian Treasure-seeking Milieu

Although Lucy's history was recounted long after the events occurred, Joseph's histories and the first-person accounts of his brother William also refer to an angel, messenger, and/or personage.[58] In light of the crucial role that the angel played in the events that Lucy recounted, we can ask whom she thought the angel was and how he was characterized by others. Although the later tradition identifies the angel as Moroni, one of the ancient Nephites, he remains unnamed in Lucy's draft history. Joseph's 1838 account of the angel's appearance, which was inserted into the edited version, indicates "his name was Nephi."[59] Since Lucy reports that Joseph regaled the family with accounts of the "ancient inhabitants" of the Americas that the angel had presumably recounted to him, Lucy probably assumed that the angel was an ancient Nephite, whether Nephi or Moroni. She also indicated that an "ancient Nephite," presumably also an angel, brought the plates to the grove so that the eight witnesses could handle them.[60]

There has been extensive discussion of whether Smith initially understood the personage who he claimed appeared to him in 1823 was an angel, a spirit, or a treasure guardian.[61] Willard Chase testified in 1833 that:

> [t]n the month of June, 1827, Joseph Smith, Sen., related to me the following story: 'That some years ago, a spirit had appeared to Joseph his son, in a vision, and informed him that in a certain place there was a record on plates of gold, and that he was the person that must obtain them.'[62]

---

56. *EMD* 5:347.

57. *EMD* 1:370-71, 1:391.

58. For Joseph's references, see *EMD* 1:28-30 (1832), *EMD* 1:44 (1835), and *EMD* 1:66 (1838); for William's, see *EMD* 1:478-79 (1841) and *EMD* 1:496 (1883).

59. For evidence that Joseph used the names Nephi and Moroni interchangeably as late as 1838, see D. Michael Quinn, *Early Mormonism and the Magic World View*, Rev. and enlarged ed. (Salt Lake City: Signature Books, 1998), 198-199, 508n186.

60. *EMD* 1:395-96.

61. For an overview of the discussion, see Mark Ashurst-McGee's "Postscript" (pp. 77-100) in idem., "Moroni as Angel and as Treasure Guardian," *Review of Books on the Book of Mormon 1989–2011* 18/1 (2006), Article 6. Available at: https://scholarsarchive.byu.edu/msr/vol18/iss1/6.

62. *EMD* 2:66.

According to Chase, Smith's father said the spirit was "the spirit of the prophet who wrote this book, and who was sent to Joseph Smith, to make known these things to him."[63] Abigail Harris, Martin Harris's sister-in-law, offered similar testimony based on a conversation with Joseph's parents at Martin Harris's house in winter 1828. According to Abigail, the Smiths said that "the report that Joseph, jun. had found golden plates, was true, and that he was in Harmony, Pa. translating them." Joseph's parents explained that the plates were "revealed to him by the spirit of one of the Saints that was on this continent, previous to its being discovered by Columbus."[64] Quinn also cites local newspaper accounts from 1829 that reported that Smith claimed to have been visited by a "spirit."[65]

Mark Ashurst-McGee points out, however, that Jesse Smith's letter of 1829[66] is the earliest relevant source. Jesse's letter indicates that in 1828, either Joseph or his father had written that "the Angel of the Lord has revealed to him [Joseph] the hidden treasures of wisdom & knowledge, even divine revelation, which has lain in the bowels of the earth for thousands of years."[67] As Michael Quinn notes and others generally agree, "it was not customary to use 'angel' to describe a personage who had been mortal, died, and was returning to earth to deliver a message to someone."[68] Although insiders' initial characterizations may have vacillated between "spirit" and "angel," the earliest sources nonetheless indicate that by the time the plates were recovered, Joseph and his parents viewed the messenger as the spirit of a long-deceased person—an ancient Nephite—who was in some way connected to the Lord, whether as a prophet, saint, or an angel, on the one hand, and to "hidden treasures of wisdom & knowledge," on the other.

The Smiths' claims did not go uncontested. Two alternative interpretations of what they had found or done allow us to embed the process of discernment more deeply in the revival context: thus, some claimed that he had simply found treasure, which led them to characterize the supernatural presence as a "treasure-guardian" or "treasure-spirit." Others claimed that he was engaging in necromancy, which led them to characterize it as a "ghost."

Some of Smith's fellow treasure-seekers held the first view which, according to Lucy's history, Smith had to renounce in order to recover the plates. When Willard Chase and other local treasure-seekers bought in a "conjuror" to help find the plates,[69] and when Willard's sister Sally Chase claimed to have found the plates with

---

63. *EMD* 2:67.

64. *EMD* 2:31-32.

65. Quinn, *Early Mormonism*, 138.

66. *EMD* 1:552.

67. Ashurst-McGee, "Moroni as Angel and as Treasure Guardian," p. 56.

68. Quinn, *Early Mormonism*, 140.

69. *EMD* 1:331.

her "green glass,"⁷⁰ they were viewing the plates simply as "gold treasure" (not as a "gold bible") and using established folk practices for locating it. From a treasure-seeking perspective, the supernatural entity that revealed and guarded the treasure was likely conceived as a "treasure-spirit" and Smith's initial inability to recover the plates chalked up to "enchantment."⁷¹ Treasure seekers did not necessarily view their efforts as antithetical to Christianity. The Chases were Methodists, and it does not appear that they viewed treasure seeking per se as incompatible with their religion.⁷² For orthodox Christians, the heterodoxy lay in Smith's claim that he had recovered a "gold bible" and, thus, new scripture.

Others viewed Smith as engaging in necromancy, i.e., as attempting to conjure up the spirits of the dead. This was the view of some in the Smith's extended family, including Emma's Methodist cousins, Joseph and Heil Lewis, and Joseph's devoutly Calvinist uncle Jesse. Emma's cousins, who were slightly younger than Joseph, lived near her parents in Harmony when Joseph and other treasure seekers boarded at the Hales' in 1825 and when Joseph and Emma returned to live there from December 1827 until June 1829. Her cousins, like the rest of her family, were Methodists, and her cousins' parents hosted class meetings in their home. When Smith attended one of these Methodist class meetings in June 1828 shortly after the death of his son, he apparently added his name to the Methodist "class book." Emma's cousins were appalled. As they wrote many years later, "[they] thought it was a disgrace to the church to admit a practicing necromancer, a dealer in enchantments and bleeding ghosts" and told him that they would initiate an investigation of his conduct if he didn't withdraw his name from the Methodist class book.⁷³ Joseph's uncle Jesse had similar thoughts. In his 1829 letter⁷⁴ to Joseph's brother Hiram, Jesse claimed the "gold book [was] discovered by the necromancy of infidelity, & dug from the mines of atheism." The issue for Jesse Smith was not so much what Joseph claimed to have found, but his claim to have interacted with, and perhaps even to have conjured up, spirits of the dead that Jesse viewed as "of the Devil" rather than "of the Lord."

Whether they initially used "spirit" and "angel" interchangeably, the immediate Smith family clearly shifted to "angel" as the preferred designation for the manifestations of long-dead "ancient Nephites," who had once inhabited the Americas. They

---

70. *EMD* 1:342-342.

71. On treasure-seeking and enchantment, see (e.g.) the 1826 court record (Dan Vogel, *Early Mormon Documents*, vol. 4 [hereafter *EMD* 4; Salt Lake City: Signature Books, 2002], 254) and the account of Smith's father-in-law, Isaac Hale (*EMD* 4:284).

72. Lucy Smith indicates that Willard Chase was a Methodist class leader (*EMD* 1:331). After the Wesleyan Methodists broke with the Methodist Episcopal Church in 1844, Chase was ordained as a Wesleyan Methodist preacher (Dan Vogel, *Early Mormon Documents*, vol. 2 [hereafter *EMD* 2; Salt Lake City: Signature Books, 1998], 64).

73. *EMD* 4:311.

74. *EMD* 4:311.

did so, most likely because references to "spirits" more easily conjured up notions of "necromancy," while "angel" and especially "angel of the Lord" emphasized the messenger's connection to the deity. Angels, however, were still intermediaries and I think that the real-time evidence offered by the earliest recorded revelations suggests that it was in 1829 that Smith began recounting revelations that he claimed came directly from the Lord rather than through intermediaries.

If we look at the first recorded revelation, which Smith proclaimed in July 1828 in the wake of the loss of the manuscript, we find that the speaker does not disclose its identity. It addresses Smith directly in the first person but refers to God and the Lord in the third person. The speaker refers ambiguously to "my People the Nephities [sic] & the Jacobites & the Josephites & the Lamanites."[75] If "my people" refers only to the Nephites and not to all the peoples listed, it suggests that the speaker is a Nephite. In subsequent revelations announced by Smith in March and April 1829, the speaker explicitly self-identifies as the Lord, God, or Jesus Christ,[76] leading some to assume that this Lord was speaking in the first revelation as well.[77]

According to the passage already quoted from Lucy's history, however, Joseph told her that when he returned to Harmony and humbled himself in prayer "before the Lord" asking to be forgiven for all that "[he] had done which was contrary to his will[,]...*an Angel stood before me and answered me* saying that I had sinned in that [I] had delivered the manuscript into the hands of a wicked man."[78] After recounting this appearance of the angel, Lucy inserted the text of the 1844 version of D&C 3. In his 1838 history, Smith himself indicated that "*the former heavenly messenger*" mediated this first revelation by appearing and handing him "the Urim and Thummin [sic]," which then enabled him to "enquire [sic] of the Lord through them."[79]

Rather than viewing the appearance of the intermediary and the revelation as two separate events, I think it is more likely that the text of the July 1828 revelation was obtained through a prayer-induced visionary experience of "a heavenly messenger." Such an interpretation is congruent with the third-person references to "God" and "the Lord" in the recorded revelation, with Lucy's account of an angelic appearance, and Joseph's account of the appearance of "the former heavenly messenger," that is, the ancient Nephite who appeared in his 1823 vision.

If this reconstruction is accurate, there is then a marked difference between the first recorded revelation and those Smith proclaimed in March and April 1829. In July 1828, I am suggesting, Smith portrayed his revelation as being *from* an ancient

---

75. *JSP*, D1:9.
76. *JSP*, D1:39.
77. For a fuller discussion, see Taves, *Revelatory Events*, 26-33.
78. *EMD* 1:369–70; emphasis added.
79. *JSP*, H1:246; emphasis added.

Nephite (aka a "heavenly messenger" and "an angel of the Lord") much as he did in September 1823. By the following spring, his revelations were portrayed instead as coming directly from the Lord, God, or Jesus Christ, thus receiving revelations *like* an ancient Nephite.

Other scholars, including Jan Shipps, Richard Bushman, and Dan Vogel, also view the crisis precipitated by the loss of the manuscript as a major turning point.[80] However, they note the shift in Smith's status and self-understanding without linking it to a shift in the identity of the supernatural speaker and, by extension, the source of the revelation. If we don't assume that Smith claimed from the outset that he was in direct communication with the deity—as the later introduction of the first vision suggests, we can detect a shift in who was communicating in early 1829. Prior to that time, the Smiths and their close collaborators were directly engaged with lesser beings—intermediaries—whose identity was hotly disputed by others. When the translation resumed in 1829 with the arrival of Oliver Cowdery, Smith began reporting revelations that came directly from the Lord. Lesser beings still appeared to Smith and his followers, but the authenticity of such appearances could be checked by directly inquiring of the Lord himself.

To conclude, historians have acknowledged that Joseph's self-understanding changed over time, that he made a transition first from a village seer to a Seer who was greater than a prophet or revelator, and then to a Prophet. But, under the weight of Joseph's histories, which launch the church's history with the first vision, they haven't acknowledged that the supernatural beings who were said to appear changed over time as well. Lucy's history brings this to the fore and suggests that the Lord began speaking directly in 1829, not 1820. This shift in who was speaking—I am arguing—led in time to a re-imaging of Mormon origins such that the Lord—not an angel—spoke to Smith directly from the start.

ANN TAVES is Distinguished Professor of Religious Studies at the University of California at Santa Barbara. She is the author of numerous books and articles, including *Fits, Trances, and Visions: Experiencing Religion and Explaining Experience from Wesley to James* (Princeton, 1999); *Religious Experience Reconsidered: A Building Block Approach to the Study of Religion and Other Special Things* (Princeton, 2009); and, most recently, *Revelatory Events: Three Case Studies of the Emergence of New Spiritual Paths* (Princeton, 2016), which includes Mormonism as one of the three emergent paths.

---

80. See Jan Shipps, "The Prophet Puzzle: Suggestions leading to a more comprehensive interpretation of Joseph Smith," *Journal of Mormon History* 1 (1974): 17; Bushman, *Joseph Smith: Rough Stone Rolling,* 69: Vogel, *Joseph Smith: The Making of a Prophet,* 129.

The Palmyra Revival of 1824-25, From Methodist, Presbyterian and Baptist Records: Its Impact on the Restoration Movement

H. Michael Marquardt

Introduction

SHORTLY AFTER THE Joseph Smith Sr. family reunited in the town of Palmyra, New York, the Western Presbyterian Church of Palmyra was incorporated in March 1817.[1] The family eventually made arrangements to purchase about one hundred acres in Farmington (later named Burt and Manchester). The oldest son of the family, 25-year-old Alvin, worked with Russell Stoddard in building a frame home for his parents, brothers, and sisters. Soon thereafter, Alvin died unexpectedly.

The Smith family held Christian beliefs and used the Bible in their religious teachings at home. Joseph Sr. had visionary experiences and avoided organized religion. The elder Smith also believed in treasures buried supernaturally in the earth that could be obtained only through magic rituals.

Palmyra Revival

In Lucy Mack Smith's draft of her history, she relates the family's sorrow after Alvin's death in November 1823. She said, "we could not be comforted because he was not;" she adds a short statement, subsequently crossed out: "[a]bout this time their [sic] was a great revival in religion and the whole neighborhood was very much aroused to the subject and we among the rest flocked to the meeting house to see if their [sic] was a word of comfort for us that might releive [sic] our over charged feelings."[2] Her history continues:

---

2. Lucy Mack Smith, History, 1844-1845, book 4, Church History Library, Church of Jesus Christ of Latter-day Saints, Salt Lake City, UT; Lavina Fielding Anderson, ed., *Lucy's Book: A Critical Edition of Lucy Mack*

[t]here was <at this time> a man then laboring in that place to effect a union of all the churches that all denominations might be agreed to worship God with one mind and one heart This I thought looked right and tried to persuade My Husband to join with them as I wished to do so myself and it was the inclination of them all [her children] except Joseph he refused from the first to attend the meeting with us He would say Mother I do not wish to prevent you from going to meeting or joining any church you like or any of the Family who desire the like only do not ask me to go <do so> for I do not wish to go But I will take my Bible and go out into the woods and learn more in two hours than you could if you were to go to meeting two years.

While no date is given in her recollection, Lucy Smith placed the "union of all the churches" after Alvin's death. There were a number of churches holding services in the Palmyra area, *viz.*, Methodist, Presbyterian, Baptist, and Quaker. While the Methodists held camp meetings in the general area of Palmyra, there had been a revival among the Presbyterians during the earlier winter of 1816-17.

Except for the local Baptist Church of Palmyra, there are no known lists of members who joined other churches during the Palmyra revival and excitement of 1824-25. The revival that impacted Palmyra and other towns was but a small part of the Great Awakening in western New York. What follows is a reconstruction of the Palmyra revival among Methodists, Presbyterians, and Baptists.

First Methodist Episcopal Church of Palmyra

The membership records of the Methodist Church are not available as they were reported as having been destroyed in a fire at Rochester, New York in 1933. Palmyra was on the Ontario circuit within the Ontario district. The local Palmyra newspaper of September 15, 1824 showed the progress of the work of the Methodist Church:

A reformation is going on in this town to a great extent. The love of God has been shed abroad in the hearts of many, and the outpouring of the Spirit seems to have taken a strong hold. About twenty-five have recently obtained a hope in the Lord, and joined the Methodist Church, and many more are desirous of becoming members.[3]

In January 1825 a report by Rev. George Lane, presiding elder of the Ontario district, was published in the *Methodist Magazine* of April 1825 concerning the Lord's work in Palmyra and vicinity. It "commenced in the spring, and progressed moderately until the time of the quarterly meeting, which was held on the 25th and 26th of September" 1824. Rev. Lane wrote:

Smith's Family Memoir (Salt Lake City: Signature Books, 2001), 356-57, words above the line included in brackets. Another portion crossed out included: "[t]he circumstance of this Death aroused the neighborhood to the subject of religion" (355).

3. "Communication," dated "Palmyra, 11th Sept. 1824," *Wayne Sentinel* 1 (September 15, 1824):3, Palmyra, NY.

[f]rom Catharine [circuit] I went to Ontario circuit, where the Lord had already begun a gracious work in Palmyra...About this time [September 25 and 26, 1824] it appeared to break out afresh. Monday evening, after the quarterly meeting, there were four converted, and on the following evening, at a prayer meeting at Dr. Chase's, there were seven. Among these was a young woman by the name of Lucy Stoddard.[4]

(Nineteen-year-old Lucy Stoddard was a cousin of Calvin Stoddard, who would later marry Joseph Smith Jr.'s sister Sophronia.)[5]

Also of contemporary interest was a claim by Joseph Smith Sr. to have heard a rumor that his deceased son Alvin's grave had been disturbed. On September 25, along with some neighbors, he dug up the body of Alvin and found the rumor to be incorrect.[6] Lane further reported:

December 11th and 12th our quarterly meeting for Ontario circuit was held in Ontario... Here I found that the work which had for some time been going on in Palmyra, had broken out from the village like a mighty flame, and was spreading in every direction. When I left the place, December 22[n]d, there had, in the village and its vicinity, upward of one hundred and fifty joined the [Methodist] society, besides a number that had joined other churches, and many that had joined no church.[7]

By February 1825, revivals were reported in the neighboring towns of Williamson and Ontario to the north; in Manchester, Sulphur Springs, and Vienna to the southeast; in Lyons to the east; and in Macedon to the west. Even towns at a greater distance from Palmyra began to experience revival fires, with Mendon to the west and Geneva to the southeast sharing in the evangelical outpouring.

Methodist records give the total membership of the preaching points serviced by a circuit-riding preacher. The increase of 208 reported in the summer of 1825 for the previous year demonstrates that this was a banner year for the Ontario circuit on which Palmyra was located.[8]

---

4. "Revival of Religion on Ontario District," letter of George Lane, January 25, 1825, in *The Methodist Magazine, Designed as a Compend of Useful Knowledge, and of Religious and Missionary Intelligence, for the Year of our Lord 1825*, vol. VIII (New York: Published by N. Bangs and J. Emory, 1825), 8 (April 1825):158-59.

5. Calvin W. Stoddard was baptized on April 3, 1825 (Minutes of the Palmyra Baptist Church, April 3, 1825). Stoddard married Sophronia Smith, who was then a member of the Palmyra Presbyterian Church, on December 30, 1827.

6. "To the Public," *Wayne Sentinel* 2 (September 29, 1824):3, also in issues of October 6, 13, 20, 27 and November 3, 1824.

7. *Methodist Magazine* 8 (April 1825):160.

8. *Minutes of the Annual Conferences of the Methodist Episcopal Church for the Years 1773-1828*, vol. 1 (New-York: Published by T. Mason and G. Lane, 1840), the report of Ontario district in the Ontario Conference for 1824 was 417 white, 4 color (446) and the membership figure for 1825 was 627 white 2 color (471). (1825).

Palmyra Presbyterian Church

The first volume of the Palmyra Presbyterian Church's minutes has been missing since at least 1898. But the records of the Geneva Presbytery, to which the local church belonged, are still extant, and these clearly reflect the revival in the Palmyra congregation. The minutes show that by September 21, 1825, when figures were in for a revival over the winter of 1824-25, "99 have been admitted on examination." As early as February 1825, the Presbytery was called on to:

> bless the Lord for the displays of sovereign grace which have been made <within our boundaries> during the past year. In the congregation of Palmyra, the Lord has appeared in his glory to build up Zion. More than a hundred have been hopefully brought into the kingdom of the Redeemer. The distinguishing doctrines of grace have proved eminently the sword of the Spirit, by which the rebellion of man's heart has been slain. The fruits of holiness in this revival even now are conspicuous. The exertions for the promotion of divine knowledge are greater than formerly. Sabbath Schools, Bible classes, Missionary & Tract Societies are receiving unusual attention, & their salutary influence is apparent.[9]

The *Religious Advocate*, a Presbyterian publication printed in Rochester, was cited in the March 2, 1825 issue of the *Wayne Sentinel*:

> a revival of religion had taken place in the town[s] of Palmyra, Macedon, Manchester, Phelps, Lyons and Ontario, and that more than 200 souls had become hopeful subjects of Divine Grace, &c. It may be added, that in Palmyra and Macedon, including Methodist, Presbyterian and Baptist Churches, more than 400 have already testified that the Lord is good. The work is still progressing.[10]

James Hotchkin wrote, "a copious shower of grace passed over this region in 1824, under the labors of Mr. Stockton, and a large number were gathered into the church, some of whom are now pillars in Christ's house."[11]

---

9. Geneva Presbytery "Records," September 21, 1825, Book D:40; Geneva Synod "Records," October. 6, 1825, 431, both in the Presbyterian Historical Society, Philadelphia, PA. In the Presbytery's Report to Synod, the Palmyra church reported for the year between September 10, 1824, and September 23, 1825, additions of 103 members and a membership jump from seventy-nine to 178 members (130% increase) with forty adult baptisms. See "Presbyterial Reports to the Synod of Geneva," Presbyterian Historical Society. For the quotation, see Geneva Presbytery "Records," February 2, 1825, Book D:27-28.

10. "Religious," *Wayne Sentinel* 2 (March 2, 1825):3, see also p4.

11. James H. Hotchkin, *A History of the Purchase and Settlement of Western New York and of the Rise, Progress, and Present State of the Presbyterian Church in that Section* (New York: Published by M. W. Dodd, 1848), 378.

Palmyra Baptist Church Records

Membership rolls of "the first Baptized [sic] Church in Palmyra," which had a frame meetinghouse west of the village of Palmyra in Macedon Township, includes the names of those added to the membership record. The awakening began on October 20, 1824, when church minutes show that:

> Michael Egleston, Erastus Spear, Lorenzo Spear, Abagail Spear, Belena Byxbe, Minerva Titus, Sophia Rogers, and Harriot Rogers told their Christian experience to the Church and were fellowshipped by the Church and on Thursday following were Baptized by Elder Bradley and Received into the Church.

The minutes of November 20 mention eight more individuals baptized; the November 25-26 minutes name an additional twelve. In December 19 more were added by conversion. In the first four months of 1825, there were 44 additional baptisms. During the months of May-August, there were only three baptized. For the period from October 1824 to August 1825, a total of 94 persons were received on profession of faith and baptized, and an additional 14 were added by letter. The local membership of the church was 132 in 1824 and had grown to 219 by 1825, an increase of 87 over the one-year conference period.[12] This 1824-25 revival received write-ups in a number of publications.[13]

Abraham Spear wrote:

> <in 1824> A Powerful work of the Holy Spirit took place on the hearts of the impenitent, Saints rejoiced and Sinners trembled Several hundred professed to have passed from death to life and out of the number who professed to have obtained a hope in Christ 118 [sic; 108] were added to the Baptist Church under the ministry of James C Barret and Baruch Beckwith."[14]

---

12. "A Book of Records for the First Baptized [sic] Church in Palmyra" (1813-1859), includes minutes for October 16; November 20, 24; December 4, 5, 18, 1824; January 1, 15, 29; February 19; March 5, 19; and April 3, 1825. Original Palmyra Baptist records, American Baptist Historical Society, Atlanta, GA. See also *Minutes of the Ontario Baptist Association, Convened at Penfield, on the 28th and 29th of September 1825* (Rochester: Printed by Everard Peck, 1825), 5.

13. For example, *New-York Religious Chronicle* 2 (November 20, 1824): 154; 3 (April 9, 1825): 58; *Western New York Baptist Magazine* 4 (February 1825): 284; *Western Recorder* 1 (November 9, 1824): 90; 2 (March 29, 1825): 50; *Boston Recorder* 10 (April 29, 1825): 70; 10 (May 20, 1825): 82; *Baptist Register* (Utica), December 3, 1824; March 11, 1825, 7; *American Baptist*, February 1825; *Zion's Herald* 3 (February 9, May 11, 1825), a Methodist weekly in Boston; *American Baptist Magazine* 5 (April 1825):124-25; and the *New York Observer*, May 7, 1825.

14. "A brief History of the <Rise and Progress of the> Baptist Church Formerly Palmyra Now Macedon Wayne Co. and state of New York," 3, reproduced in *First Baptist Church of Macedon, A History of the First Two Hundred Years 1800-2000* (n.p.: Bicentennial Committee of the Church, 2001), 14.

Moving the Palmyra Revival

The first Latter Day Saint publication regarding the Palmyra revival appeared in the letters of Oliver Cowdery during 1834-35 at which time changes in the chronology were being made for theological and financial purposes. This included changing the name of the church, altering the designated site where it had been organized, and revising the text for about a third of the recorded revelations that Joseph Smith had proclaimed. Emphasis was now being placed on priesthood restoration and the establishment of a firm foundation toward a retrospective view of a New Testament church. Altering those original revelatory messages would also permit a revised story of the events in the early life of Joseph Smith Jr.[15]

Oliver Cowdery, evidently obtaining his information from Joseph himself, wrote about "a great awaking [sic]," and Methodist elder George Lane, who had visited the Palmyra area. But rather than placing the ministry into the latter part of 1824 as Lane had done, Cowdery's 1834 letter placed it into 1820 or 1821:

> I shall, therefore, pass over that, till I come to the 15th year of his life. It is necessary to premise this account by relating the situation of the public mind relative to religion, at this time: One Mr. Lane, a presiding Elder of the Methodist church, visited Palmyra, and vicinity. Elder Lane was a tallented [sic] man possessing a good share of literary endowments, and apparent humility. There was a great awakening, or excitement raised on the subject of religion, and much enquiry for the word of life. Large additions were made to the Methodist, Presbyterian, and Baptist churches.—Mr. Lane's manner of communication was peculiarly calculated to awaken the intellect of the hearer, and arouse the sinner to look about him for safety—much good instruction was always drawn from his discourses on the scriptures, and in common with others, our brother's mind became awakened...In this general strife for followers, his mother, one sister, and two of his natural brothers, were persuaded to unite with the Presbyterians.[16]

Cowdery wrote that Joseph's mother united with the Presbyterians, paralleling the event cited in Lucy Smith's own history about joining a church. In his following letter, printed in February 1835, Cowdery made what he terms a correction "in the type" of the excitement in Palmyra as having occurred in 1823, off by one year but still at variance with the earlier 1820-21 date portrayed in his December letter:

> You will recollect that I mentioned the time of a religious excitement, in Palmyra and vicinity to have been in the 15th year of our brother J. Smith Jr's, age—that was an error in the type—it should have been in the 17th.—You will please remember this correction

---

15. H. Michael Marquardt, "Changing Revelatory Messages: A Mormon Example," *John Whitmer Historical Association Journal* 33 (Spring/Summer 2013):122-39.

16. "Letter III. To W. W. Phelps, Esq.," *Latter Day Saints' Messenger and Advocate* 1 (December 1834):42, Kirtland, OH.

as it will be necessary for the full understanding of what will follow in time. This would bring the date down to the year 1823.[17]

It is not known why this change was made, but Cowdery's new claim would now bring new focus to the evening of September 21, 1823, almost two months before Alvin's death.

Names of Smith Family Members Who Joined the Palmyra Presbyterian Church

In 1838 and the following year, a further account by Smith himself placed the revival to an even earlier time period with an expanding emphasis on theology, mentioning by name members of the Smith family who joined the Western Presbyterian Church of Palmyra. The following is an extract relating to the excitement:

> Sometime in the second year after our removal to Manchester, there was in the place where we lived an unusual excitement on the subject of religion. It commenced with the Methodists, but soon became general among all the sects in that region of country, indeed the whole district of Country seemed affected by it and great multitudes united themselves to the different religious parties, which created no small stir and division among the people, Some crying, "Lo here" and some Lo there. Some were contending for the Methodist faith, Some for the Presbyterian, and some for the Baptist...I was at this time in my fifteenth year. My Fathers family was proselyted to the Presbyterian faith and four of them joined that Church, Namely, My Mother Lucy, My Brothers Hyrum, Samuel Harrison, and my Sister Soph[r]onia...I attended their several meetings as occasion would permit. But in [the] process of time my mind became somewhat partial to the Methodist sect[18]

The fact that the names of Joseph's mother and brothers appear later as members of the Western Presbyterian Church of Palmyra (later dropped for nonattendance) is further evidence that the revival Smith had in view involved the local Presbyterian Church.[19] Joseph would have been a man of eighteen years in 1824.

Prior to the time of the Palmyra revival, Orsamus Turner noted Joseph's presence at a Methodist camp meeting and found him "a very passable exhorter."[20] Smith

---

17. "Letter IV. To W. W. Phelps, Esq.," *Latter Day Saints' Messenger and Advocate* 1 (February 1835):78.

18. Manuscript History, Book A-1: 1-2, Church History Library; Karen Lynn Davidson, David J. Whittaker, Mark-Ashurst-McGee, and Richard L. Jensen, eds., *Histories, Volume 1: Joseph Smith Histories, 1832-1844* (Salt Lake City: Church Historian's Press, 2012), 208. First printed in "History of Joseph Smith," *Times and Seasons* 3 (March 15, 1842):727, Nauvoo, IL.

19. "Records of the Session of the Presbyterian Church in Palmyra," 2:11-13, original located at the Western Presbyterian Church of Palmyra, Palmyra, NY.

20. O[rsamus]. Turner, *History of the Pioneer Settlement of Phelps and Gorham's Purchase* (Rochester: Published by William Alling, 1851), 214.

FIGURE 1: *Timeline of the Three Churches in the Palmyra Revival of 1824–25*

METHODIST EPISCOPAL CHURCH	WESTERN PRESBYTERIAN CHURCH	BAPTIST CHURCH
Genesee Conference Ontario District Ontario Circuit	Geneva Synod Geneva Presbytery	Ontario Baptist Association
Palmyra	West Palmyra	First Baptized Church in Palmyra
The work started in the spring of 1824 Sept. 25–28: appeared to break out afresh Dec. 11–12: broke out from the village like a mighty flame		Oct. 20–21, 1824: awakening began, 8 baptized; Nov. 20: 8 baptized; Nov. 25–26: 12 baptized; Dec.: 19 baptized
208 increase in district (Minutes for 1825) Palmyra: about 77 (by Jan. 1825)	99 admitted on examination (Sept. 21, 1825)	Jan.–Apr. 1825: 44 baptized; May–Aug. 1825: 3 baptized; 94 baptized, 14 by letter; Total 108 added names in minutes and also on membership list (Sept. 28–29, 1825)
Location of meeting house: on Vienna Street near the cemetery, 1822–?	*Location of Union church: on Church Street near the cemetery, 1811–32*	*Location of meeting house: on Quaker Road near the cemetery, 1810–35 in Palmyra until 1823, then in Town of Macedon*

About 270 or more individuals joined the three churches during the revival.

also attended the local Methodist class in which members were to "bear one another's burdens." But since "there was no prerequisite for Methodist membership other than a desire for salvation, the societies were open to all, regardless of their spiritual state."²¹ In his earlier 1832 history, Smith had never included the background of a revival in his religious quest, though he did mention his "intimate acquaintance with those differant [sic] denominations."²²

In his climactic 1838-39 history, Smith reported primarily about the discord rather than any harmony among the three Christian churches and affirmed the religious excitement having occurred by 1820. This latest account, written during a time of persecution, was specifically tailored to be faith-oriented in the telling. Smith did not join any of the local churches in this account, "having been forbidden to join any of the religious sects of the day." A visionary experience and the Palmyra revival were two separate events. Placing the revival years earlier created a forewarning episode in Smith's theological quest to explain, in part, why he would not join a church.

Conclusion

The records of the Methodist, Presbyterian, and Baptist churches have dates relating to the revival in Palmyra and surrounding towns occurring during 1824-25. Oliver Cowdery and the Joseph Smith history both claim an earlier background event to clarify Smith's religious development. Churches of the Restoration Movement that refer to the revival usually cite the 1820 date reported in the 1838-1839 account (first published later in the *Times and Seasons*).

The placing of the Palmyra revival before a vision makes this a theological history portraying a religious experience. Topics include such matters as confusion over which church to join and persecution for telling about a vision. Although historians cannot provide evidence for a religious claim, they can indeed tell if such an event fits the historical context. By reinterpreting and moving the historical Palmyra revival mentioned by Lucy Smith, Oliver Cowdery, and Joseph Smith to dates before Alvin Smith's death creates a distinct historical problem.

Joseph Smith's description of his personal history has significance to those in the Restoration movement. His story explains what he regarded as important being a religious leader. A prophet need not be a historian.

H. MICHAEL MARQUARDT (research@xmission.com) is an independent historian and research consultant. He is on the editorial board of the *John Whitmer Historical Association Journal*. He is the compiler of *Early Patriarchal Blessings of The Church of Jesus Christ of Latter-day Saints* (Smith Pettit Foundation, 2007); *Later Patriarchal Blessings of The Church of Jesus Christ of Latter-day Saints* (Smith Pettit Foundation, 2012); author of *Joseph Smith's 1828–1843 Revelations* (Xulon Press, 2013) and co-author with William Shepard of *Lost Apostles: Forgotten Members of Mormonism's Original Quorum of Twelve* (Signature Books, 2014).

How the Erie Canal Corridor Became the Burned-over District: Rochester and the Advent of Mormonism

Bruce W. Worthen

HISTORIANS HAVE long characterized the early nineteenth century as a time when Americans began to abandon subsistence farming in favor of commercial agriculture. This sea change was a principal component of the market revolution that reshaped the nation. This included transformations to the ordering of society, the way people lived, the way they worked, and the way they worshipped.[1] In more recent years, however, historians have called into question just how radical this market revolution really was.[2] They contend that farmers in British North America had been engaged in home and market production simultaneously since the late seventeenth century. Only the ratio of household to commercial production varied, with those living closest to the port cities of the Atlantic devoting the largest percentage of their resources to market uses.[3] While commercial agriculture eventually came to dominate farm production, this change took place over several decades—a pace that does not seem to qualify as a revolution.[4]

In some areas of the country, however, the transformation from household to market production was truly revolutionary in nature. One of these regions was a narrow string of villages in Western and Central New York that formed the opening

---

1. Charles Sellers, *The Market Revolution: Jacksonian America, 1815-1846* (New York: Oxford University Press, 1991), 5–6.

2. Daniel Walker Howe, *What Hath God Wrought: The Transformation of America, 1815-1848* (New York: Oxford University Press, 2007), 5.

3. Richard Lyman Bushman, "Markets and Composite Farms in Early America," *The William and Mary Quarterly* 55 (Summer 1998): 351-374. See also Howe, *What Hath God Wrought*, 40–41.

4. Howe, 525–527. See also Richard Lyman Bushman, "Markets and Composite Farms in Early America," *The William and Mary Quarterly* 55 (Summer 1998): 374.

section of the Erie Canal Corridor. Starting in 1819, villages from Rochester to Utica underwent a transformation that occurred so swiftly that it overwhelmed the ability of society to cope with the sudden change. This was particularly true of Rochester, a small but economically promising village in 1818 that would become the fastest growing city in America in the 1820s. Rochester also became the nation's first boomtown by pulling the neighboring villages of Mendon, Manchester, Canandaigua, and Palmyra into its economic orbit. Soon, Rochester resembled the port cities of the Atlantic and struggled to cope with a burgeoning working class that was young, poor, defiant—and in need of control.[5]

This article argues that the Erie Canal corridor became the Burned-over District when business interests centered in and around Rochester began to promote institutional religion as a means of controlling an increasingly unruly working class. It challenges the conventional narrative that portrays the Second Great Awakening as a movement aimed at rekindling the spiritual fire of a nation that had forgotten God. To the contrary, this article asserts that nineteenth century Americans were a deeply spiritual people who were concerned about their fate in the hereafter. The real religious battle in the Burned-over District was between professional clergy of the institutional churches and the lay practitioners of Christian folk religion. In the 1820s, this conflict spread throughout the Erie Canal corridor—laying the groundwork for Mormonism.

Distance, the First Enemy

It is not surprising that the Burned-over District and the Erie Canal corridor occupied the same general space. The construction of this 365-mile artificial waterway dramatically altered every settlement that it touched. In western and central New York, change came with surprising force as once-small farming villages began to resemble the cultural character of Atlantic port cities. Where once the great distances between backcountry farms and the markets of the East had carried an implacable economic enmity, a continuous waterway from New York's interior to the Atlantic Ocean was now paving the way for the interior's full participation in the market economy.[6]

This great transportation revolution had its roots in the economic ambitions of early nineteenth century New Yorkers who sought to supplant the expensive and unreliable system of overland transportation with a network of interconnected waterways. In 1810, canal commissioner and future Governor DeWitt Clinton embarked

---

5. Paul E. Johnson, *A Shopkeeper's Millennium: Society and Revivals in Rochester, New York, 1815-1837*, 25th Anniversary Edition. (New York: Hill and Wang, 2004), 37–38.

6. Howe, 41.

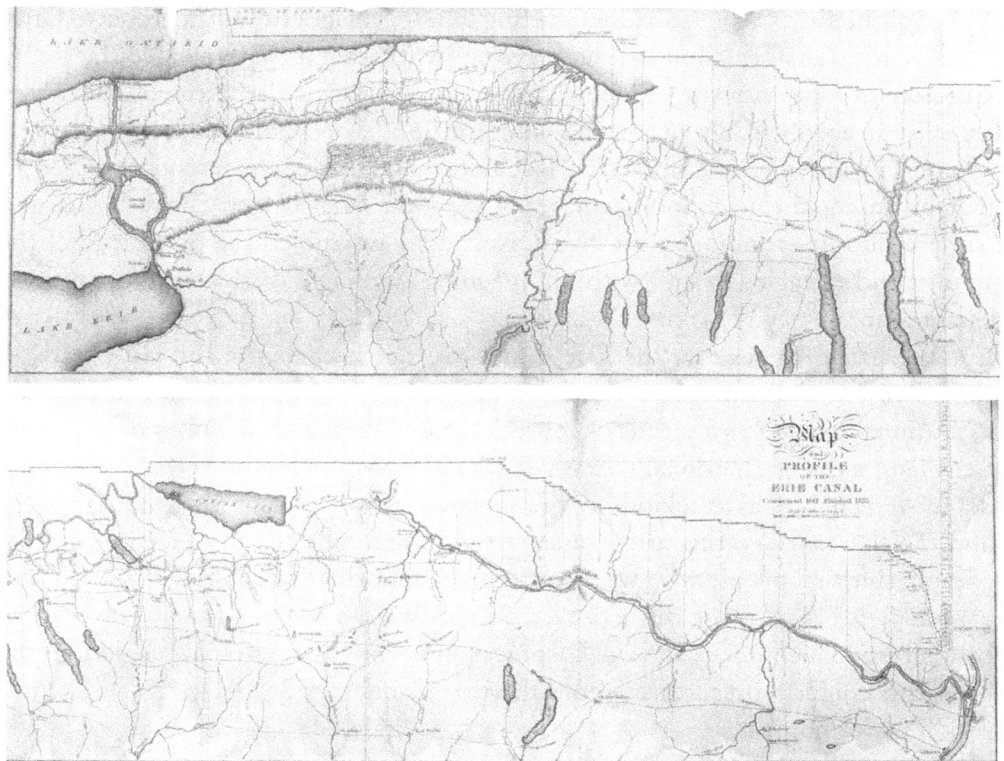

FIGURE 1: *Map and Profile of the Erie Canal. Originally published in: Laws of the State of New York, in relation to the Erie and Champlain canals / Published by authority, under the direction of the Secretary of State (E. and E. Hosford, printers, Albany, 1825).*

on a journey through central and western New York in search of a route for an ambitious artificial waterway that would connect the Hudson River to Lake Erie.[7]

On July 9, 1810, Clinton arrived at Utica—a prosperous village in New York's interior that had benefited from an earlier experiment in providing improvements to the navigable waterways of the region. In 1788, Utica had been a small farming village with only a handful of residents living in shanties. The fortunes of the town improved considerably between 1791 and 1796, however, when a private company built a series of canals and locks on the Mohawk River from Little Falls to Rome. These improvements had eliminated the need to unload cargo and carry it overland past the rapids and falls of the Mohawk—creating a continuous waterway from the Hudson River to Utica and Rome.

These improvements to the Mohawk River were relatively modest, but they had an immediate impact. Utica experienced a dramatic drop in transportation costs and

---

7. Carol Sheriff, *The Artificial River: The Erie Canal and the Paradox of Progress, 1817-1862* (New York: Hill and Wang, 1996), 19.

a corresponding increase in prosperity for the residents of the township.[8] As a result, Utica became the crossroad for trade between the Atlantic and the interior of New York State.[9] By the time of Clinton's 1810 visit, Utica had grown into a prosperous commercial hub with 1,650 residents, 300 houses, four churches, two newspapers, a bank, and a post office.[10] This stood in stark contrast to other townships further west that did not have the benefit of a continuous waterway.

As Clinton travelled deeper into the interior of New York in 1810, transportation became more difficult, the villages became smaller, and the residents less prosperous. He also noticed an increase in the number of squatters and the absence of many of the social, economic, and political institutions that were the hallmarks of his state's more settled cities. This included the absence of organized religious denominations and an increase in apostolic gatherings that included itinerant preachers who emphasized individual worship over institutional religion.[11]

FIGURE 2: *DeWitt Clinton.*
Libary of Congress.

On July 25, 1810, near the village of Lyons, New York, Clinton encountered a Methodist camp meeting in a wooded area with some two hundred people in attendance. Clinton described the scene in his journal saying, "In one place, a man had a crowd around him to listen to his psalm singing; in another, a person was vociferating his prayer." In yet another place a man had his arm around the neck of a second man and was strongly admonishing him to repent of his sins. Clinton noted that the man listened to these exhortations anxiously—"with tear-suffused eyes." Later, Clinton described how four itinerant preachers took turns "preaching up the terrors

---

8. M. M. (Moses Mears) Bagg, *Memorial History of Utica, N.Y.: From Its Settlement to the Present Time* (Syracuse, N.Y.: D. Mason, 1892), 362–363.

9. DeWitt Clinton and William W. Campbell, *The Life and Writings of De Witt Clinton* (New York: Baker and Scribner, 1849), 50. Clinton later indicates that Rome, New York, about sixteen miles to the northwest, could have been a trading crossroads as well, but the policies of the principal landowner responsible for the sale of lots had restricted the growth of the area. See Clinton and Campbell, *The Life and Writings of De Witt Clinton*, 53.

10. Bagg, *Memorial History of Utica, N.Y.*, 21. See also Clinton and Campbell, 47–50.

11. Clinton and Campbell, 58–68.

of hell." Meanwhile, on the road leading to the camp were "persons with cakes, beer, and other refreshments for sale."[12]

On July 26, 1810, Clinton arrived in Canandaigua and encountered another religious curiosity. It seemed that a preacher named Jemima Wilkinson was visiting the town. Clinton wrote in his journal that Wilkinson had some forty followers at nearby Crooked Lake. "She is opposed to war, to oaths, and to marriage; and to her confidential friends she represents herself as Jesus Christ."[13] Wilkinson was but one of several charismatic evangelists in the backcountry of New York.[14]

After a short stay in Canandaigua, Clinton continued his journey west, noting the worsening condition of the land. On the evening of July 27, 1810, after travelling some twenty miles, he stopped at a tavern. In his journal, Clinton wrote that the sign above the establishment contained masonic emblems. He later learned from the owner that these markings were intended "to prevent his debtors from seizing the house." As he settled in for dinner, Clinton discovered that the owner of the tavern was something of a preacher. Instead of engaging in a conventional religious discourse however, he "presented me with a masonic sermon."[15] It seemed that the region was replete with lay preachers and those who claimed membership in Christ's church but did not belong to any particular religious denomination.[16] Much the same phenomenon was present throughout the country at the time.

By the dawn of the nineteenth century, scarcely five percent of the population of America belonged to a church—even though millions regularly attended religious gatherings.[17] Their suspicions of organized religion had their roots in colonial times when churches were often little more than government agencies, and the clergy were primarily patronage appointees. After the Revolutionary War, Americans had largely abandoned these denominations and had become engaged in the practice of folk religion—a form of Christianity that emphasized the spiritual power that ordinary people could claim for themselves. As a result, visions, revelations, speaking

---

12. Clinton and Campbell, 106–107.

13. Clinton and Campbell, 110. See also William N. Fenton, "The Journal of James Emlen Kept on a Trip to Canandaigua, New York," *Ethnohistory* 12 (Autumn 1965): 289.

14. William N. Fenton, "The Journal of James Emlen Kept on a Trip to Canandaigua, New York," *Ethnohistory* 12 (Autumn 1965): 293-295.

15. Clinton and Campbell, 111.

16. Clinton and Campbell, 60–61.

17. Several Methodist preachers commented on the lack of formal church membership in the first generation following the American Revolution. One minister suggested that for every person who joined the church there were a dozen more who simply attended activities open to the public. See John H. Wigger, *Taking Heaven by Storm: Methodism and the Rise of Popular Christianity in America* (New York: Oxford University Press, 1998), 4. See also Gordon S Wood, *Empire of Liberty: A History of the Early Republic, 1789-1815* (Oxford; New York: Oxford University Press, 2009), 50–52.

in tongues, and other forms of individual worship abounded.[18]

This was also a time when apostolic religious movements such as the American Methodism of Francis Asbury, little noted before the Revolutionary War, took the backcountry by storm.[19] Itinerant preachers brought a dynamic form of proselyting to the region, drenching it in spiritual fire.[20] They claimed that their authority came from visions, revelations, and the Bible.[21] Followers of this new religious expression felt empowered to determine the meaning of scripture for themselves and to fashion their own salvation.[22] They refused to allow institutional religions or college-educated clergy to come between them and heaven.[23] With access to the divine so accessible, it was not surprising that formal church membership had fallen into disuse. In the post-revolutionary

FIGURE 3: *Francis Asbury*. Originally published in William Peter Strickland, *The Pioneer Bishop: Or, The Life and Times of Francis Asbury* (New York, Carlton & Porter, 1858), 10.

---

18. Gordon S. Wood, "Evangelical America and Early Mormonism," *New York History* 61 (October 1980): 10. Wood argues that the spiritual enthusiasms of the period had always been present but had been politically suppressed. The American Revolution set these practices free so that Christian folk religion would soon dominate religious worship in the new nation, especially in the West.

19. There were approximately 1,000 Methodists in 1774; nonetheless, it grew to become America's largest single denomination in just a generation. See Wigger, *Taking Heaven by Storm*, 3.

20. Nathan O. Hatch, *The Democratization of American Christianity* (New Haven: Yale University Press, 1989), 5–6. See also Edward Pessen, *Jacksonian America: Society, Personality, and Politics*, Revised edition. (Urbana: University of Illinois Press, 1985), 70.

21. Hatch, 10–11. Methodist preacher Freeborn Garrettson declared, "I also know, that both sleeping and waking, things of a divine nature have been revealed to me." See also Hatch, 79. The author quotes Baptist preacher Joseph Thompson who claimed that the Prophet Isaiah had appeared to him at age sixteen and called him to the ministry.

22. Gordon S. Wood, "Evangelical America and Early Mormonism," 18. See also Hatch, 162.

23. Americans did not tie religiosity to membership in an institutional church during this period. Churches that attracted members tended to call themselves "denominations" rather than "sects," suggesting an egalitarian rather than elitist orientation. See Wood, *Empire of Liberty*, 579–582.

world, Americans had democratized Christianity and practiced a form of religion that historian Nathan Hatch calls "of the people, by the people, and for the people."[24]

Meanwhile, for those seeking the community and structure of an institutional church, Freemasonry offered a practical substitute.[25] Professional men and middling sorts often turned to Masonic lodges for the sake of fraternity, mutual business interests, and a discussion of moral principles while holding fast to their right to interpret scripture for themselves and to approach God directly.

The lives of the people in New York's interior would soon undergo a drastic change, however. While most people would conform to life in the market economy, one notable family would seek to swim against the social, economic, and religious currents. The family of Joseph and Lucy Smith would one day produce a new social order with its own distinct character, but on arrival in the corridor area, they could not have been more typical of the families in the region.

The Smith Family in Palmyra

When Joseph Smith Sr. and his wife Lucy moved their family to the Palmyra area in the winter of 1816-17—just before the groundbreaking of the Erie Canal—they adopted the traditional economic practices of the frontier settlement. They hired out their labor and engaged in home industry to raise funds to purchase a farm.[26] By July 1820, the family had contracted for unimproved acreage in nearby Manchester and had begun clearing the land and preparing it for cultivation and habitation.[27] The Smith family members seemed to fit in well with the social, economic, and religious conventions of the region, well-suited as they were to the apostolic traditions of life at the edge of settlement.

Lucy's brother Jason had been an itinerant preacher who eschewed organized religion and felt that the "gifts of the spirit" were within the grasp of lay Christians.[28] Lucy shared both her brother's convictions and his skepticism about the teachings of the traditional denominations of the day. She attended church services of various congregations during her early life, but chose not to join any of them. "I concluded that my mind would be easier if I were baptized and I found a minister who was

---

24. Wigger, 104–110.

25. Wood, *Empire of Liberty*, 50–52.

26. Richard L Bushman, *Joseph Smith: Rough Stone Rolling* (New York: Alfred A. Knopf, 2005), 30–32.

27. H. Michael Marquardt and Wesley P Walters, *Inventing Mormonism: Tradition and the Historical Record* (San Francisco]; Salt Lake City: Smith Research Associates; Distributed by Signature Books, 1998), 4–6.

28. Bushman, *Rough Stone Rolling*, 12–13.

FIGURE 4: *Methodist Camp Meeting, 1819. Libary of Congress.*

willing to baptize me and leave me free from membership in any church," Lucy would write years later.[29]

Meanwhile, Joseph Smith Sr. had certain doubts about organized religion that he had gleaned from his father Asael, who felt that none of the denominations of his day taught doctrine that was consistent with scripture. While willing to visit religious gatherings, Joseph Sr. had no interest in converting.[30] This led the Smith family, like most in the backcountry, to gravitate toward religious movements that did not require formal membership, like the Methodists.

By 1820, some 250,000 people claimed to be Methodist adherents, but church leaders estimated that fewer than ten percent of them were formal members. Nonetheless, Methodists were accommodating of these non-member adherents and even allowed them to assume certain roles in the church.[31] This included becoming an "exhorter" who engaged in public sermonizing. While technically an exhorter required a license to engage in preaching, church leaders did not strictly enforce the

---

29. Lucy Smith, *Lucy's Book: A Critical Edition of Lucy Mack Smith's Family Memoir* (Salt Lake City: Signature Books, 2001), 279–281.

30. Dan Vogel, *Religious Seekers and the Advent of Mormonism* (Salt Lake City, Utah: Signature Books, 1988), 26–27.

31. Wigger, 3–5.

requirement.[32] Methodists also valued personal religious experiences, such as visions and prophetic dreams, while downplaying the importance of college training in theology.[33] In addition, the Methodists embraced the religious enthusiasms of the day, including speaking in tongues, displays of ecstasy, and the sharing of supernatural experiences. This contrasted with the traditional pre-American Revolution denominations that had denounced and suppressed such expressions.[34]

Even in the face of the discouragement of the traditional denominations of British North America, the early Smith family had embraced religious enthusiasms before the Revolution and were continuing to practice them generations later in Palmyra. As a teenager, Joseph Smith Jr. had the reputation of being an effective exhorter who freely shared his visionary experiences while staying aloof from church membership.[35] His fellow residents practiced and valued these traditions as well. It would not be long, however, before fierce resistance would arise against this rich and widely accepted religious tradition.[36]

In nearby Rochester, unforeseen social disorder among the workers was getting out of hand, much to the dismay of the landowners and trade masters who had little means of control. But the city's business leaders quickly saw the wisdom in turning to the socializing influence of professional ministers to reform these unruly workers. It is not surprising that this chain of events began soon after New York's artificial waterway opened for business.

Clinton's Big Ditch

On July 4, 1817, the construction of the Erie Canal began in earnest. Instead of breaking ground near the Hudson River or Lake Erie, however, work began at the midpoint of the proposed canal in Rome, New York.[37] The plan was to join the villages of Central and Western New York to the Mohawk River at Utica, which would quickly turn the canal into a money-making operation. It proved to be a wise choice.

---

32. Wigger, 29–31.

33. Wigger, 19.

34. Wigger, 104–124.

35. Dan Vogel, *Early Mormon Documents* (Salt Lake City: Signature Books, 2000), 3:50. It is unlikely that Joseph Smith Jr. addressed an entire camp meeting but was most likely one of those on the periphery that DeWitt Clinton described in his journal who expressed their faith for those who wished to listen. See Clinton and Campbell, 106–107.

36. Wigger, 29–30.

37. Sheriff, *The Artificial River*, 9. See also "New York Grand Canal," *Daily National Intelligencer* (Washington), July 22, 1817.

Figure 5: *Rochester, circa 1827.* Originally published in William F. Peck, History of Rochester and Monroe County, New York: From the Earliest Historic Times to the Beginning of 1907 (New York: The Pioneer Pub. Co., 1908), 53.

Within a year, the rapid progress of building the canal had largely silenced the critics. The following year saw long sections of the canal opened to regular traffic.[38]

On October 22, 1819, passengers boarded a canal boat at Rome, New York, to make the first sixteen-mile journey to Utica.[39] By the end of October, another section running west to Syracuse was navigable, producing a dramatic impact on its local economy.[40] Soon, the cost of shipping five bushels of salt from Syracuse to Utica had dropped from one dollar to 31 cents.[41]

With the financial success of the project now assured, the canal commissioners planned the remaining sections of the waterway. By the end of October 1819, they had decided that the Erie Canal would pass through Palmyra and then on to Roch-

---

38. "The Grand Canal," *Rochester Telegraph*, July 21, 1818. This article reported the confidence people now had in the canal project saying that "not a solitary doubt now remains of its complete success." Compare with "Small Fry," *The National Advocate* (New York), July 1, 1817. This editor called the Erie Canal "a wild scheme" and predicted that "the state will have to abandon it."

39. "The Canal," *Daily National Intelligencer* (Washington), November 2, 1819. See also Peter L Bernstein, *Wedding of the Waters: The Erie Canal and the Making of a Great Nation* (New York: W.W. Norton, 2005), 102.

40. "Extract of a Letter from One of the Acting Canal Commissioners, to the President of the Board," *St. Louis Enquirer*, December 8, 1819.

41. "We Understand that Contracts are Already Entered into," *Providence Patriot* (Rhode Island), November 10, 1819.

ester.[42] The move would soon open distant markets to these villages as well, dropping the cost of shipping bulk goods to five percent of what they had been when overland transportation had been the only option.[43] It would also cause a whirlwind of changes as the region moved abruptly from subsistence farming to commercial agriculture.

On July 4, 1820, just three years after construction of the canal had begun, it was opened to Montezuma, New York—thirty miles east of Palmyra.[44] Twice a week, boats made the journey of one hundred miles to Utica, charging passengers four dollars for the two-day trip, including lodging and provisions. Once in Utica, the Mohawk River could transport passengers and cargo to the Hudson River and from there to New York City. Soon residents began to see how valuable the canal would become.[45] Meanwhile, both the Erie Canal and the business of building it were drawing increasing numbers into the working class. During a time when most of the country was still suffering from the economic collapse of 1819, employment opportunities were booming in the corridor with 2,500 workers making good wages while constructing the middle section of the canal.[46]

The partially completed canal also allowed residents in the region to export bulk goods to neighboring villages for a fraction of what it would have cost overland. One resident of Utica noted that a single horse could draw as much weight on the canal as sixty horses on the old rutted roads. This allowed loggers to transport 440 tons of lumber twenty miles on the canal for $50 instead of $1,600 for overland transportation. There were similar savings in the shipping of wheat, salt, and gypsum.[47]

On November 15, 1821, amidst great fanfare, the first canal boats sailed from Palmyra, New York. This initial section had progressed only twenty-eight miles before winter weather had halted construction. By April 15, 1822, however, boats were carrying Palmyra produce all the way to New York City.[48] Palmyra was no longer an isolated village dependent on subsistence farming. It was quickly becoming integrated into the market economy.

On June 19, 1822, the leading newspaper of the village changed its name from *The Western Farmer* to *The Palmyra Herald and Canal Advertiser* and began promot-

---

42. "Speech of his Excellency DeWitt Clinton," *Palmyra Register* (New York), January 19, 1820. See also New York State Canal Commissioners, *Annual Report of the Canal Commissioners, Communicated to the Legislature, February 18, 1820*. (Albany, New York: Websters and Skinners, 1820), 22.

43. Bernstein, *Wedding of the Waters*, 22.

44. "The Fourth of July," *Waterloo Gazette* (New York), July 19, 1820.

45. "Boats–Montezuma & Oneida Chief," *Ontario Repository* (Canandaigua, New York), July 11, 1820.

46. "The Grand Canals," *Maryland Gazette and Political Intelligencer* (Annapolis, Maryland), October 25, 1821. See also Bernstein, 198.

47. "Transportation on the Erie Canal," *Ontario Repository* (Canandaigua, New York), August 1, 1820.

48. "The Launch," *Western Farmer* (Palmyra, New York), November 21, 1821. See also "Internal Navigation," *Western Farmer* (Palmyra, New York), April 17, 1822. For a map of Palmyra with the location of the Erie Canal see Bushman, *Rough Stone Rolling*, 34.

ing Palmyra as an emerging center of commerce with a wealthy and sophisticated population of some 800 residents.[49] The newspaper noted the grist mills, sawmills, and carding machines on nearby Mud Creek, suggesting that the village could soon become a major manufacturing center. It also pointed to the amenities that were appearing in the village, including the existence of a Presbyterian meeting house and the plans to add a Methodist hall as well.[50] Not surprisingly, similar changes were occurring in other villages along the corridor. However, the most dramatic transformation was taking place 25 miles west of Palmyra in Rochester.

By October 23, 1822, boats from Rochester began navigating the canal as well,[51] quickly transforming this once-struggling village into a growing metropolis much like those of the Atlantic port cities.[52] The High Falls of the adjacent Genesee River supplied inexpensive hydropower that allowed Rochester to operate lumber mills, flour mills, and carding machines so much larger and more powerful than those of nearby villages. Thus, it became more profitable for neighboring farmers to ship grain to Rochester for milling rather than doing it themselves.[53] Soon, villages such as Palmyra were growing "wheat up to the doorway" and sending it via the canal both to Rochester for milling and thence to the coastal cities for delivery.[54] The sudden economic transformation of these villages would soon have a dramatic impact on how residents lived, worked, and worshipped.

The Burned-over District

By the 1820s, the Erie Canal had turned the Genesee Valley into one of the largest grain-producing regions of the world. Though Palmyra was an important participant in this economic revolution, Rochester was the epicenter. Thanks to the abundance of hydropower, Rochester was buying large quantities of grain from surrounding villages, milling it, and exporting hundreds of thousands of barrels of flour a year. Much of the money the region's farmers made from selling their grain to Rochester

---

49. "Our Readers Will Perceive," *Palmyra Herald and Canal Advertiser* (New York), June 19, 1822.

50. "Palmyra Village," *Palmyra Herald and Canal Advertiser* (New York), June 19, 1822.

51. "Erie Canal," *Palmyra Herald and Canal Advertiser* (New York), October 23, 1822.

52. "Letters from the North and West, written to a Friend," *Palmyra Register* (Palmyra, New York), October 13, 1818. "Rochester presents a striking instance of the rapid growth of this country. Six years since, what is now a village of one hundred houses was a wilderness. The stumps of trees are still standing in the streets, and the ground remains unlevelled around them." The article notes the advantages of Rochester's waterfalls for powering "a vast number of mills." The author predicts, "This village must, in time, become a large commercial and manufacturing town." See also Sheriff, *The Artificial River*, 10–15.

53. Donald Worster, *A River Running West: The Life of John Wesley Powell* (Oxford; New York: Oxford University Press, 2000), 15–17. The Powell family moved to Palmyra around 1830. They saw wheat fields and lumberyards all along the Erie Canal as residents sought to capitalize on the new link to the industrial center of New York City.

54. Harry L Watson and Eric Foner, *Liberty and Power: The Politics of Jacksonian America* (New York: Hill and Wang, 1990), 27–28.

Figure 6: *Opening of the Erie Canal.* Originally published in Harper's New Monthly Magazine, *June 1893.*

mills was spent in the city. As a result, Rochester became a booming manufacturing center—supplying villages along the canal with clothing, farm tools, and household products. Where once almost everyone in Rochester had made their living from farming, now the majority of adult men were involved in either manufacturing or day labor.[55] These men worked for wages and were no longer dependent on trade masters or landowners for their upkeep—or for their behavior.

With no one exerting a restraining influence over their action, blue-collar workers were soon wreaking havoc over what had once been an orderly society.[56] While the commercialization of agriculture had created prosperity in the region, it was also generating turmoil in the lives of those who had grown up knowing only the familiar rhythms of family farm life.[57] Although binge drinking was the most common response to these conflicts, some communities were also experiencing social unrest, labor violence, and structural poverty.[58] Employers needed a means of controlling the working class if they wanted to maintain their businesses. They soon found an ally in the profession-

---

55. Johnson, *A Shopkeeper's Millennium*, 18–19. See also Sheriff, *The Artificial River*, 149–150.

56. Johnson, 38.

57. Joyce Oldham Appleby, *Inheriting the Revolution: The First Generation of Americans* (Cambridge, Mass.: Belknap Press, 2000), 51. The first generation of post-revolution Americans faced a difficult challenge. On the one hand, universal male suffrage provided men a sense of real voting power, but when they were at work, the fact that they were wage-earners created a master-slave relationship with their employers. This recognition occurred with some suddenness in Rochester, New York. See Johnson, 13. See also Pessen, *Jacksonian America*, 84–86.

58. The members of the new working class were typically landless and dependent on wages, placing them in a precarious situation. See Sellers, 23–26. The insecurity of the working class manifested itself in a variety of antisocial activities of which binge drinking was the most prominent. See Wood, 336–339. For a description of these phenomena in the area where Mormonism was born, see Johnson, 37–42.

al clergy, who were seeking to reclaim religious influence from the itinerant preachers and those practicing folk religion.[59]

Since Rochester was home to thousands of working-class people who resisted the control of their employers, it is not surprising that the city soon became the hub of America's religious revival movement. Soon, as Joseph Smith Jr. famously remembered, "there was an unusual excitement on the subject of religion" that shook the entire region.[60] Professional preachers invaded townships such as Palmyra looking for new converts.[61] And, as they began relaying their message, the growing fear of divine disapproval for working class improprieties began to replace those celebrations of ecstatic experiences of the revival gatherings.[62] The professional clergy then began to sway followers away from itinerant preachers to appropriate the power of religious devotion to themselves in the effort to reform the working class. Business owners supported these efforts and increasingly made piety, as evidenced by church membership, a prerequisite for employment and respectability.[63]

Where once settlers had enjoyed religious gatherings without feeling pressure to join a denomination—now church membership was becoming a necessity for obtaining employment. Moreover, the process of joining and participating in a church required converts to reform their lives. In the Methodist faith, ongoing membership required at least weekly attendance at church-sponsored classes—not Bible study but meetings centered on reforming behavior. Withdrawal of membership for

---

59. Organized religion was a key ally in the social reform movement of the early nineteenth century. See Appleby, *Inheriting the Revolution*, 205–215. Wealthy merchants funded the activities of reformers such as Charles Finney. See Pessen, 71.

60. Church Historian's Office, History of the Church, pp 1-2, Church History Library, Church of Jesus Christ of Latter-day Saints, Salt Lake City, Utah. (hereafter CHL)

61. Johnson, 94–95.

62. Sellers, 28. Sellers argues that by the late eighteenth century, religion had already become divided between those favoring the market-oriented economics of the Atlantic seaboard and the subsistence-oriented economics of the interior. The Second Great Awakening brought market-oriented religion to the interior as well. See Gordon S. Wood, "Evangelical America and Early Mormonism," *New York History* 61 (October 1980): 20. See also Charles Grandison Finney, *Lectures on Revivals of Religion* (New York: Fleming H. Revell, 1868), 9. Revivalist minister Charles G. Finney declared that God had found it necessary to use people's passions to, "produce powerful excitements among them, before he can lead them to obey." He saw this exercise as a temporary expedient, however.

63. Gordon S. Wood, "Evangelical America and Early Mormonism," 13. See also, Johnson, *A Shopkeeper's Millennium*, 120–128. In this study of Rochester, New York, workers who did not belong to a church had difficulty finding a job. Employers desired sober, obedient workers. The author argues that business interests in Rochester saw organized religious institutions as a useful way to control the working class. See also Sellers, *The Market Revolution*, 230–231. Sellers documents the alliance between businessmen and evangelists in the Erie Canal corridor. This phenomenon spread throughout the trans-Appalachian West. See Thomas Ford, *A History of Illinois, from Its Commencement as a State in 1818 to 1847* (Chicago: S. C. Griggs & Co., 1854), 92–94. Former Governor Thomas Ford of Illinois described the conflict between the itinerant preachers and the college-educated professional clergy who were trying to convert the formers' adherents.

drunkenness or antisocial behavior was the penalty for non-adherence and could result in loss of employment.[64]

Soon the professional clergy, with the aid of business interests, were successfully replacing "The Democratization of Christianity" with a new movement they called "The Second Great Awakening."[65] They preached a gospel of obedience, reliability, and sobriety. It was not long before appeals from competing sects had reached a crescendo, turning the Erie Canal corridor into the "Burned-over District."[66] One religious movement, in particular, refused to go along with these plans.

Mormonism and the Working Class

Joseph Smith Jr. took a very different approach to the turmoil of the 1820s than what the professional ministers employed. In many ways, his religious teachings rejected the principles of market capitalism at a time when popular evangelists were embracing them.[67] Mormonism steered a middle course between the era's Evangelical Reform Movement and the Christian folk religion of the past. It was a movement that responded to the changing social, political, and economic landscape of the country but in a way that did not reject belief in dreams, visions, speaking in tongues, or the pursuit of individual communion with the divine. It also honored the rich Methodist tradition of a lay clergy, while disparaging any value of university-trained ministers.[68]

Smith also disputed the value of teaching the workers themselves to cope with the anxieties of the age, opting instead to attempt to reform the institutions of society that he felt were responsible for the turmoil.[69] Soon, Smith was denouncing the

---

64. Wigger, 80–103.

65. Johnson, 93–94. While revivalism appeared in colonial America under the banner of the "The Great Awakening," many historians today argue that later generations of ministers, in trying to spark revivals of their own, exaggerated the significance of the former rival movement. See John Butler, "Enthusiasm Described and Decried: The Great Awakening as Interpretative Fiction," *Journal of American History* 69 (1982): 305-25. See also Jon Butler, *Awash in a Sea of Faith : Christianizing the American People* (Cambridge, Mass.: Harvard University Press, 1990), 164–165. Frank Lambert argues that these exaggerations originated in the writings of eighteenth-century ministers. See Frank Lambert, *Inventing the "Great Awakening"* (Princeton, N.J.: Princeton University Press, 1999), 4–6. See also Sellers, 216–225.

66. Organized, institutionalized religion was not a feature of frontier societies but emerged only during the industrialization process. See Whitney R Cross, *The Burned-over District; the Social and Intellectual History of Enthusiastic Religion in Western New York, 1800-1850.* (Ithaca: Cornell University Press, 1950), 70.

67. Sellers, 216–225. Sellers sees Joseph Smith and Charles Finney at opposite ends of the spectrum when it came to supporting market principles.

68. Gordon S. Wood, "Evangelical America and Early Mormonism," 21-22.

69. For a comparison of Joseph Smith and Alexander Campbell on the subject of biblical rationalism see RoseAnn Benson, "Alexander Campbell: Another Restorationist," *Journal of Mormon History* 41 (October 2015): 3. For a comparison of Alexander Campbell and Joseph Smith on the subject of market reforms see Bushman, *Rough Stone Rolling,* 149, 155.

competition for converts in the Burned-over District as an abomination rather than a glorious Great Awakening.

While most in Palmyra succumbed to the pressure to join a church, Smith demurred. He testified that since God had told him that the trained ministers seeking new members were corrupt,[70] he would institute a new form of Christian republicanism that could restore the original structure of Christianity. Against the Bible-based arguments of his detractors, he presented a new book of scripture whose sacred storyline of Hebrews in early America would resolve many disputed theological issues of the day. This Book of Mormon's vivid narrative and its author's charisma would persuade a rapidly growing group of working-class followers to join his movement.[71]

Smith and his followers then boarded the ships at Palmyra and travelled the Erie Canal to bring his new religion to other disordered towns in the Burned-over District. Soon Mormonism would spread to Ohio, where Smith sought to establish an American Zion with a novel form of Christian communalism using a system of "stewardships" and "consecrations" to redistribute wealth.[72],[73] His religion seemed a combination of spiritual fire and organizational innovation with its "School of the Prophets" to assist its leadership.[74] Not surprisingly, the movement attracted a host

---

70. Church Historian's Office, History of the Church, pp. 2-3.

71. The classically trained preacher Alexander Campbell was furious that the new book posited Smith's own answers to the most pressing doctrinal questions of the day. He wrote, "This prophet Smith, through his stone spectacles, wrote on the plates of Nephi, in his book of Mormon, every error and almost every truth discussed in N. York for the last ten years. He decides all the great controversies - infant baptism, ordination, the trinity, regeneration, repentance, justification, the fall of man, the atonement, transubstantiation, fasting, penance, church government, religious experience, the call to the ministry, the general resurrection, eternal punishment, who may baptize, and even the question of freemasonry, republican government, and the rights of man. All these topics are repeatedly alluded to." See *Millennial Harbinger*, February 1831, p. 93. The "Golden Bible" proved especially popular with those disillusioned with Methodists' doctrines and Campbellites' scriptural debates. See Wigger, 19. Where the Baptists often argued over doctrine, the Methodists emphasized piety and personal religious experience.

72. Richard S. Van Wagoner, *Sidney Rigdon: A Portrait of Religious Excess*, 1st ed. (Salt Lake City: Signature Books, 1994), 85–87. Joseph Smith used stronger organizational techniques in his United Firm than was present in more typical communal societies. Rather than literally "having all things in common," a Mormon Bishop assigned stewardships over material wealth to specific individuals and collected donations or "consecrations" of property.

73. Mark Ashurst-McGee, "Zion Rising: Joseph Smith's Early Social and Political Thought," (Tucson, Arizona: Arizona University Press, 2008), 201–206.

74. Kirtland Council Minute Book December 1832–November 1832, January 22, 1833, CHL. This document contains minutes of Church meetings as well as the deliberations of the Latter-day Saint leadership. The minutes of a January 22, 1833 meeting record, "Great and Glorious were the divine manifestation of the Holy Spirit. Praises were sung to God & the Lamb besides much speaking & praying, all in tongues." See also the entry for January 23, 1833. For information on the School of the Prophets see Kirtland Council Minute Book December 1832–November 1832, May 4, 1833, CHL. In this meeting the leadership of the Church discussed "the necessity of building a school house" to educate the Elders of the Church. This was pursuant to a Joseph Smith revelation to "become acquainted with all good books, and with Languages, Tongues & people &c. &c." See Joseph Smith, Robert J Woodford, and Steven Craig Harper, *The Joseph Smith Papers: Revelations and Translations Volume*

of working-class followers; most of them from the ranks of disaffected Apostolic Methodists and Campbellite Reformists.[75]

Conclusion

While Mormonism is often seen as an esoteric religion from Palmyra based on iconoclastic principles, it can perhaps be better understood as a working-class movement that emanated from the social upheaval of the greater Rochester community. The same is true of the Second Great Awakening—which historians have usually cast as a revival of religious fervor rather than as an attempt to re-enthrone institutional religion as a means of social control. Most importantly, perhaps, is the fact that seeing the revival movements of this period in working-class terms reveals that what was burning in the Burned-over District was not a renewed interest in religious doctrine per se—but a fierce debate over which spiritual paradigm was best adapted to the turmoil of the age.

BRUCE W. WORTHEN is an independent researcher from Salt Lake City, Utah. He holds a PhD in American History from the University of Utah. His is currently writing a biography of John Milton Bernhisel entitled *Out of the West: John M. Bernhisel and Art the of Mormon Diplomacy*. This is his second article for the *John Whitmer Historical Association Journal*.

---

1 : *Manuscript Revelation Books* (Salt Lake City: Church Historian's Press, 2011), 383. Original in Kirtland Revelation Book 2, March 8, 1833, CHL.

75. John G Turner, *Brigham Young, Pioneer Prophet* (Cambridge, Massachusetts; London, England: The Belknap Press of Harvard University Press, 2012), 27, 32.

Layered Grief in the Burned-over District: Religious Ecstasy as a Healing Balm

Russell L. Osmond

WHY DO PEOPLE in a religious context so often simply continue to "believe" despite all evidence that disputes the very foundation of those beliefs. Leon Festinger answered this question in 1957 with his book-length treatise *When Prophecy Fails* in which he introduced the concept of "cognitive dissonance."[1] Unfortunately, cognitive dissonance does little to explain the intensity or frequency of the "ecstatic" religious excitement in the burned-over district. This paper will explore an alternative dynamic: that the common denominator of the era was not religious revival at all but was instead *constant chaos*.

Surviving any form of constant chaos is akin to dying and starting over and perceiving constant chaos with the expectation of more to come might be termed "forever-grieving," i. e. being confronted with new "layers" of grief stacked on top of the previous ones. It thus becomes a kind of "grief-layer-cake."

Coping with constant chaos equates to enduring what Kubler-Ross[2] defined as the "grief process." The sequence is predictable and universally experienced in five steps as follows:

1. Denial (almost instantly)
2. Anger
3. Bargaining
4. Depression
5. Acceptance

---

1. Leon Festinger, H.W. Riecken, and S. Schacter, *When Prophecy Fails: A Social and Psychological Study of a Modern Group that Predicted the Destruction of the World.* (Minneapois: University of Minnesota Press, 1956).
2. Elisabeth Kübler-Ross, *On Death and Dying* (New York: MacMillan, 1969).

The five steps are additive, and all affected persons move through them sequentially at variable paces. But when another traumatic event strikes in the middle of the steps, the five automatically begin all over again, starting with fresh denial. The result is that a person submerged in chaos can be experiencing multiple grief levels at the same time, becoming even more disorganized. The concept is simple and the clinical science is well established.

In this way, understanding the Kubler-Ross grief cycle may help to illuminate the origins of the explosive ecstasy that so typified the burned-over district, that period which became the fountainhead of Mormonism (Smith-Rigdon Movement). The "burned-over" term was best characterized by Whitney Cross in his classic study,[3] and the era continues to be revisited by scholars such as Linda K. Pritchard and Ann Taves.

This country was barely forty years old when it went stumbling awkwardly westward with what would later become justified as America's manifest destiny. God was on the side of America and the multitude pressing ever further into the Northwest Territory felt there was no limit to the opportunity to build a better future. All could simply keep moving à la *Pilgrim's Progress* (one of the few books possessed by the bulk of those in constant motion) whose premise was that "we win in the end."

As a result, the 1820s experienced a totally new form of constant chaos in conjunction with the building of the Erie Canal. Once the first shovel of dirt was moved from "Clinton's Ditch," as its critics called it, chaos ensued eastward toward Albany and westward toward Buffalo/Rochester all at once. An urgent, topsy-turvy migration of "different folk" piled up all along its route as immigrants with multiple languages and limited means became the workforce. Boomtowns became the canal's trademark, and speed was of the essence. Nothing remained stable from the Mohawk Valley to the Finger Lakes to Lake Ontario, even after the canal's completion on October 26, 1825. Change and chaos were the only constants.

Unique to this growth spurt in American westward movement was the ubiquity of setbacks and disappointments experienced by all involved in the canal's construction. As engineers figured out new ways to fabricate something never before built, the human cost in injury and destruction became the price of entry for nearly all involved. One is hard-pressed to find many printed materials illuminating the immensity of human suffering during the canal's construction; instead, the written record was heavily focused on the canal's progress and promise.

Personal setbacks suffered by the builders and their families were celebrated as something to be taken in stride with a "never let them see you sweat" attitude. As would be described in Upton Sinclair's *The Jungle*[4] a century later, there would always

---

3. Whitney Rogers Cross, *The Burned-over District: The Social and Intellectual History of Enthusiastic Religion in Western New York, 1800–1850* (Ithaca: Cornell University Press, 1950).

4. Upton Sinclair, *The Jungle* (New York: Doubleday, 1906).

be new hands to replace those who stumbled and, for those who did stumble by whatever means, it would represent personal failure.

Enter the Kubler-Ross five steps. In the chaos of the burned-over period, before anyone could process through all steps of one grief experience, too often another would unexpectedly strike. This would lead to layer upon layer of unprocessed grief piling upon one another, leading to the denial-anger-bargaining-depression-acceptance sequence restarting over and over again with each new disappointment. The resulting cacophony would frequently disrupt the evolving grief process of each previous setback until the sufferer would be overwhelmed with conflicting emotions/reactions.

Enter Ecstasy as the Antidote

When one is emotionally overwhelmed, the pursuit of a safe refuge becomes paramount in importance. It's the drowning person hoping against hope for a last-minute life vest to appear. The grasping for anything that could bring "escape" from the fear of cataclysm heightens the intensity to seek whatever balm becomes available. As individuals thus "grasp at straws," they may often find respite in the release of ecstasy, however it may be found. Most of the religious expressions portrayed in the burned-over district's photos and monographs describe a "whirling dervish" kind of extreme ecstasy. Indeed, the coiner of the phrase "burned-over district" was a Protestant pastor in the Rochester area (a frustrated Charles G. Finney), who was angry about how all this explosive religious ecstasy detracted from his ability to conduct a sensible religious service!

Simply put, it was not revivals *per se* that induced the outpouring of ecstatic religious experience in the 1820s in central New York. It was *emotional exhaustion*. The revivals merely provided a rapturous escape medium for those whose grief-layer-cakes were piling up tier upon tier. Statistics of church membership for the period indicate that folks did not join churches so much as they chased after them to find temporary relief.

This, then, is an alternative interpretation to Joseph Smith's version of how the story happened. Even so, his repeated ecstasy-stimulating healings, angelic visitations, and continuous revelations through the ensuing fourteen years of wearisome confrontation and resettlement did, in fact, result in his church's impressive growth, migration, and metastability all the way to 1844. It was his own charismatic genius that produced those rapturous releases that his followers would embrace and emulate through their own flights from hopelessness.

The Kubler-Ross schema is also helpful in understanding why the various divergences in the Smith-Rigdon Movement blew apart upon Smith's unexpected death. Without the living presence of their charismatic prophet providing those excursions into ecstasy, the transformative magic was gone, along with the much of the hope that it had promised.

The mountain and prairie groups that would come into being reacted in different fashion to Smith's loss during their respective first centuries, and neither would be in the ecstatic tradition. Brigham Young chose to focus on the early Christians' martyrdom/persecution narrative to stir the emotions of his followers (complete with the Salt Lake Valley's very own Jordan River and Dead Sea). Joseph Smith III, however, chose a more emotionally subdued mien to build his organization in a spirit of pragmatism.

The Utah group survived against all odds because of its resilience and because its members were ever reminded that their persecutions merited temporal blessings in proportion to their personal worthiness. Every mention of "pioneer heritage" and every annual Pioneer Day would be celebrated with reference to that "veil of tears." This fortress mentality, the prevailing "us vs. them" approach to problems, became a hardwired feature of the collective Mormon psyche. Brigham Young, the Lion of the Lord, ruled with a velvet-covered iron fist, fortifying his church against the "Gentiles" until the 1950s when President David O. McKay turned the membership outward beyond "the valleys of the Rockies" to face the world beyond.

The Midwestern group took a different approach. Its first century defined those burned-over years ahistorically, refusing to accept its rival group's version of events. To govern the church, the so-called "pragmatic prophet," Joseph Smith III, chose a variation of Robert's Rules of Order to build in a set of rational steps to create a consensual church.

In the process, both groups found ways to proselyte and grow using very different techniques: Brigham's nostalgic emotionality vs. Joseph III's rationality. The latter buried its grief-layer-cakes in small, close-knit communities that would ultimately unify in proximity to the larger Christian body, hence its new name *Community* of *Christ*. Its redirected focus on "correct factual history as legitimate legacy" has largely assuaged the lingering torment of the 1980s. Ecstasy has never been an antidote for chaos for these church families whose annual Reunion traditions kept the spirit alive absent the charismatic zest of their burned-over past.

The Intermountain faction, in contrast, has kept its "suffering servant" narrative alive through updated media presentations of whatever setbacks are faced and overcome. The multi-media expertise of the church has received numerous awards for its creativity in keeping this narrative vibrant across different cultures, including those of the Third World. But ironically, the connectivity of the internet has deprived the church leadership of its customary control of the narrative it once possessed, and the resulting spike in member resignations has often left many of these former followers in internal disarray, forcing them to deal with their emotional crises without their previous community support as they encountered the scholarship of an amended historical paradigm.

In conclusion, it is reasonable to assume that the missing link in understanding the origins of the burned-over district's fervor lies in the cacophony of so many uprooted lives who found themselves digging not only a ditch but a veritable grave of grief as well.

It isn't easy being grieved.

Russ Osmond, PhD, is founder and president of Change Strategies International, Inc., founded in 1987 in Atlanta, Georgia. An internationally published author in three disciplines, his lifetime focus has been why people do what they do, believe what they do, and change what they do. Behavior modification "how to" is his primary focus.

The Family that Built Canals

Vickie Cleverley Speek

Introduction

Sometimes you stumble upon a story that is so rich and full, you can't let it go.[1] I first came across the David Sanger family about twenty years ago when I was researching and writing my book about James Strang, one of the proposed heirs to Joseph Smith Jr. after Smith died in 1844.[2] I knew that Strang's father-in-law had worked as a contractor on the Illinois and Michigan (I&M) Canal. A portion of that canal is located only a couple of miles from our former home in north central Illinois, so my husband and I took a field trip down the waterway to check out the sites.

The I&M Canal, which was built from 1836 to 1848, is mostly abandoned now, but in Ottawa, Illinois, about thirty miles west of our home, we found the remains of an amazing stone aqueduct that was built over the Fox River in 1842.[3] At 464 feet of length, it was the greatest engineering feat of the entire ninety-six-mile long canal. The aqueduct was from four-to-six feet deep, and canal boats up to one hundred feet long floated in the water over top of this river, kind of like a long modern-day water slide. A boardwalk ran beside it where a mule and mule driver walked to pull the boat along. A sign along the riverside park said this aqueduct was built by David Sanger and his sons.

A short time later, I read some letters from a highly intelligent, disabled woman named Louisa Sanger who had corresponded with James Strang in the 1840s. Louisa and her family had lived in Ottawa, Illinois, and were Mormons. The connection was obvious.

Intrigued, I began to research the family. I soon learned the Sangers are considered some of the most important leaders in the early settlement of northern Illinois and in the development of Chicago. In addition to their work on the I&M Canal and the Erie Canal, the Sangers purchased stone quarries and built many famous buildings, including the Joliet Penitentiary and the Chicago Water Tower. The family also invested in a line of stagecoaches that monopolized the entire Midwest, including the stagecoach that brought Joseph Smith to safety after his arrest in Dixon, Illinois, in June 1843. One of the Sanger sons, Lorenzo, built more than 450 miles of railroads in Illinois, Missouri, and California and, at the time of his death in 1875, was arranging a huge partnership with a new company called the Union Pacific Railroad.[4] Lorenzo and his brother James supplied northern troops during the Civil War and partnered in building four ironclad, monitor-class ships for the U. S. government.[5]

The women in the Sanger family are particularly important to this article.[6] Mary Palmer Sanger, David's wife and mother of his children, was their connection to the Church of Jesus Christ of Latter-day Saints.[7] Mary Louisa Sanger, called Louisa, one of David's daughters, was well acquainted with James Strang, Brigham Young, James Brewster, and many other intellectuals of the day.[8] LDS records show she was sealed as a plural wife to Hyrum Smith, brother of Joseph Smith Jr.[9] David's daughter Harriet and a daughter-in-law were married to prominent physicians,[10] and one of David's granddaughters married George Pullman, the Chicago millionaire who invented the Pullman Palace Railroad Sleeping Cars.[11]

The Sanger family is representative of the expanding United States and exemplifies the pioneering spirit of the mid-nineteenth century. The family participated in the religious fervor that embodied the "Second Great Awakening," and several members joined the Church of Jesus Christ of Latter-day Saints.[12] Although they investigated the claims of James J. Strang and other would-be prophets after Joseph Smith's death, none of the immediate family stayed active in the church. They instead chose to express their beliefs individually and turned their interest to service organizations such as the Knights Templar, the Freemasons, and women's organizations.

---

4. *Magazine of Western History*, November 1890-April 1891, 13:707-11.

5. "James is down the Mississippi River at Memphis, and Vicksburg, and all along the country, buying cotton and speculating in various things." Louisa Sanger to My Dear Friends, February 18, 1863. Eliza Rich Correspondence. The ships were the *Tuscumbia, Indianola, Chillicothe,* and the *Etlah,* the last being a full-blooded monitor. See Steel, "William Alexander Steel (1836-1879)," University of Mississippi, http://home.olemiss.edu/~mudws/family/wasteel.html, citing *History of Will County, Illinois* (Chicago: Wm. Le Baron Jr. & Co., 1878; digitized version, Urbana: University of Illinois, 2007), 712-14, https://archive.org/details/historyofwillcouoochic/page/712/mode/2up.

6. This article does not name all the Sanger children. See Steel for genealogical information.

7. See Steel. Mary (Polly) Palmer was born December 31, 1783, in Plainfield, Sullivan, New Hampshire, to Aaron Palmer and Mary Sherman Reed. She married David Sanger on July 8, 1806 in Littleton, New Hampshire.

8. See Steel. Louisa was born in New Hampshire on March 26, 1813. See also, Louisa's obituary in the *Ottawa Free Trader*, Saturday, August 18, 1877. She was never (legally) married and had no children.

9. Susan Easton Black, comp., "Membership of the Church of Jesus Christ of Latter-day Saints, 1830-1848," Ancestry, https://www.ancestry.com/search/collections/5333/.

10. See Steel. The daughter was Harriet Aurelia Sanger. She was born May 1, 1819, and married Dr. John A. Henricks (1811-1876) of South Bend, Indiana. She died before 1854. Mary Miles Sanger was the wife of Dr. William Alonzo, the second son in the Sanger family.

11. See Steel. Harriet Amelia Sanger (1843-1922) was the daughter of David's third son, James Younger.

12. The early church has had several name changes over the years, and there were several offshoots, so the members of the organizations will all be called Mormons in this article.

Some Mormon history researchers have restricted their focus to the relationship family members had to the church. Had I done that, I would have missed out on learning of a remarkable family's many historically important experiences.

David Sanger started his family's long westward migration from New England. "He followed the work of building canals, a task that included felling trees, removing stumps, excavating the channel (often through solid limestone), and building locks and aqueducts."[13] Incidentally, since Alfred Nobel did not invent dynamite until 1867, the Sangers were limited to black powder in their endeavors. Only a few canals were operating in the United States at this time, and none of them were connected to major waterways. In 1810, Congress voted to fund a series of canals across the country, including the Erie and the Illinois & Michigan. David Sanger worked on both of these and many more.[14]

Influence of the Erie Canal

The 363-mile-long Erie Canal was a significant freight route that went from New York City and the Atlantic Ocean to Buffalo and the Great Lakes. The original channel was forty feet wide and four feet deep with dirt heaped along each side to form a ten-foot-wide walkway known as a towpath. Horses or mules pulled the boats along the towpath, led by a mule driver called a hoggee. When completed in 1825, the Erie was the second-longest canal in the world.[15] "At a time when bulk grounds were limited to pack animals (250 pound maximum) and there were no railways, water was the most cost-effective way to ship bulk goods. It was estimated that four horses could pull one ton of goods twelve miles a day over an ordinary road, but in the same period they could pull 100 tons of goods twenty-four miles by water.[16]

The Erie Canal increased population in existing towns and initiated the construction of exciting new ones. It provided a rapid migration route for settlers wanting to go west. The Louisiana Purchase became a territory of the United States in 1803, only thirteen years before the canal was begun, and Americans were anxious

---

13. David Sanger was born in 1782 in Framingham, Massachusetts, the son of David Sanger (1751) and Rheuhama Nutt (1753). Steel. There is circumstantial evidence David learned canaling in Massachusetts, where the Middlesex canal was constructed between 1793 and 1803. The 27-mile long Middlesex Canal played a significant role in the early industrialization of Massachusetts. "Middlesex Canal Archeological Reconnaissance Survey, Massachusetts," Middlesex Canal, September 1998, www.middlesexcanal.org/Report.html.

14. Ron Vasile, "The Start of Chicago's Maritime History–The I&M Canal," I&M Canal National Heritage Area, http://www.canalcor.org/CCA2005/alngcnl.html.

15. Construction on the Erie Canal started July 4, 1817, at Rome, New York and was completed on October 26, 1825. The canal was first used in 1821. The longest canal was in China. See "Erie Canal," Wikipedia, https://en.wikipedia.org/wiki/Erie_Canal.

16. Archer Butler Hulbert, *Historic Highways of America: The Erie Canal* (Library of Alexandria, 1904), 38-46. https://books.google.com (many vols.). Also, Mary M. Root, "The Building of the Erie Canal," Survey History, http://www.surveyhistory.org/building_the_erie_canal.htm.

Figure 1. *Erie Canal and Towpath.*

to reach those new lands and markets.[17] A trip that could have taken six weeks prior to canal construction now took less than a week and cost a tenth as much. In 1825, the first year the canal was completed, more than 40,000 people were passengers. The canal also served as the last leg of the Underground Railroad, ferrying runaway slaves to Buffalo at the US/Canada border.[18]

A portion of the Erie Canal passed through the center of Palmyra, New York. Construction on that section began in 1817 and was completed in 1822. As a young man, Joseph Smith would have watched the construction of Lock E29 being built in his hometown. Two miles away, a feeder waterway, the Cayuga and Seneca Canal, ran in front of the Smiths' home and connected to the Erie Canal at Macedon.

Members of the early Mormon church in New York took the canals on their moves to Kirtland, Ohio, and Nauvoo, Illinois. Under the leadership of Newel Knight, a group of about sixty people, the "Colesville Saints," departed for Ohio from what is now Ninevah (Broome County in the southcentral part of New York) in early April 1831. They traveled northwest, mostly by water, to reach the Erie Canal and then sailed west on the Erie Canal over 160 miles to Buffalo. From Buffalo, they

---

17. The United States purchased 828,00 square miles of new land at a cost of $15 million or approximately $18 dollars per square mile. "Louisiana Purchase," Wikipedia, https://en.wikipedia.org/wiki/Louisiana_Purchase.

18. "All Hail the Erie Canal," July 9, 2017, CBS News, https://www.cbsnews.com/news/all-hail-the-erie-canal-200th-anniversary/.

Figure 2. *Erie Canal at Palmyra, New York, 1918*

took a Lake Erie steamer south 150 miles to Fairport, Ohio, only eleven miles from Kirtland, in May. Lucy Mack Smith, Thomas B. Marsh, and Martin Harris also led groups of Mormon travelers to Kirtland along the same route.[19]

The Sangers

No place in New York benefited more from the canal than the little town of Rochester. In 1815, Rochester contained just 331 inhabitants; by 1830 it had 9,207 and was still growing at a phenomenal rate.[20] The Sangers were among them. In 1817 David began working on the first aqueduct over the Genesee River in Rochester. The stone structure was huge for its time: 802 feet long and seventeen feet wide and supported by eleven arches.[21] David also built the locks near the terminus of the Erie Canal at Buffalo. This western country was so new that only three steamboats were running on Lake Erie. Twelve-year-old Lorenzo P. Sanger worked on one of them, the *Pioneer*, as a steward.[22] When David's contract on the Erie Canal was finished in

---

19. Stanley B. Kimball, "The First Road West: From New York to Kirtland, 1831," Church of Jesus Christ of Latter-day Saints, https://www.churchofjesuschrist.org/study/ensign/1979/01/the-first-road-west-from-new-york-to-kirtland-1831?lang=eng.

20. Richard L. Bushman, *Joseph Smith and the Beginnings of Mormonism* (Urbana: University of Illinois Press, 1984), 45-46.

21. The aqueduct leaked, so it was later replaced by what is today known as the Broad Street Bridge.

22. *History of Will County, Illinois*, 712, https://archive.org/details/historyofwillcou00chic/page/712/mode/2up.

the fall of 1826, he moved his family to Pittsburgh, where construction of the Pennsylvania Canal system was underway. The project lasted five years.[23]

The four young Sanger sons, Lorenzo, William, James, and Lucian, learned canal building from their father and became successful contractors and businessmen on their own. Lorenzo was known as the "boy contractor," having won his own contract to build a lock near Livermore, Pennsylvania, when only 20 years old.[24] About 1831, Lorenzo and his partner unwittingly struck oil while digging a salt well in Freeport, Pennsylvania. "After drilling several hundred feet, they struck a large flow of salt water, and with it what the salt men termed 'that infernal American or Seneca oil,' since known as petroleum; and as the value of the oil was not then known, the well was abandoned."[25]

Since the second son, William Sanger, suffered from a lung ailment all his life, he became a prominent physician, merchant and farmer instead of a contractor. In family correspondence he is simply called "the doctor."[26] James Young Sanger, the third son, was also brought up in the business. After the family moved to Pittsburgh, James began working in a mercantile establishment where his design of a new method of inventory made him head clerk at the age of 14. He would also contract on his own to build canals in Ohio and Indiana.[27] The youngest Sanger son, Lucian, became a businessman and part owner of a successful stagecoach company.[28]

On completion of the Pennsylvania Canal, the Sanger family continued westward to Ohio and Indiana where the Ohio and the Wabash Canals were opening. In 1835, they moved to St. Joseph, Michigan, and helped to build the first stone bridge over the St. Joseph River. They also had a large merchandise and warehouse business. There is some evidence they also built steamboats to transport their products.[29]

---

23. See Steel.

24. *History of Will County, Illinois*, 712.

25. See Steel. Lorenzo Palmer Sanger was born March 2, 1809 in Littleton. He married Rachel Mary Denniston (1809-1870) in Westmoreland Co., Pennsylvania on February 3, 1830.

26. See Steel. William Alonzo Sanger was born in Littleton August 9, 1810. He married Mary Miles (born 1812) in Newburgh, Ohio in 1833. See also [Mary Palmer Sanger to Phoebe Palmer Graves Bent], January 26, 1851, Eliza Rich correspondence.

27. James Young Sanger was born in Sutton, Vermont on March 26, 1814. He married Mary Catherine McKibben (1818-1904) in Lockport, Illinois, on April 5, 1841. Their daughter Harriet Amelia Sanger (1843-1922) married industrialist George M. Pullman in Chicago on June 13, 1867. Steel. See also *Magazine of Western History*, 707-11.

28. See Steel. Lucian Palmer Sanger (sometimes written Lucien), was born in Perry, New York, on March 14, 1816. He married Elizabeth B. Reynolds (born 1830) in Ottawa, Illinois, on September 17, 1851.

29. "In 1835, he started in the then fashionable way of traveling, viz., on horseback, to St. Joseph, Mich., and joined Gen. Hart L. Stewart, now of Chicago, in merchandising, warehousing, and steam-boating on the St. Joseph River." *History of Will County, Illinois*, 711-12. Also, Newton Bateman, Paul Selby, Josiah Seymour Currey, *Historical Encyclopedia of Illinois: Biographical, Memorial* vol. 1 (n.p.: Munsell, 1920), 462-63.

Figure 3. *A canal aqueduct*

In 1836 the Sangers obtained a huge contract to build locks and an aqueduct on the Illinois and Michigan Canal that would connect the small settlement of Chicago to LaSalle on the Illinois River.[30] From that small town near Ottawa, the canal boats would be replaced by river steamers to sail down the Illinois River to the Mississippi and from there to New Orleans and the Gulf of Mexico.[31] David and his sons began in the rocky sections near Lockport and Joliet and continued westward to LaSalle. Their main accomplishments were Lock 15 and the aqueduct that carried the canal over the Fox River at Ottawa. This project, begun in 1838, was the pinnacle of David Sanger's career.[32]

The family may have been introduced to Mormonism through the efforts of Phoebe Palmer Graves, the sister of David's wife Mary.[33] In the early 1830s, Phoebe and her two daughters met Mormon missionaries in Erie, Pennsylvania, and were baptized.[34] One of the missionaries, Charles C. Rich, later married Phoebe's daugh-

---

30. Speek, "Forgotten Waterway." "Until recently, the I&M Canal has been a forgotten chapter in American history. Most people have heard of the Erie Canal, but few are familiar with the I&M, which was just as significant. It made Illinois the grain-basket of the country and provided safe transport for northern troops and supplies during the Civil War. It also provided easy access to New Orleans and the Gulf of Mexico."

31. John Lamb, "The Illinois and Michigan Canal and Town Development in Northern Illinois," *Proceedings of the Canal History & Technology Symposium* 3 (Easton, PA.: The Center for Canal History and Technology, March 31, 1984): 3-11. Chicago had a population of only 150 people in 1833. By the spring of 1837, the population had increased to 4,170. See Milo Quaife, *Chicago Roads and Highways* (Ann Arbor: University of Michigan, 1923), 26.

32. See Steel.

33. Phoebe Palmer (1788-1858) was divorced from Ruben Graves. They had three children together: Eliza Ann Graves (1811); Mary Palmer Graves (1818); and a son. See Mary L. Gibby, "History of Ann Eliza Graves Rich, Pioneer of 1847," FamilySearch.org.

34. Black, "Membership." This was probably 1835-1836 when Rich was living in Kirtland, Ohio.

ter, Eliza Ann Graves.[35] Phoebe's other daughter, Mary Graves, married a cabinet maker, George Bratton, and the extended family moved west to Ottawa, Illinois, where their relatives, the Sangers, lived.[36]

William Sanger and his wife Mary had also become Mormons, probably in Ohio or Indiana.[37] William was baptized in 1839 and ordained a seventy.[38] In early 1843, David Sanger moved his household from Ottawa, Illinois, to the Mormon settlement of Nauvoo, where on June 12, 1843, David, his wife, and his daughter Louisa were baptized.[39] David was issued a high priest license on June 17, 1845.[40] Either then or a short time later, William and Mary also moved to Nauvoo. All were quickly enveloped within the upper levels of Nauvoo society—and into the secret inner workings of the church.[41]

When his contract was finished on the I&M Canal, Lorenzo Sanger turned his attention to railroad construction and stage lines. In March 1843, he and his brother Lucian joined a partnership to purchase the Frick and Walker stage company with the goal of operating a line of coaches from Chicago to Galena, Illinois, by way of Dixon.[42] In June 1843, stage-driver Lucian witnessed an arrest of Joseph Smith Jr. The Mormon founder had been visiting his wife's relatives in Dixon when he was unexpectedly accosted by a Missouri sheriff and an Illinois constable, who charged him with treason against the state of Missouri.

Having seen the arrest from his perch atop a stagecoach,[43] Lucian asked what had happened. Smith stated the following, as quoted later in the *History of the Church*:

> ...that the sheriff intended to drag me [Joseph Smith] away immediately to Missouri and prevent my taking out a writ of habeas corpus...Sanger soon made this known to Mr. Dixon, the owner of the house, and his friends, who gathered around the hotel door, and gave Reynolds to understand that if that was their mode of doing business in

---

35. Bessie Porter Brough, "Mary Graves Bratton Porter, Pioneer of 1852," FamilySearch.org.

36. George Bratton was baptized in Nauvoo in 1842 and ordained a seventy. He was endowed on December 19, 1845. See Black, "Membership; and Seventy Quorum Membership, 1835-1846," Ancestry.com.

37. See Steel. They lived during the 1830s in Medina, Ohio, and Lima (now Howe), Indiana.

38. "Early Church Information File, 1830-1900 (Church of Jesus Christ of Latter-day Saints)," FamilySearch, https://www.familysearch.org/wiki/en/Early_Church_Information_File_(ECIF).

39. "Early Church Information."

40. Black, "Membership."

41. George and Mary Bratton also moved to Nauvoo. Phoebe and Eliza Graves lived with them. See Brough, "Mary Graves."

42. Quaife, *Chicago Roads*, 156. Frick and Walker had held a virtual monopoly on stages in the Midwest for many years. In 1847, Lorenzo joined with several others in forming the Northwestern Stage Company that would serve Michigan, Indiana, Illinois, Wisconsin, Iowa, and Missouri. *History of Will County*, 712; and Bateman, *Historical Encyclopedia of Illinois*, 462-63.

43. Quaife, *Chicago Roads*, 153. In the 1830s and 40s, the stage driver or operator was a much-respected man in the community.

Missouri, they had another way of doing it in Dixon. They were a law-abiding people and Republicans, and gave Reynolds to understand that he should not take me away without giving me the opportunity of a fair trial, and that I should have justice done me; but that if he persisted in his course, they had a very summary way of dealing with such people.[44]

Smith then hired Lucian to convey him and his attorneys to Quincy, Illinois, some 260 miles away, to appear before Judge Stephen A. Douglas.[45] Lucian was also in the procession when Joseph Smith later rode triumphantly into Nauvoo."[46]

A detachment of about twenty-five men stayed at the David Sanger home in Ottawa while on their way from Nauvoo to Dixon to rescue Joseph Smith:

> General Rich left the company about an hour before sunset, and about dusk crossed the Illinois river into Ottawa, and put up at Brother Sanger's. There he learned positively that Joseph...had returned to Dixon and obtained another writ of habeas corpus, and... that Lucien P. Sanger had taken his stage-coach to convey Brother Joseph to Quincy.[47]

The Nauvoo city council later commended Lucian Sanger for his "bold and decided stand taken against lawless outrage and the spirit of mobocracy."[48]

Despite his actions supporting Joseph Smith and the Mormons in Nauvoo, Lucian had not been a member of the church at the time. There is some indication in the early church membership files that Lucian might have joined the church since he had been given a patriarchal blessing by William Smith on July 30, 1845. However, a copy of that blessing states the following:

> Beloved friend—[it] is therefore thy duty inasmuch as thou hast not yet been baptized for a remission of sins that thou shalt follow the example of thy Savior and obey his precepts...although temptations have arisen to entice thee to disbelieve, yet there is a Spirit that tells thee that these things are true and that it is thy duty to obey the Gospel of Christ.[49]

Most of the other members of the Sanger family also received patriarchal blessings: William on April 2, 1845; Mary Miles Sanger on April 4, 1845;[50] and David

---

44. E. Southwick to Joseph Smith, July 29, 1843, CHL. Also, Brigham H. Roberts, ed., *History of the Church of Jesus Christ of Latter-day Saints 1844-1872* vol.5 (Salt Lake City: Deseret News, 1912), 442.

45. Ibid., 448.

46. Ibid., 458.

47. Ibid., 487.

48. Ibid., 474.

49. H. Michael Marquardt, comp., *Early Patriarchal Blessings of the Church of Jesus Christ of Latter-day Saints* (Salt Lake City: Smith Pettit Foundation, 2007), 364-65.

50. Black. "Membership." William's blessing is listed under the last name Langer instead of Sanger.

Sanger and his wife, Mary Palmer, on June 11, 1845.[51] David and Mary were endowed in the Nauvoo temple on December 18, 1845, and were sealed on January 29, 1846,[52] the same day as William and his wife.[53] Louisa, at 32 years of age, was a total invalid. She had a spinal disability which required her to have a special chair, yet she had:

> an active and vigorous mind, and keen literary tastes. Her bodily informities [sic] only seemed to exalt and refine the mental part. Simple, unaffected, and engaging in her manners, her conversation was often an intellectual treat. With the rest, she cherished a taste for poetry, and the columns of the [Ottawa] *Free Trader*…were often enriched with contributions from her pen.[54]

Louisa Sanger received a patriarchal blessing at Nauvoo on September 17, 1843, from Hyrum Smith.[55] Louisa's physical disability was mentioned in her patriarchal blessing: "Thou hast seen much affliction. But [dismay] not of thy pain and be cheerful for the day of thy deliverance is at hand…Thou shalt have every blessing which thy heart desires and be able to accomplish every purpose of thy heart."[56]

On June 27, 1844, Joseph and Hyrum Smith were murdered. Their deaths set up a leadership succession crisis that drove members of the church apart as they debated who should replace Joseph as their prophet. The Sanger family was also divided for a time. "Alienated by what they perceived as the wicked and unholy leadership at Nauvoo," David and Mary Sanger completed their endowments and sealing in the temple, sold their properties in Nauvoo, and moved back to Ottawa.[57] David died there on May 1, 1852, and Mary in 1854.

Louisa stayed in Nauvoo with her aunt Phoebe Graves but grieved both the Smiths' deaths and her separation from her parents. She had apparently developed a close relationship with the church patriarch John Smith, Hyrum Smith's uncle and successor in that office. On May 17, 1845, she wrote in verse to John Smith seeking a father's blessing:

---

51. *Patriarchal Blessings* vol. 9, pp. 224, 679 and 680.

52. Devery S. Anderson and Gary James Bergera, eds., *The Nauvoo Endowment Companies, 1845-1846* (Salt Lake City: Signature Books, 2005), 525.

53. Lisle G Brown, comp., *Nauvoo Sealings, Adoptions, and Anointings* (Salt Lake City: Smith Petit Foundation, 2006), 268. William A. Sanger and his wife Mary received their endowments in the Nauvoo temple on December 18, 1845.

54. James wrote: "I wish you would call on Linch and Trask [?] & get Louisa's chair & have it shipped on the Illinois." James Sanger to A. H. Evans, April 8, 1840, Augustus H. Evans Papers. See also Louisa Sanger obituary, the Ottawa *Free Trader*, Saturday, August 18, 1877.

55. *Early Church Membership*. Black, "Membership," reports Louisa's patriarchal blessing: "(probably) Dec 1844 by John Smith in Nauvoo."

56. An actual copy of Louisa's blessing can be read at: "Patriarchal Blessing of Louisa Sanger," n.d. Eliza Rich Correspondence.

57. Property transactions in Nauvoo, Hancock County, Illinois and surrounding communities (1839-1859), FamilySearch,

Dear Father I have waited with a sad yet patient heart
For the visit that you promised, for I know you could impart
Some words of consolation that would cheer and comfort me
And my heart when I am sorrowful has often turned to thee.

I have been a child of sorrow, every earthly hope is gone
And amidst my desolation I can look to you alone
As a counsillor [sic] and father, you can tell me what to do
You can guide me and direct me, and I can appeal to you.

Dear Father I remember that you promised you would be
A Father to the orphan and a counsillor to me
And now I claim your promise do not turn away my prayer
For if you should forsake me you would leave me in despair.

I am desolate and lonely there is none to comfort me
And I want a Father blessing, may I ask for one from thee?
My heart is full of sorrow and my spirit is oppressed
But bless me O my Father and I shall indeed be blessed.[58]

Louisa was sealed posthumously to Hyrum Smith as a plural wife on January 27, 1846; however, she may have been sealed to him during his life. She was also "sealed for time" on that day to her longtime friend Reuben Miller, who acted as Hyrum's proxy.[59] Louisa's parents and her brother William were in Nauvoo on that date and may have witnessed the sealing. There is no evidence that Louisa ever lived with Miller as his plural wife or that the marriage was consummated.[60]

Louisa's relatives Phoebe and Eliza Graves became plural wives themselves on January 14, 1846. Phoebe was sealed to Samuel Bent, and Eliza to Charles C. Rich. Both men were prominent leaders in Nauvoo and members of the Council of Fifty. Eliza later immigrated to Utah where her husband became an LDS apostle.[61] Phoebe's other daughter, Mary Graves, wished to go to Utah, but her husband, "could not see as she did…so they decided to separate." George Bratton took his family as far as Council Bluffs but would not continue to Utah.[62] In May 1852, Mary and her

---

58. Louisa Sanger to Pres. John Smith, May 17, 1845. John Smith Papers, CHL.

59. See Gary James Bergera, "Identifying the Earliest Mormon Polygamists, 1841-44," *Dialogue: A Journal of Mormon Thought 38*, no. 3 (Fall 2005): 28.

60. Reuben Miller immigrated to Salt Lake City with the bulk of the Mormons. Louisa and Reuben corresponded infrequently but never saw each other again.

61. Phoebe Palmer Graves was endowed December 19, 1845, in Nauvoo. Her second husband Samuel Bent died in Garden Grove, Iowa Territory, in 1846. See *Nauvoo Community Project (BYU Center for Family History and Genealogy)*, Ancestry.com. See also Charles Coulson Rich, Biography, JosephSmithPapers.org.

62. Gibby, "Ann Eliza Graves Rich." George Bratton subsequently settled in Nebraska Territory.

mother, with Mary's family of four little girls, left Winter Quarters in a company of fifty wagons led by a Captain Brim.[63]

By the middle of 1845, none of the Sangers had accepted the prophetic succession claims of Brigham Young. Nor did any of them decide to follow Young to Utah. William and Mary Sanger left Nauvoo and moved to Lima (now Howe), Indiana, where they had lived in the 1830s. They later moved to several communities in Illinois where William remained a doctor and prosperous farmer.[64]

Despite their separation from the Mormons who had gone on to Utah, William, Lucian, and Louisa maintained a deep belief in the principles of the faith and defended all who believed in it. In 1845 T. Walter Nixon, acting as an agent for Brigham Young, attempted to round up disaffected members in Ottawa to urge them to go west. "I…received an insult from Brother Anti-Mormon Sanger—who opposed me in a forceable manner, stating the measures I had taken were not legal and contrary to the church. Also, it would injure the revival amongst the Saints," he wrote.[65] It is not clear which brother Sanger Nixon was speaking of, but Louisa had written that William had no faith in Young's twelve apostles and was more likely to be living in Ottawa at that time.[66]

William, Lucian, and Louisa were emotionally close and often shared their faith privately with each other. After their parents died, Louisa, who would remain an invalid all her life, lived at different times with her siblings but was most comfortable living with William or Lucian and their wives. "If there is a righteous couple on earth, it is them [William and Mary], and I can say the same of Lucian and wife," she wrote to her cousin Eliza. "Lorenzo and James are too much absorbed in business to think much of anything else, but they are both kind-hearted and mean to be good, and they are both good men."[67]

Lucian wrote to his aunt:

> If only I knew that the teachings at the [Salt Lake] Valley were right in the sight of God. I would be willing to sacrifice almost everything for the truth, the Living Truth. But Oh I am at a great loss. I know not what is right but we are informed if we do his will we shall know of the doctrines whether it be of God. Now I ask you what can a person

---

63. Brough, "Mary Graves Bratton Porter." Mary later married John President Porter Sr., as his second wife. His first wife was a sister of Charles C. Rich.

64. See Steel. Francis Hendriks Sanger, the six-month-old child of William and Mary Sanger, died in Nauvoo on July 16, 1845. *Nauvoo Neighbor*, July 16, 1845. William died on December 11, 1887, in Florence, Kansas.

65. T. Walter Nixon to Bro. Brigham Young, February 13, 1844 [45], CR 12341, Brigham Young office files, CHL.

66. Louisa to James Strang, July 15, 1846, letter 37, James Strang papers, Beinecke Library, Yale University, New Haven, Connecticut.

67. n.d., MS338, folder 1, no. 3, Eliza Rich Correspondence.

do that is consciously desiring to do right and our teachers tell us that we must do that which we have reason to suspect is wrong? What shall we do?[68]

One of the several claimants to the leadership of the church was James Jesse Strang of Burlington, Wisconsin. He had claimed to have received a letter from Smith instructing that he, Strang, should become the church's prophet should something happen to Smith. Louisa appears to have doubted Strang's succession claims at first. He wrote to her thanking her for her kindness when they had first met but then accused her of telling people that the so-called letter of appointment he had received was in his own style of writing. "Well, you have heard me read a few pages of my own writing," he admitted, then added:

If on such small means of judging. you have ventured to charge me with the crime of forgery, including…that of imposture and blasphemy & making my life a living lie, Still Louisa, [for] your kindness when without acquaintance you confided in and taught me, I forgive you."[69]

Perhaps due to the influence of her friend Reuben Miller, who had initially supported Strang's claims, Louisa eventually became interested in Strangism. Only two months after she was sealed to Hyrum Smith for eternity and to Miller for time, she left Nauvoo with Miller and apostle John E. Page. It was rumored she was going with them to Strang's home in Voree, Wisconsin. The two men did travel to Voree, but Louisa stopped and remained in Ottawa where she once again began living with her parents.[70]

She maintained a lengthy correspondence with Strang from her home in Ottawa. Insisting that he answer her questions and give evidence of his appointment to be a prophet of God:

You know that I desire truth above all things and in order to prove all things it is necessary that we should examine both sides of every question…You know that I was more slow to believe [in you] than he was…for in the days of Joseph [Smith] I had many days of doubt and perplexity and I expected it would be so with you…[but] I cannot give you up yet for if I do, I must give up my Last and only hope, for with my present feelings I can [not] think of going back to the Twelve—Indeed I am satisfied that if theirs is the celestial law, I do not possess a celestial spirit, for I can never abide that law and have no desire to inherit that glory.[71]

However, in another letter Louisa chastised Strang for taking George J. Adams, John C. Bennett, and William Smith as counselors. "I am sure you cannot be sur-

---

68. [Lucian Palmer Sanger to Phoebe Palmer Graves Bent], January 26, 1851, Eliza Rich Correspondence.
69. James Strang to Louisa Sanger, December 5, 1844, CR 1234, CHL.
70. Joseph L Heywood to Bro. Heber [C. Kimball], March 17, 1846, CR 1234, CHL.
71. Louisa Sanger to James Strang, July 15, 1846, letter 37, James J. Strang papers. Beinecke.

prised that we are so unwilling to fellowship men whose moral character is so bad that the Twelve would not take them."[72]

Although she had accepted polygamy in Nauvoo, she apparently regretted it:

I do wish you would not let Wm. [William] Smith disgrace your paper by making the awful disclosures which he threatens to do…such disclosures can do no good to anyone. The Saints know it all now, and the world has no right to know it. It is putting weapons into their hands which they will be sure to use [against us]…If he will make such disclosures, don't send the paper to us for I shall be ashamed to have it directed to us.[73]

By August 1859 Louisa was completely disillusioned with organized religion. She wrote to Strang:

Really I am one of the most highly favored beings on the earth! Within the last week I have had the honor of receiving letters from two Prophets—to say nothing of kind priests and elders, and several of the sisterhood—belonging to three different parties, all of them claiming to be the true church, and the only true church on earth! Save me from my friends! While the world is perishing for lack of knowledge, I am in great danger of perishing for knowing too much![74]

She scolded:

You know of course what terrible things I have heard of you. Enough if half are true to sink you to the lowest pit. But I have learned long ago to pay no attention to man reports. It was your own actions, your own writings that destroyed my confidence in you—Bro Miller's influence had nothing to do with it, nor did it come all at one—one grain after another was thrown in the scale against you until it finally turned over and since then I have felt perfectly indifferent to you, and all your saying and doing.–I have never been your enemy because I considered if you are a decision, you are utterly unworthy of a thought … I could not stoop so low as to hate a willful religious imposter.[75]

Through the remainder of her life, Louisa maintained an interest in obtaining knowledge about all things in the world. She was especially interested in the "scientific" principles of "magnetism" [hypnosis], psychology, and phrenology and had participated in the "Cleveland water cure" to restore her health.[76] She also believed

---

72. Ibid.

73. Ibid.

74. She did not name the two prophets. One was undoubtedly Strang, and the other may have been Brigham Young, Sidney Rigdon, or James Brewster. She added that the only church she was drawn to was, perhaps, Brewsterism. Louisa Sanger to James Strang, August 19, 1849, letter 55, James Strang Papers, Beinecke.

75. Letter 55.

76. Louisa said magnetism was "simply the old gospel principle of laying on of hands." Louisa to Eliza, January 15, 1868. Eliza Rich Correspondence.

in and practiced spiritualism[77] and was an advocate for social causes. Although she detested the Civil War, she hoped good would come from it:

> By this war, <u>Slavery</u> will be overthrown, and the way will be prepared for universal <u>liberty</u> for all classes, and all races of men, And then I expect the way for the Millennium will be prepared and the redemption of <u>women</u> will be the next great step in the Redemption of the world.[78]

Still, she maintained her belief in the basics of Mormonism:"Now I suppose you want to know how I feel about Mormonism and everything connected with it," she wrote to Eliza:

> so I will tell you truly and candidly. I still believe the Book [of Mormon] and all connected with the foundation and organization of the church. All this I never doubted for a moment when in the darkest times I have ever seen. I believe it was and <u>is</u> true revelation and restoration and arrival of the gospel dispensation & covenant. The dark spot that comes next I shall pass over in silence, but I confidently expect that this period of darkness cannot last forever and when it passes I expect the light shall be brighter than it has ever been before, and there will be no more doubt and uncertainty.[79]

Louisa was fond of her brother Lucian and often used him to carry private letters to the post office. He worked as a land agent and speculator but experienced heavy losses when banks failed in the 1850s and 60s.[80] "It seems very hard that one who has toiled so hard all his life, one so good, charitable, and honorable in every way as he has been, should have such a hard time all through life. But so it always is, the best always fare the worst."[81] He then moved to Joliet, Illinois, where he constructed and sold agricultural equipment.

Ironically, later in his life Lucian Sanger did move to Salt Lake City. Sometime after 1870 the family moved to Utah Territory where Lucian became involved in the mining business. His wife Elizabeth[82] was among a group of prominent non-Mor-

---

77. Letter 55; also n.d., MS338, folder 1, no. 3, Eliza Rich Correspondence. See Louisa to Dear Cousin, January 7, 1867, Eliza Rich Correspondence.

78. Louisa Sanger to My Dear Friends, February 18, 1863, Eliza Rich Correspondence.

79. Louisa to Dear Aunt and Cousins, August 28, 1852, Eliza Rich Correspondence.

80. Louisa Sanger to My Dear Friends, February 18, 1863, Eliza Rich Correspondence.

81. n.d. MS 5338, folder 1, number 3. CHL

82. See Steel. Lucian married Elizabeth B. Reynolds (born in 1830) on September 17, 1851. She was the daughter of Martin Reynolds and Elizabeth Hitt.

mon women who founded the Ladies Library Association.[83] Eventually, the family moved to San Francisco, California, where Lucian died on August 1, 1881.[84]

Louisa was desperate to keep Lucien's wife from knowing that she had participated in polygamy. Louisa warned her cousin Eliza Rich in Utah to be careful what she said to Lucian's wife, "She is very strongly prejudiced against your peculiar institutions and you must be very careful not to say anything before her that the whole world may not know. Especially be very careful not to say anything about <u>me that I don't want her to know</u>."[85] Louisa died August 3, 1877.

Lorenzo Sanger never became a Mormon. He served as state senator from Galena, Illinois, (a lead-mining area) for several years, where he was noted as one of the most active and influential members and a warm and intimate friend of Stephen E. Douglas.[86] In 1857 Lorenzo's firm contracted to build the western division of the Ohio & Mississippi Railroad. After its completion he gained the contract for building the North Missouri Railroad from St. Louis to Macon, Missouri. He then moved to Joliet, Illinois, and obtained the contract to build the state penitentiary at Joliet. The 1860 census, taken when the Joliet penitentiary was nearing completion, lists Lorenzo and his family living in a house on the prison grounds.[87]

During the Civil War, Lorenzo Sanger and his son-in-law William A. Steel contracted with the US government to build four ironclad, Monitor-class warships: the Tuscumbia, Indianola, Chillicothe, and Etlah. In July 1865 Lorenzo and William founded the largest quarries in the country, which would prove to be the best limestone yet found in America.[88]

About 1873, in failing health, Lorenzo traveled to Salt Lake City where he spent more than a year living with his brother Lucian. He then went to Oakland, California, where he died in 1875.[89] Lorenzo's body was embalmed and taken by railroad back to Joliet where his was "one of the most imposing funerals ever witnessed in

---

83. See Steel. "They settled in Ottawa, Joliet, and later in Frankfort, Illinois, where he operated an iron foundry making corn shellers and agricultural implements."

84. Joliet *Herald News*, July 30, 1881. Lucian's estate in Utah was valued at only $750 when it was probated in Salt Lake City Salt Lake *Evening Democrat*, March 2, 1887.

85. Louisa to My Dear Cousin, February 25, 1877, Eliza Rich Correspondence. See also Louisa Sanger to My Dear Eliza, July 28, 1863, Eliza Rich Correspondence.

86. See Steel.

87. Louisa Sanger lived with them and wrote a letter to her cousin on paper printed with the prison letterhead. *History of Will County*, 712. Eliza Rich Correspondence.

88. Steel. "W. A. Steel."

89. Joliet *Herald News*, March 27, 1875; also, *History of Will County*, 711-13. Lorenzo P. Sanger's obituary in the *Oakland Tribune*, March 24, 1875, read, "Sanger, although a man of unyielding purpose and rugged character, was kind-hearted in his public dealings, and exceedingly tender in the private and domestic relations of life."

Joliet. Knights Templar took charge of his funeral—he was a member—and the impressive ceremonies of the order were observed."[90]

James Young Sanger associated with his brothers in railroad construction in the Midwest. In 1857 James went to California where he built the state's first railroad, the California Central.[91] After completing the pioneer railroad of the Pacific Slope, a line which extended from Sacramento to Maysville in less than two years,[92] he returned to Illinois where he partnered to build and operate the Joliet Penitentiary. In 1866-67 he partnered with Lorenzo to excavate the rocky portions in the widening of the Illinois and Michigan Canal (now known as the Joliet Sanitary and Ship Canal). Exposure to the wet and cold on the project resulted in the sickness from which he died.[93]

When the Civil War broke out James contracted with the government to provide supplies of various types. After the war he became involved in efforts to construct a large portion of the Union Pacific Railway, but ill health forced him to give up his portion of the contract. He returned to Chicago where he died on July 2, 1867.

James Sanger is listed as:

> one of the most prominent citizens of Illinois whose efforts contributed as much as those of any other toward the growth and development of the State. The influence of the enterprises with which he was identified upon the commerce of the West is incalculable. The 450 miles of railroad in the construction of which he was largely instrumental, were built at an out lay of $12 million...He was widely known, not only in commercial, but also in social circles, and was a prominent member of the Masonic order. His success in life was due to his fertility of resource, his wonderful ability to recover from pecuniary embarrassments, and his indomitable energy.[94]

Conclusion

The I&M canal is mostly abandoned now, but in Ottawa, Illinois, about thirty miles west of my old home, I found the remains of an amazing stone aqueduct and, more importantly, I discovered the story of America exemplified in one extraordinary family.

In addition to their work on the transportation canals across frontier America, the family invested in stagecoaches that ran across the entire Midwest and built more than 450 miles of railroads in Illinois, Missouri and California. They built ironclad ships for the Civil War. They took up mining in Colorado, Utah, and California. The

---

90. Ottawa *Free Trader*, April 10, 1875.
91. *History of Will County*, 711.
92. Ibid., 710
93. Ibid.
94. *Album of Genealogy and Biography, Cook County, Illinois*, 2nd edition (Chicago: Calumet Book & Engraving, 1895; reprint, LaCrosse, WI: Brookhaven Press, 2000), 440-41.

Sangers built some of the most famous buildings in America. The final project James and Lorenzo Sanger took on returned them to their roots. They blasted away the stone along the I&M Canal they had labored to construct nearly forty years early, widening the waterway so ships could transport commodities down the Mississippi River to the Gulf of Mexico. As Louisa wrote: "It seems like old times."

The Sanger family even took up the cause of literacy. Non-Mormon Mary Miles Sanger helped develop the first library in Salt Lake City, and a Sanger son-in-law donated several thousand of his personal books to start the public library in Joliet, Illinois.[95] They were interested in religion and social causes, especially Louisa. I laughed and cried when I read her letters. She was a highly intelligent woman who never let her spinal disability overcome her spirit or her mind. I think I shall always recall the advice she wrote in one of her last letters to Eliza, who had complained about a former friend of theirs leaving the Mormon church. Louisa wrote: "It is a small comfort to know that when the saints are judged, God, will judge himself, and not leave us to be judged by the standard of man's judgement. It would go rather hard with everybody I guess, if we were judged by such prejudiced creations."[96]

Sometimes you never expect a story to be so rich and full. To me, the story of the family that built canals is really something special.

VICKIE CLEVERLEY SPEEK is a new resident of Port Charlotte, Florida, where she is excited to search for fossil shark's teeth and learn how to garden with exotic plants. She is the author of *God Has Made Us A Kingdom: James Strang And The Midwest Mormons* (Signature Books, 2006) and worked as a ghostwriter for *The Amazing Jimmi Mayes: Sideman to the Stars* (University Press of Mississippi, 2013).

---

95. Steel. "W. A. Steel."

96. Louisa Sanger to My Dear Friends, February 18, 1863, Eliza Rich Correspondence.

Thomas A. Lyne, the Latter-day Saints, and the American Theatre: Confluences and Influences, 1844–1904

Lee Krähenbühl

We enter the Holy of Holies to worship; we go to the theatre to learn the everyday lessons of practical life and to study character for a knowledge of human nature; nor is it a little singular in this man, Brigham's life, that though he put on the capstone of the Nauvoo temple, he also at Nauvoo played the High Priest to our T. A. Lyne's Pizarro… The Mormon theatre was conceived in Nauvoo in Joseph's day. It is as orthodox as the Temple. Thomas A. Lyne was Joseph's actor…[1]

—Edward Tullidge, Historian of Utah and Biographer of Brigham Young, 1886

The Latter-day Saints were, in 1844, the very first English-speaking religious body in North America to sanction theatre as an activity appropriate for its parishioners to both attend and produce. Other American faith traditions would not follow suit for another forty years.[2]

This indisputable fact is curiously absent from studies and reference books ranging from the two volumes of the *Cambridge History of American Theatre* to Stephen Mansfield's relatively recent book *The Mormonizing of America*.[3] The paucity of references to theatre in the latter work is particularly puzzling because of its ambitious

---

1. Edward William Tullidge, *History of Salt Lake City* (Salt Lake City: Star Printing Company, 1886), 740f.

2. See Claudia Durst Johnson, *Church and Stage: The Theatre as Target of Religious Condemnation in Nineteenth Century America* (Jefferson, NC & London: McFarland, 2014).

3. Stephen Mansfield, *The Mormonizing of America: How the Mormon Religion Became a Dominant Force in Politics, Entertainment, and Pop Culture* (Franklin, TN: Worthy Books, 2012).

subtitle: *How the Mormon Religion Became a Dominant Force in Politics, Entertainment, and Pop Culture.*

Brigham Young's Salt Lake Theatre was one such display of dominant cultural force in the nineteenth century. It was the most splendid such venue west of the Mississippi when built in 1862.[4] Every major theatrical star in America played there through the 1880s, and its mostly Latter-day Saint company was the early training ground of not only the mogul of Melodrama who will be profiled later in this article, but also of MAUDE ADAMS (1872-1953), the highest-paid American actress of her day and, in 1904, the very first to play Peter Pan on Broadway.[5]

Dramatis Personæ of the Burned-over District

Other nineteenth-century American actors, lesser-known in our day but nonetheless significant in their own, also had backgrounds among the Latter-day Saints. Four will be particularly characterized here. Two were children of prominent leaders in Joseph Smith's lifetime: J. W. (Jared) CARTER, JR. (1838-1874) and C. V. (Cortland van Rensaaler) HESS (1838-1887) had been boys together in Nauvoo in 1844, the place and time in which the first Mormon theatre company performed. Two others were converts: the siblings CAROLINE JENKINS COGGESHALL (1834-1895), and WILLIAM JENKINS COGGESHALL (1836-1906), to be discussed later under their most widely recognized stage names: CARRIE CARTER and W. J. COGSWELL.

A dramatic spark within the Latter-day Saint movement was apparent in the sheer *theatricality* of its origin in what came to be called the "Burned-over District"—that part of Western New York State that was scorched by the fire-and-brimstone revivalism of the Second Great Awakening during the 1820s. A chief architect of the fervent tent meetings that gave the region its nickname was the eventual founder of Oberlin College, CHARLES GRANDISON FINNEY (1792-1875), the *de facto* dean of public performance for the purpose of proselytizing. A pragmatic theologian, he sought to present Christianity to the masses in an engaging manner. The enthusiasm of the revival meeting was, Finney wrote, "not a miracle, or dependent on a miracle in any sense." Rather, revival was "a purely philosophical result...of the *right* use of the appropriate means."[6] "Ministers," he insisted, "ought to know *what measures* are best calculated to aid in accomplishing the great end of their office, the salvation of

---

4. See esp. George D. Pyper, *The Romance of an Old Playhouse* (Salt Lake City: Seagull Press, 1928); John Shanks Lindsay, *The Mormons and the Theatre, or The History of Theatricals in Utah, with Reminiscences and Comments Humorous and Critical* (Salt Lake City: Century Printing, 1905).

5. See esp. Armond Fields, *Maude Adams: Idol of American Theatre, 1872-1953* (Jefferson, NC & London: McFarland & Co., 2004); "The Life Story of Maude Adams and Her Mother," *The Green Book Magazine*, June 1914, 884-900; "Recollections of Maude Adams," *The Green Book Magazine*, July 1915, 164-172.

6. Charles Grandison Finney, *Lectures on Revivals of Religion* (Cambridge, MA: Harvard University Press, 1960) 12f.

souls[7]...The object," he concluded, "is to get up an excitement, and bring the people out."[8]

Among those who were "brought out," and who in turn "brought out" many after them, were personalities that loomed large in the various branches of the Restoration movement. Most of them have seldom, if ever, been examined in the theatrical limelight that this article will cast upon them. In no particular order, they are:

- AMASA LYMAN (1813-1877), advisor to Joseph Smith and, after his death, member of Brigham Young's advisory group of the First Presidency;

- GEORGE A. SMITH (1817-1875), Joseph Smith's first cousin, also a twelve and First Presidency member; later, the first official historian of the Latter-day Saints, and the redactor of Joseph Smith's journals into the *History of the Church*;

- HEBER C. KIMBALL (1801-1868), member of the Council of Twelve and Council of Fifty in Nauvoo, First Counselor to Brigham Young who later appointed him Governor of the provisional state of Deseret, and a Utah Territorial Legislator at the end of his life;

- ERASTUS SNOW (1818-1888), another member of the twelve, active missionary, LDS colonizer of the West, and adviser to Brigham Young;

- BRIGHAM YOUNG himself (1801-1877), with whom readers are familiar;

- HIRAM B. CLAWSON (1826-1912), a jack-of-all trades: architect, stonemason, businessman, master of debate, actor, and close associate of Brigham Young—in fact, Young's son-in-law, taking two of Young's daughters as his last plural wives; also the first manager of the Salt Lake Theatre;

- JARED W. CARTER SR. (1801-1849), a counselor close enough to Joseph Smith to have been named in several sections of the Doctrines and Covenants, and believed to have been one of the architects of the vigilante Danites; repeatedly in and out of favor with Joseph Smith Jr. until his murder, upon which he became a Strangite for a time, only to return quietly to the Brighamites for a few years before his death in 1849 in Illinois;

- his son, the aforementioned JARED W. CARTER JR. (1838-1874), who became an itinerant actor;

---

7. Frank Otto Gatell and John M. McFaul, eds., *Jacksonian America 1815-1840: New Society, Changing Politics* (Englewood Cliffs, NJ: Prentice-Hall 1970) 51.

8. Gatell and McFaul, *Jacksonian America*, 52.

- the aforementioned siblings William Jenkins Coggeshall (1836-1906), known by his stage name W. J. "Bill" Cogswell, and his sister Carrie Coggeshall (1834-1895), first married to actor Thomas A. Lyne—then, in an extremely awkward turn of events, leaving Lyne for Jared Carter Jr. in 1862; and

- Lincoln Jared Carter (1865-1926), son of Carrie and Jared, the spectacularly successful actor, playwright, theatrical manager, producer, and inventor of patented theatrical effects still in use today; who became known as "King of the Melodrama" until the introduction of cinema eclipsed his brilliant career.

"Joseph's Actor:" T. A. Lyne and the Succession Crisis

All of these colorful characters spent time in the crucible of New York's Burned-over District.[9] But, of particular interest, is a then-prominent tragedian named Thomas Ackley Lyne[10] (1806-1890, fl. 1829-1885), who toured extensively through the Burned-over District both before and after his involvement with the Latter-day Saints in Nauvoo. Lyne shared the stage with the nineteenth century's most renowned theatrical personalities. At the time of his death in 1890, he was acknowledged as "the oldest actor in America" by a theatrical press that kept careful track of such things.[11] It has long been known that Lyne raised a company of amateur LDS actors to support his dramatic repertoire in Nauvoo from April through June 1844, including a benefit for Joseph Smith's legal-defense fund that also featured members of his inner circle, including Brigham Young in a fabled but non-speaking cameo as a Peruvian high priest.

Historical memory of Lyne and his work has faded significantly in the 130 years since his death. However, over a quarter-century of archival digging has revealed Lyne to be the true, if inadvertent, father of theatre and elocution among the Lat-

---

9. In chronological order: Clawson was born in Utica in 1826; Jared Carter, Sr. was baptized into the Latter-day Saints in Colesville in 1832; Young and Kimball were baptized the next year on the same day, at the same meeting at Mendon. 1834 was a banner year for this crowd in the District: George A. Smith was baptized a Latter-day Saint in Potsdam; Snow was an LDS missionary in the vicinity at the same time; Lyman was baptized by an LDS missionary that same year in New Hampshire, then rushed westward into the Burned-over District, only to find that Joseph Smith had relocated the Saints to Pennsylvania, eventually catching up to them in Kirtland, Ohio. Carrie Coggeshall, a young actress whose family (including brother William) had migrated from Massachusetts to Buffalo in the 1850s, would return to the Niagara area again and again with her second husband to perform, and to retire there at the end of her life. Jared Carter was performing in Rochester, where the two were staying with Carrie's sister, when she gave birth to their son Lincoln on April 15, 1865 (which should give us some clue as to why he was given that first name).

10. See esp. Noel D. Carmack, "The Seven Ages of Thomas Lyne: A Tragedian Among the Mormons," *The John Whitmer Historical Association Journal*, vol. 14 (1994) 53-72.

11. See e.g. "The Oldest Actor Gone," *The World* (New York, NY), April 2, 1890, p. 2, col. 6, item 2; *Weekly Register-Call* (Central City, CO), May 2, 1890.

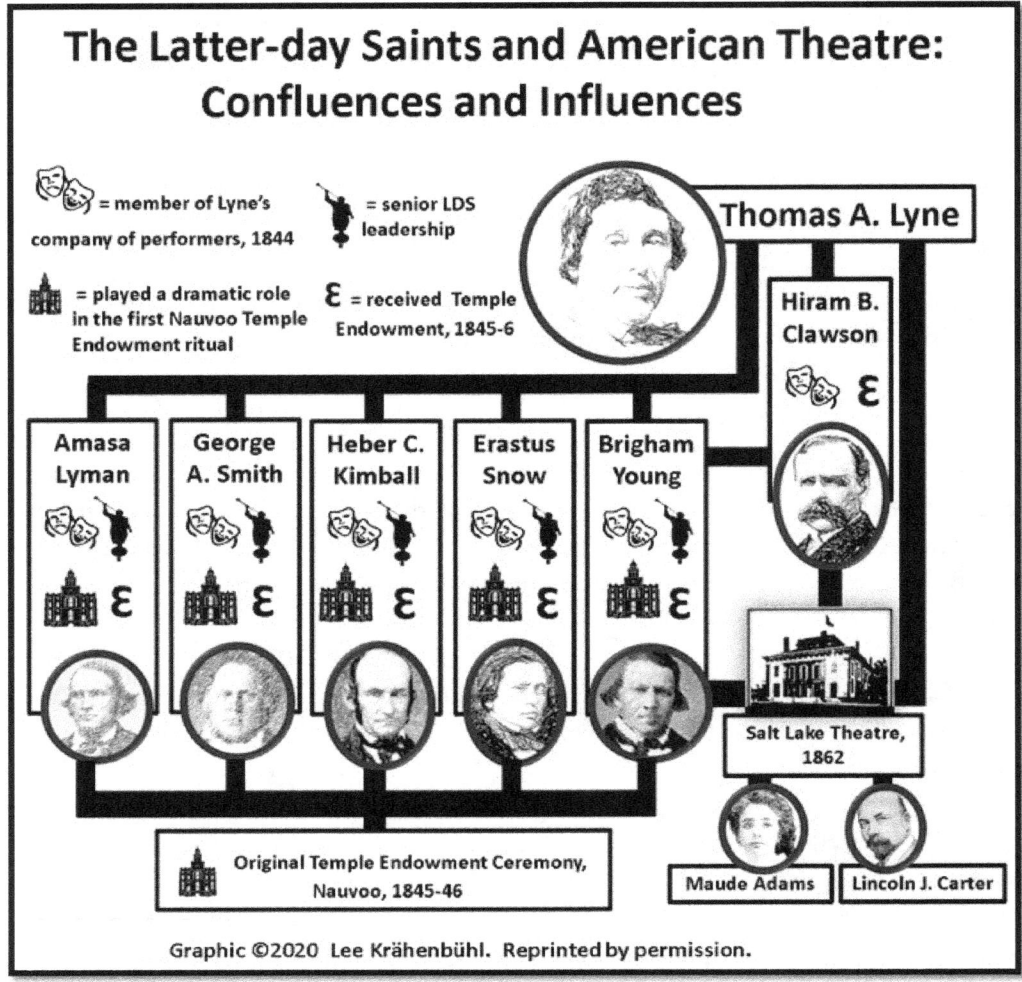

FIGURE 1. *Confluences and Influences: Latter-day Saints and American Theatre*

ter-day Saints, and thereby of the earliest professional productions sanctioned by any English-speaking religious community. Evidence of Lyne's surprising influence on later developments in Mormon ritual also emerges, as diagrammed in Figure 1. Lyne's indirect connection with the Nauvoo Temple endowment ceremony is ironic in light of his later battle against Brigham Young's authority, which would consume him thereafter, both during his nemesis's lifetime and beyond his passing.

Why, then, is so little remembered of Thomas A. Lyne? How is it that this prominent American tragedian, this significant presence in Nauvoo during the Spring of 1844, this member of the entourage of the soon-to-be-murdered Mormon founder, has receded into obscurity? The answer can be found in the Succession Crisis of

Summer 1844, the power struggle created by the murders of Joseph and Hyrum Smith.

The short version of a very long story is that Lyne found himself in non-Brighamite company after the assassination, though he was not immediately aware of the imminent danger from his former colleagues that this posed. He joined forces with two men who would prove to be his undoing. One was his brother-in-law GEORGE J. ADAMS (1811? or 1813?-1880), a failed tailor/actor/former-Methodist convert who had introduced Lyne to the Restoration.[12] The other was Joseph Jr.'s brother WILLIAM SMITH (1811-1893), who supervised a proselyting tour of Boston, Bedford, and New York with Lyne and Adams in September and October 1844. What Lyne had not known was that William Smith had secretly been teaching the secret doctrine of polygamy. When Lyne wrote a very public editorial cautioning Mormon women against the advances of anyone who held such views,[13] the younger Smith apparently feared that exposure was imminent—and promptly excommunicated him *in absentia*.[14]

Confused and embittered, Lyne threw his support to SIDNEY RIGDON (1793-1876), Joseph Smith's vice-presidential running mate in the abandoned 1844 U.S. election campaign. But within two years, Rigdon's movement imploded. Lyne half-heartedly lent his histrionic efforts to the Strangites until both the leader of that movement and his lieutenant, George J. Adams, were also exposed as polygamists, at which point Lyne abandoned all involvement with any Restoration movement for the next decade.

As a result of Lyne's rejection of the Brighamites and subsequent support of Rigdon and Strang, the narrative of the Latter-day Saints has gradually ossified into the mistaken legend that it was Joseph Smith himself who organized a theatre troupe in Nauvoo in 1844. Lyne appears in that narrative only as an incidental character, when he appears at all. A closer look reveals that the story in its present form did not, however, emerge until some six decades after the events in question. Even so, the fallacy persists not only in popular Mormon writing,[15] but also in modern theses,

---

12. See Reed M. Holmes, *The Forerunners*, 2nd ed. (Pepperell, MA: Reed and Jean Holmes, 2003); *Dreamers of Zion: Joseph Smith and George J. Adams: Convection, Leadership, and Israel's Renewal* (Brighton: Sussex Academic Press, 2012).
13. *The Prophet*, October 5, 1844, 2-3.
14. *The Prophet*, November 2, 1844, 2.
15. Stahle, "Good Theater is Part of Good Life," *Church News*, June 19, 2003, https://www.thechurchnews.com/archives/2003-06-21/good-theater-is-part-of-good-life-101748, accessed Feb. 26, 2020

dissertations, and scholarly studies.[16] It was asserted again as late as 2016 in a major historical work about Mormons during the Civil War.[17]

But—ironically enough, because he bitterly opposed the institution and hierarchy of the LDS for the last quarter-century of his life—it was truly T. A. Lyne (not Joseph Smith) who introduced the practice of professional theatre to the Latter-day Saints.

Confluences and Influences between the Earliest LDS Theatre and First Temple Endowment

Lyne was theatrical director and elocutionist to a company of amateur players in Nauvoo in the spring of 1844, some of whom were prominent officials in the Church of Jesus Christ of Latter-day Saints. What has never before been acknowledged is that his work therefore influenced the eventual execution of the very first temple endowment ceremony held in the Nauvoo Temple in the winter of 1845-46, long after Lyne had departed the scene.

Consider the six men pictured in the middle row of Figure 1: Young, Smith, Kimball, Snow, Lyman, and Clawson. All were members of the loose collection of amateurs whom Lyne gathered around him to perform plays in May and June 1844, one of which was a benefit for Joseph Smith's legal defense fund. The first four were members of his Council of Twelve, the most powerful men in Nauvoo after Smith himself. The fifth, Lyman, joined the council after Smith's death. Interestingly, all six took part in the earliest Temple endowment ceremony in Nauvoo. Young, Lyman, Smith, Kimball, and Snow *all assumed dramatic roles in that original version of the ritual* in 1845; a teenaged Hiram Clawson received his endowment in the ceremony, enacted by his fellow players from Lyne's former company in February 1846. There can be no doubt that each played specific roles in the ceremonies, based upon documentation within the respective journals of William Clayton, Amasa Lyman, Heber C. Kimball, and others.[18]

Jonathan Stapley noted in 2018 that, in the months leading up to his assassination, Joseph Smith had begun sublimating written revelation proclamations "in favor

---

16. See e.g. Harold Ivan Hansen, "A History and Influences of the Mormon Theatre from 1839-1869," unpublished doctoral dissertation, State University of Iowa, 1949, 8ff; Nola Diane Smith, "Reading Across the Lines: Mormon Theatrical Formations in Nineteenth Century Nauvoo, Illinois," unpublished doctoral dissertation, Brigham Young University, 2001, 28ff; Lori Hurd, "Theater as a Means of Moral Education and Socialization in the Development of Nauvoo, Illinois, 1839-1845," unpublished thesis, California State University Dominguez Hills, 2004, 19ff.

17. See John Gary Maxwell, *The Civil War Years in Utah: The Kingdom of God and the Territory That Did Not Fight* (Norman, OK: University of Oklahoma Press, 2016) 120f.

18. See e.g. William Clayton, *An Intimate Chronicle: The Journals of William Clayton*, George D. Smith, ed. (Salt Lake City: Signature Books, 1995), entries for December 15ff, 1845-46. Lyman's and Kimball's journals corroborate Clayton's detailed assignations of dramatic roles to each participant.

of his living oracle. Instead of a systematic written liturgy," Stapley writes, "Smith introduced ritual concepts and people learned to participate in them through proximate example and oral instruction. Each ritual was thus performative in the sense that church members and leaders learned it together."[19] After Smith's death, Brigham Young picked it up from that point, formalizing the endowment ceremony as it commenced in the uncompleted Nauvoo Temple in the winter of 1845-46, building on Joseph Smith's model of ritual-through-performative example.

Considering the fact that Young, Kimball, George A. Smith, Lyman, and Snow rehearsed the dramatic sketch at the heart of the temple endowment that winter and that Hiram Clawson received his endowment in that same ceremony the following February, the question must be asked: Whose lessons were being remembered as they "learned it together," refining the endowment into a repeatable ceremony? Before coming to Nauvoo, none of these men from the Burned-over District would in their wildest nightmares have entertained the idea of receiving dramatic training because the social risk would have been too great.[20] Yet, in the Spring of 1844, they appeared onstage together. Who had given them their six-week course in how to stand, how to transition from one scene into the next, how to convert an empty room into a theatrical space, how to move as individuals and a group, and how to articulate, enunciate, and project their spoken roles? Their acting coach and elocutionist had been Thomas A. Lyne, tragedian. While never himself involved in the temple endowment ceremony, he had surely trained those who first staged it.

Thus, Lyne's preparatory work during the Spring of 1844 became woven into the very fabric of Mormon temple practice by the winter of 1845-46. To say that this is significant is an understatement. As Stapley writes, "The Nauvoo Temple introduced a radically expanded cosmology, and the entirety of Mormonism realigned itself to accommodate"[21]—and at the heart of this realignment was a ceremony performed by actors trained by T. A. Lyne.

Ironies abound. Lyne was exiled from the main body of the "Brighamites" in the Fall of 1844 by Joseph Smith's erratic brother William Smith, who would soon have his own problems with Brigham Young. This drove Lyne to the Rigdonites, completely out of touch with the LDS community in Nauvoo. Therefore, not one of the performers in that original temple endowment in 1845 and '46—not Brigham Young, George A. Smith, Heber C. Kimball, Amasa Lyman, Erastus Snow, or any of the others whom Lyne had coached—ever afterward acknowledged the fact of Lyne's influence as they rehearsed, blocked, and staged the new temple endowment.

---

19. "Smith's revelations were heavy on exhortation and extremely light on polity." Jonathan A. Stapley, *The Power of Godliness: Mormon Liturgy and Cosmology* (NY: Oxford University Press, 2018) 6.

20. See esp. Johnson, *Church and Stage*, for striking examples of this stigma and its social effects in the nineteenth century.

21. Stapley, *Power of Godliness*, 6.

It would never have occurred to them to do so. Moreover, because the endowment was a secret ceremony, Lyne would forever be unaware that he had a hand in shaping the performative liturgy of a new American religion. In 1844 Lyne had provided onstage thespian tutelage to Brigham Young, who within two decades would in turn establish the grandest theatrical venue west of the Rockies. Yet the two men would spend the last active decades of their lives in a very public dispute with one another, in a setting neither of them could have imagined.

Once the Brighamites had established themselves in Salt Lake City, Young commissioned the building of the Salt Lake Theatre. To manage the business side of the venue, Young selected his son-in-law Hiram Clawson—the precocious young actor Thomas A. Lyne had drafted into his original company in Nauvoo eighteen years earlier.

By this time in late 1862, Lyne was down on his luck and stranded in Colorado Territory with two small children in his care while his third wife, Carrie, was on tour of Rocky Mountain towns in a company with Jared W. Carter Jr. Lyne was well aware at the time that Carrie was about to leave him for Carter.[22]

When an associate tipped Lyne off about the opening of the Salt Lake Theatre, Lyne wrote a letter to Brigham Young requesting employment[23] and Hiram Clawson convinced his father-in-law to give him a chance. Lyne departed for Salt Lake City, acted as elocution coach to the company, and appeared in all his signature classical roles there until the rift between him and Young became insurmountable. He opposed Young's authority to the end of his long life in Salt Lake City, and outlived Young by thirteen years—almost out of sheer spite.

And there are yet deeper layers of irony to explore.

As noted earlier, Carrie Coggeshall was to leave Lyne in early 1863 to become the new Mrs. Carter. To explore the remarkable connections here, the story returns to Nauvoo, Illinois, in the Spring of 1844, when Lyne was performing with his company of amateurs at the Masonic Hall. It is most likely that he was lodging at the City Hotel[24] during his three-month stay in the city. During the first week of April, Lyne was baptized a Latter-day Saint by Amasa Lyman. Down the next block, less than a minute's walk from his hotel, his neighbors were Sidney Rigdon, who had run the Nauvoo post office out of his home for a time, and Joseph and Emma Smith, who had just moved into the new Mansion House, part of which also stands in Old Nauvoo as part of Community of Christ's historic homestead.

---

22. See Melvyn Schoberlin, *From Candles to Footlights: A Biography of the Pike's Peak Theatre, 1859-1876* (Denver: The Old West Publishing Co., 1941) 110ff.

23. T. A. Lyne to Brigham Young, November 11, 1862.

24. The building, which served as a boarding house, tavern, and Masonic meeting place under several names, still stands in historic Nauvoo at the northwest corner of Main and Sidney streets.

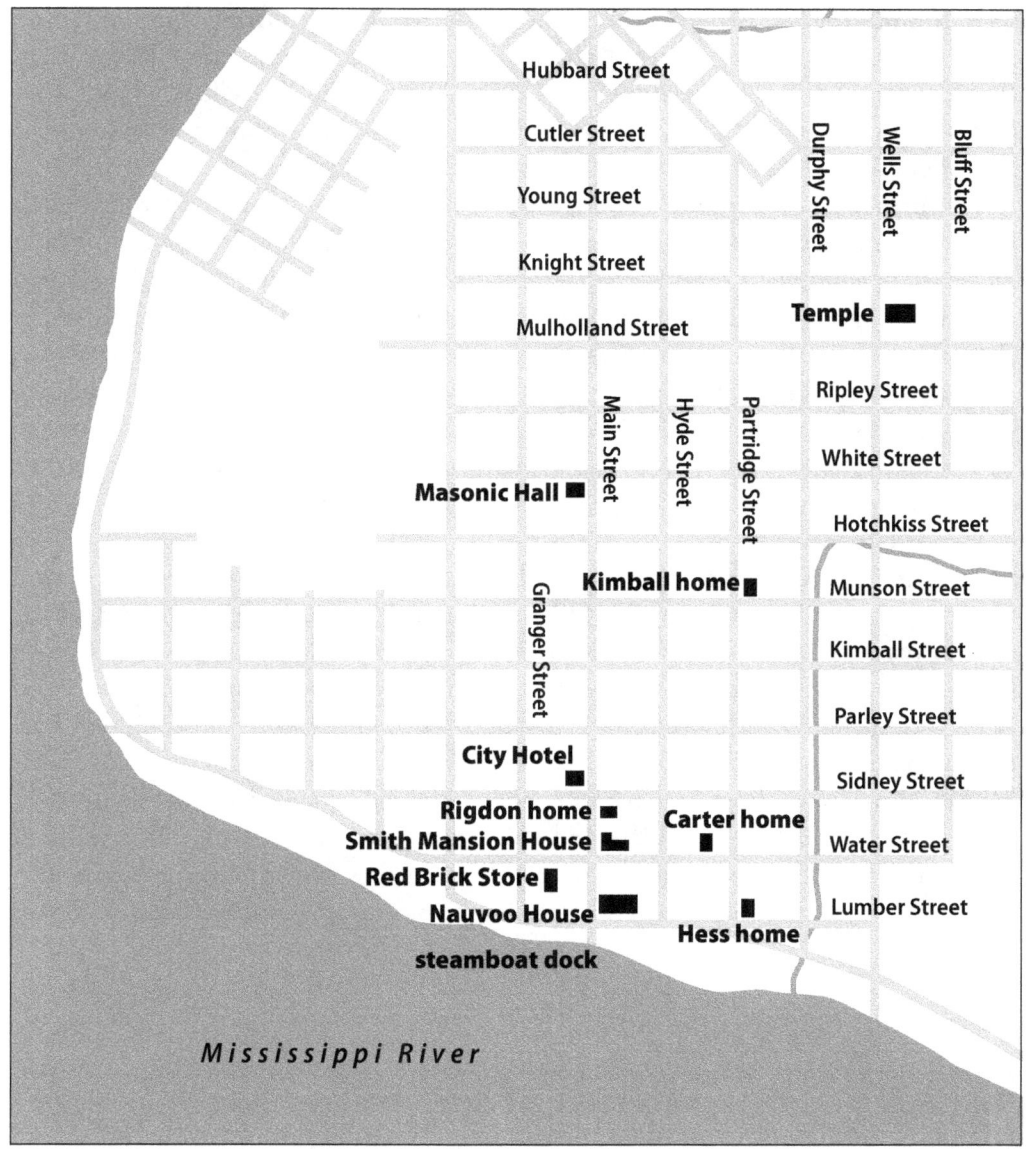

FIGURE 2. *Thomas A. Lyne's Nauvoo. Map by John Hamer.*

Upon arriving at Nauvoo in April 1844, Lyne had immediately divorced his first wife, Mercy Adams, *in absentia*.[25] Circumstances and later events lead to the conclusion that because Lyne was eager to become a Latter-day Saint and Mercy was apparently refusing to leave New York City to join him, Amasa Lyman, who baptized him, assured him that divorce was not only acceptable but necessary. Joseph Smith's entourage (i.e. Adams, Lyman, Kimball, and others) even had a second

---

25. *Nauvoo Neighbor*, May 1, 8, 15, 1844, 4, col. 5 item 2.

wife in mind for him whom Lyne immediately set about courting.[26] It was MARY ANN HARLAN HESS (1824-1852), the daughter of the recently transplanted LDS high priest of Philadelphia, PETER HESS (1799-1877) and his wife MARIA LEIDY (1805-1879), who lived in the same neighborhood, just a five-minute walk from the Mansion House.

A further irony becomes apparent upon tracing Lyne's steps past the Rigdon home, turning eastward at Joseph and Emma Smith's Mansion House onto Water Street, then southward onto Partridge Street to arrive at the house the Hesses had rented (see figure 2).[27] Each time Lyne visited Mary Ann, he passed the house of the elder Jared Carter Sr. on Water Street, just a block east of the Mansion house.[28]

And who was likely to have been playing in the yard of that house on any given sunny day? Six-year-old Jared Carter, Jr.—who was to run away with Lyne's third wife some eighteen years later—and two years after that, while staying at Carrie's sister's home in Rochester where Jared Jr. was starring, was to welcome Lincoln Jared Carter into the world.

But the ironies do not stop there. Mary Ann Hess had a little brother named CORTLAND VAN RENSAALER (C.V.) HESS (1838-1887) who, like Jared Carter Jr., was also six years old in the spring of 1844. Little Cortland and little Jared lived one block from each other in Nauvoo while Lyne was wooing Cortland's sister Mary Ann from April to June 1844. Both Jared and Cortland were youngest sons of prominent Latter-day Saints[29] and each may have even seen Lyne perform onstage at the Masonic Hall in May 1844. It is truly remarkable that *both would grow up to become actors.*

It is important to understand the significance of this fact. No parents of children in any other religious community born in 1838 would have welcomed such a decision to go on the stage; even Latter-day Saints approached theatre attendance

---

26. Circumstances seem to indicate that Lyne's courtship of Mary Ann Hess was arranged well ahead of time between Amasa Lyman, who baptized Lyne, and Peter Hess, who was a fellow Philadelphian, with the understanding that Lyne's first marriage would be annulled by the LDS leadership. Lyne's wife Mercy Adams was the sister of Joseph Smith's associate George J. Adams, who has to have been complicit in the arrangement in order for it to be approved.

27. Peter Hess is listed as a tenant in Munson Lands, block 157, south of Water Street, bounded by Hyde Street to the west and Partridge Street to the east. Historic Nauvoo Land and Records Research Center, Peter Hess, file 20184.

28. The remains of the basement of Carter's house can still be seen, fenced but unlabeled, in Old Nauvoo. See Historic Nauvoo Land and Records Research Center, Jared Carter, Sr., file 5211.

29. Carter had been an advisor to Joseph Smith for over a decade (see Historic Nauvoo Land and Records Research Center, Jared Carter, Sr., file 521100; Hess had been the local leader of the Saints in Philadelphia the previous year, and would continue in that role when he moved his family from Nauvoo back to that city after the assassination (see Walter W. Smith, "History of Philadelphia Branch" and "Local Historians," *Journal of History*, Reorganized Church of Jesus Christ of Latter-day Saints, vol. 12-13 [1919] 532ff).

with suspicion.[30] In 1846, Lyne wrote for a Rigdonite newspaper an account of his LDS conversion. He recalled his rejection at the hands of religious folk in other Protestant groups with bitter sarcasm:

> Now christians [sic], start and [gasp, "]the wicked one["]![...] Your pious pastor, in many instances, being aware there were actors near his atmosphere, has entertained his liberal auditors with denunciations, loud and angry, against the followers of Thespius [sic], till they have felt they were in the presincts [sic] of hell, instead of being in the house of charity, which is God's house. This is not an uncommon thing. Many can testify to this who would often be found in a house of worship, but the priest tells them, they are the children of the devil, and would contaminate his pure flock, of which he is the essence.[31]

Lyne went on to disclose that, with only two notable exceptions, this anti-theatrical attitude had repelled him from church attendance for over ten years before he joined the Mormons.

Two little boys born in 1838—who spent a few weeks in their childhoods watching actor Tom Lyne walk back and forth between the City Hotel and the Hess property to woo Cortland's sister—both grew up to become actors despite this powerful social stigma outside Mormon circles. And both would be reunited by a momentous later event of mid-April 1865—not in each other's presence, but certainly in history's.

Three Degrees of T. A. Lyne

It is apparent that Cortland Hess had grown up idolizing his brother-in-law Lyne. Years later, after Cortland's sister Mary Ann died suddenly in 1852 and Lyne had remarried Carrie Coggeshall, Jared Jr.'s reunion with Lyne must surely have been less than affectionate. But Lyne had by then influenced not only the formulation of the temple endowment ceremony, but also these two actors, Hess and Carter, who had their own roles to play in American theatre history on April 15, 1865. On that day, C. V. Hess was giving depositions to police in Washington, DC, because he was a member of the company of actors at Ford's Theatre and had witnessed the assassination of Abraham Lincoln.[32] And Jared Carter Jr. was welcoming his first son into

---

30. Joseph Smith laid out his own views along this line in a letter of April 1, 1843 to one "Lyman Powell" in Spring 1843, discovered by Noel A. Carmack, at the time an archival conservator at Merrill Library at the University of Utah. It was not immediately clear who this "Lyman Powell" could have been, aside from an "itinerant actor." My subsequent research reveals that the letter had actually been written by Lyne himself—as spokesman for "Lyne and Powell," the troupe he was managing at the time with his partner, John H. Powell. See Noel A. Carmack, "A Note on Nauvoo Theater," *BYU Studies Quarterly*, vol. 34 issue 1, 94-100.

31. T. A. Lyne, "Communications," *Messenger and Advocate of the Church of Christ*, Greencastle, PA, vol. 2 #8, whole #32, 509.

32. C. V. Hess was a signatory to an open letter from the company of Ford's theatre to the general public, deploring the assassination perpetrated "by a fiend named John Wilkes Booth, who has used our profession as an instrument to the accomplishment of his horrible and inhuman design..." *The New York Clipper*, May 6, 1865, 30,

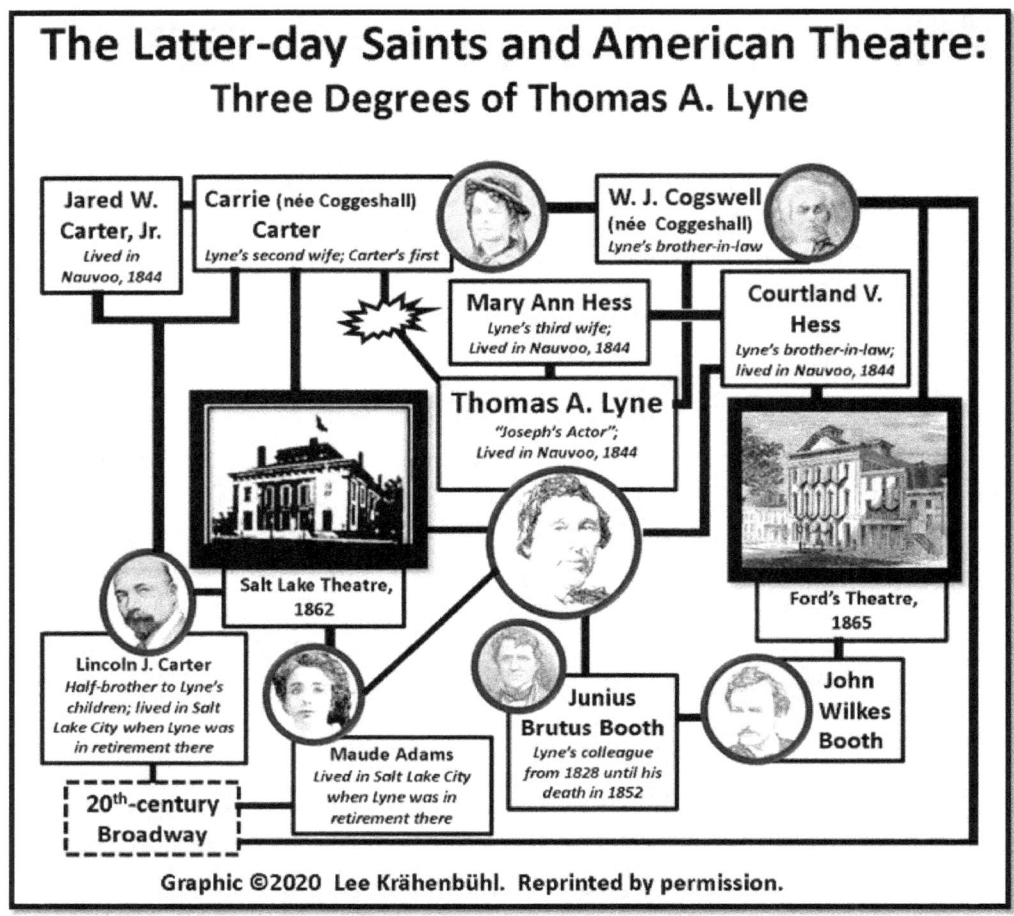

Figure 3. *The Latter-day Saints and American Theatre: Three Degrees of Thomas A. Lyne*

the world with his wife Carrie Coggeshall Lyne—a son they named Lincoln Jared Carter when news of the assassination reached them.

This is not Lyne's only connection to the resident company of Ford's Theatre. Aside from the many actors who had played opposite him and had also appeared there, one of Lyne's other brothers-in-law—W. J. "Bill" Cogswell, to whom Lyne had given his first regular acting work as a teenager in his company in Milwaukee in 1855[33]—had been an actor in the Ford's company the year prior to the Smiths' murders, playing Tressell in *Richard III* opposite none other than Junius Brutus Booth

---

col. 3; see Thomas A. Bogar, *Backstage at the Lincoln Assassination: The Untold Story of the Actors and Stagehands at Ford's Theatre* (Washington, D C.: Regnery History, 2013) 81ff, 112ff, 164, 223ff, 251, 277.

33. See e.g. *Milwaukee Daily Free Democrat*, November 3, 1855, 3, col. 3, item 6.

Jr., the son of Lyne's colleague, and friend and brother of Lincoln's assassin.³⁴ Most of Cogswell's fellow actors in the company were present the following year.³⁵

T. A. Lyne was, in fact, the center of a web of relationships in the twin worlds of the new American religion of the Latter-day Saints and the antebellum American theatre. When displayed graphically (**Figures 1 and 3**), Lyne's web of confluence and influence recalls later writer Frigyes Karinthy's concept of "six handshakes" or "six degrees of separation"³⁶—the notion that no one on earth is more than five relationships removed from anyone else. T. A. Lyne's level of connection here can be reduced to three; in most cases, in fact, he was directly involved with the significant events, movements, and people of both worlds.

Lyne's connection with Ford's Theatre and the Lincoln assassination—he was two degrees separated through C. V. Hess, and three through both W. J. Cogswell and through his close relationship with Junius Brutus Booth. Sr.³⁷—is only one instance of this web. Lyne was personally and professionally acquainted with the greatest actors of his day. Both he and the elder Booth were particularly close to EDWIN FORREST (1806-1872), the first American international superstar of the stage; Booth named a son after him, and Lyne was born the same year and in the same city as he. Others, more obscure today but household names before the Civil War, read like a roll call of theatre history: THOMAS ABTHORPE COOPER (1776-1849), MARY ANN DUFF (1794-1857), TYRONE POWER (1795-1841), ELLEN TREE (1805-1880), CHARLOTTE CUSHMAN (1816-1876), WILLIAM CHARLES MACREADY (1793-1873), and GREENBURY C. GERMON (1816 – 1854), who would go on to originate the title role in the first stage version of *Uncle Tom's Cabin*.

Carrie and Jared Carter and Carrie's brother William were all eventually leading members of the acting company at Brigham Young's Salt Lake Theatre.³⁸ Lyne was connected to all of them, and through them to Lincoln J. Carter—born in Rochester, New York, in the heart of the old Burned-over District and named for the fallen President who had been assassinated by the son of Lyne's close associate.

---

34. *Evening Star* (Washington, D. C.), October 18, 1864, 3, col. 3.

35. See Bogar, *Backstage at the Lincoln Assassination*, passim.

36. See Frigyes Karinthy, *Chain-Links (Láncszemek)*, in *Minden Másképpen Van. (Ötvenkét Vasárnap.) [Everything Is Different. (Fifty-Two Sundays.)* (Budapest: Atheneum Irodalmi és Nyomdai R.-T, Budapest, 1929) 85-91. Available in English translation at https://djjr-courses.wdfiles.com/local--files/soc180:karinthy-chain-links/Karinthy-Chain-Links_1929.pdf, accessed 13 December 2019. John Guare popularized the concept in his play (1990) and film (1993) *Six Degrees of Separation*.

37. It is even possible that Lyne met a teenaged John Wilkes while acting with the elder Booth in Baltimore, but no solid evidence of such a meeting has yet emerged. Odds are slim that any will, as the elder Booth's widow burned all his personal correspondence after his death. See Asia Frigga Booth Clarke, *The Unlocked Book* (New York: GP Putnam's Sons, 1938) 35.

38. See e.g. John Lindsay, *The Mormons and the Theatre, or the History of Theatricals in Utah* (Salt Lake City, 1905), chs. XIV-XV.

It was Lincoln J. Carter who would go on to become the most commercially successful of them all. He grew up in Ogden and Salt Lake City while Lyne was still performing there and watched his parents from the wings of Brigham Young's theatre (which had begun under the management of Lyne protegee Clawson), eventually becoming a call boy. Carter knew Lyne well; he was half-brother to Lyne's two children with Carrie Carter. He was holder of dozens of patents for stage-effect machinery, was the first stage director in America to use movies in his productions, and was known as "King of the Melodrama" from his first success, *The Fast Mail*, in 1892. He was also known through his commercial dominance of the Chicago stage, his success in the Broadway theatres of Manhattan, and through several simultaneous touring companies of a dozen subsequent plays. In sum, Lincoln J. Carter was by far the most famous and influential of any theatre practitioner with an LDS background before the advent of cinema.[39] Another alumna of the Salt Lake Theatre, Maude Adams, knew Lyne in his retirement and continued to write about him nearly a quarter-century after his death.[40] In sum, through Adams and Carter, Lyne has a third-degree connection to 20th-century Broadway.

T. A. Lyne, the Mormons, and Theatre in American Culture

As previously noted, Lyne had been drawn to the Latter-day Saints by his brother-in-law George J. Adams. It was not, however, their doctrines that had brought him to Nauvoo. As Lyne described the conversation with Adams that had led to his conversion:

> This minister of the gospel, so far forgot his piety, as to go into a coffee house, where we refreshed ourselves. I questioned the propriety of this, for such were my pharisaical notions then, oh! [...] he informed me that he was God's free man, kept a strict account with his own conscience, always preserved a ballance [sic] in his own favor, and was tolerably indifferent to the opinion of the whole sectarian world.—Honest, responded I, let us understand this doctrine, that has done so much to megamorphose [sic] you from a pretended sanctified Methodist, to a righteous, yet liberal practiser [sic]; if it bears the impress of good sense, free from the blighting mildew of priestcraft dressed in its long robes of outward osterity [sic], I will embrace it, no, I'll think of it. ["]Come and hear me lecture[," he replied]. We parted, he half sure of a convert, and I on rather favorable, terms with the world again, that a man might by accident stumble on a kindred spirit.[41]

Thomas A. Lyne did not become a Latter-day Saint because of the church's theology, which he never fully understood even when acting as an evangelist on the

---

39. See e.g. Jane Glotfelty Rhoads & Jamison David Rhoads, "The Business of Show: Lincoln J. Carter and J. J. Shubert," *The Passing Show: Newsletter of the Shubert Archive*, vol. 34 (2017-19).

40. See "The Life Story of Maude Adams and Her Mother," *The Green Book Magazine*, June 1914, 895-899.

41. Lyne, "Communications," 509.

church's behalf. He converted because he was assured by George J. Adams that, unlike in any other religious community in America, he would be accepted and respected as an actor. Had Lyne not been successful in legitimizing the vocation of the professional theatre in Nauvoo, it is highly unlikely that either Jared Carter Sr.'s widow or Peter and Maria Hess would have allowed their sons to enter the profession; neither would Lincoln J. Carter nor Maude Adams have likely joined the ranks of its successes.

And that is how professional theatre came to Nauvoo, and from Nauvoo to the Salt Lake Theatre, and through the Salt Lake Theatre to enter the mainstream of American culture. After the Latter-day Saints had not only condoned theatre attendance in 1844 but had, by the end of the century, produced nationally famous theatric professionals from among their ranks, antitheatrical resistance among other religious communities throughout the United States had begun to recede. By the twentieth century and the apex of Carter's and Adams' fame, such resistance was largely a thing of the past; Americans might object to the content of a given performance or genre, but none would again suggest that the practice of theatre was itself morally reprehensible.

It was the Latter-day Saints who had pioneered the practice of theatre among English-speaking American religious communities. A web of confluences and influences interwove their movement with the history of the American stage, and at its center was "Joseph's Actor," Thomas A. Lyne.

LEE KRÄHENBÜHL, PhD, (LKrahenbuhl@stevenson.edu) has taught theatre history and world religions at the college and university levels since 1989. He is the author of the forthcoming biography *'Joseph's Actor': Rediscovering the Life and Career of the Eminent Tragedian Thomas A. Lyne (1806-1890), Accidental Father of Theatre & Elocution Among the Latter-day Saints*. Dr. Krähenbühl is Program Coordinator and Associate Professor of Communication, Interdisciplinary, and Professional Studies at Stevenson University Online, and President of the Maryland Communication Association. He lives in Silver Spring, Maryland with his family.

Why Did the RLDS Youth Programs Disappear After a Half-Century of Success?

Sherry Mesle-Morain

FROM THEIR INCEPTION in the 1910s to their full strength in the 1940s, 1950s and 1960s, the Reorganized Church of Jesus Christ of Latter Day Saints (RLDS, now Community of Christ) enjoyed a bounty of youth programs beyond Sunday Church School. These programs served boys and girls from ages seven to older youth in their early twenties. By the end of the 1980s, most of these programs were either no longer offered or had morphed into activities very different in nature and frequency. In his *JWHA Journal* article in 2011,[1] Mark Scherer asked, "What caused the demise of the Zion's League program in the 1980s after a half-century of service to youth? Assess the history of youth work as a general church program." This paper explores both the development and the demise of these programs.

Development of RLDS Youth Programs

President Frederick Madison Smith (1914–1946) was the visionary who saw the value of a strong youth program and recognized those men who would provide such ministry. In 1917, he appointed Floyd M. McDowell as leader of the boys' movement of the church. McDowell also worked closely with Eugene Closson, the church's first full-time youth leader, and together they established the first church youth camp at Nauvoo in 1928.[2]

In the 1936 "Conference Daily Edition of The Saints' Herald" was a report by F. Henry Edwards addressed to the First Presidency:

---

1. Mark A. Scherer, "Beyond Nauvoo: Discovering the Reorganized Church Story Again for the First Time," *John Whitmer Historical Association Journal* 31, no. 2 (2011), 37.

2. Stephen K. Smith, "Nauvoo Camp and the Rise of Organized Youth Camping in Community of Christ," *John Whitmer Historical Association Journal* 39, no. 2 (2019), 15.

We are suffering severe losses among the children and young people, who are not being held to the church because of the sheer impossibility of ministering to them in our present limited quarters. We will do the best we can until we get more room, but really effective work must wait until this difficulty is removed.[3]

At that same conference, Presidential Counselor McDowell met with 200 young people over two days to discuss the "need for a church-wide program for young people of the church."[4] Though the funds were not available for full-time leadership, Closson and George C. Mesley recommended "...the full-time active service of a man who could meet the needs of young people throughout the church and give the leadership that President McDowell formerly gave to this field."[5] Zion's League was officially established, just one year later, in 1937 to serve young people in grades 9 through 12. "This movement within the RLDS Church again paralleled the larger Christian youth movement of the consolidation of denominational fellowship groups during the 1940s. This was due in part to the fear of losing denominational distinction and a diffusion of denominational loyalty."[6]

The anticipated full-time director of youth work finally arrived in 1947 when F. Carl Mesle Jr. answered the call to work with the church young people in Independence, Missouri. It was Gene Closson who had nurtured Mesle when he was a student at Graceland College in the 1930s, giving him an image of what Zionic youth work ought to be.

Mesle had spent four and a half years in professional Scouting, first as a field executive in Camden, New Jersey, and briefly in Kansas City, prior to his being called up in 1941 to serve in the United States Army. President F. M. Smith initially invited him to go under appointment before he got out of the Army in December 1945 at the end of World War II. He declined, citing a commitment he had made to H. Roe Bartle, Scout Executive of the Kansas City Boy Scout Council to serve as Field Executive for that Council. However, the next year Mesle was asked again by C. George Mesley on behalf of President Israel A. Smith to assume leadership of youth work in Independence, Missouri.[7] He was the first appointee professionally trained specifi-

---

3. F. Henry Edwards to The First Presidency, "Report of Independence and Headquarters," *Conference Daily Edition of The Saints' Herald.* Independence, MO. April 5, 1936, 25.

4. *Conference Daily Edition of The Saints' Herald.* April 9, 1936, 65-66.

5. E. E. Closson, C. G. Mesley, "Report of the Department of Religious Education, The Young People's Division," *Conference Daily Edition of The Saints' Herald,* April 5-6, 1936, 43.

6. Michael Hoffman, "The Transformation of Youth Ministry in the Church: A Historical Perspective," Unpublished seminary paper, Community of Christ Seminary, Independence, MO. June 1998, 11.

7. Carl Mesle, Transcript of an Oral History conducted by Ron Van Fleet. Independence, Mo, 1975, Oral History Interview Collection, Community of Christ Archives, 4.

cally for his assignment.[8] He assumed the role of full-time Youth Director for Center Stake and, in 1950, as General Church Youth Director.

Girls' Programs

The Oriole program for girls was begun in April of 1915, followed in 1919 by the Blue Bird program for younger girls. Estelle Lentell, appointed by the First Presidency under the leadership of President F. M. Smith, nurtured both programs for over twenty years. By 1936, 297 girls participated in the fifty-one registered Oriole circles from seventeen states, Canada, England and Australia.[9] In 1939, the first Oriole camp was held at what is now Lake Doniphan Conference and Retreat Center, Excelsior Springs, Missouri.[10] In 1950, the Blue Bird program was renamed Skylarks so as not to be confused with the Camp Fire Girls' Blue Bird program for their young girls.[11]

It was Mesle's opinion that "...of all the programs going on, the best job was being done by the Girls' Work leader. They had a church-centered program, they had a real devotion and these women were very much interested in these girls..."[12]

Edna Easter, Director of Girls' Activities from 1945, served side by side with Carl Mesle in youth work. Skylarks enjoyed activities suitable to their age and attended overnight camp at church campgrounds. To encourage them to establish good habits for daily living, each Skylark had a chart on which she checked off each day's activities such as make your bed, pick up your clothes, set the table. Orioles earned badges in a wide variety of areas from Wildflowers to Etiquette and they attended a week-long camp. The Light of Life program, written by Easter for Orioles and implemented in 1946, was analogous to the Boy Scouts' God and Country Award.[13]

One of the reasons the church established its own girls' programs was to include a spiritual component to the girls' activities, including the Light of Life award. The Girl Scouts of America "owned" their Scout troops, and spiritualization was not significant in their programming, whereas the Boy Scouts of America gave ownership of the Scout troops to the sponsoring faith groups, who were encouraged to provide the spiritualization component so long as the Scout leaders adhered to BSA program standards. Mesle had to prove to volunteer Scout leaders that this was the case

---

8. Dick Lancaster, email message to author, June 3, 2018.

9. C. B. Woodstock, "Blue Birds, Orioles and Temple Builders; Report of the Department of Religious Education," *Conference Daily Edition of The Saints' Herald*. April 5, 1936, 44-45.

10. Edna Easter, "Camping from the Ground Up," (Independence: Reorganized Church of Jesus Christ of Latter Day Saints, Christian Education Office, 1976), 10.

11. Easter, Edna, Transcript of an Oral History conducted by Ronald Van Fleet. Independence, MO, 1975. Oral History Interview Collection, Community of Christ Library Archives.

12. Mesle Oral History, 17-18.

13. Easter Oral History.

as they initially thought they were not allowed to combine religion and Scouting. Quite the opposite was true.[14]

Boys' Programs

The first Boy Scout troop west of the Mississippi River was started by W. O. Hands in 1910, the same year the Boy Scouts of America came across the ocean from its origins in England. This was Troop #1, sponsored by the Stone Church congregation.[15] Floyd McDowell, always active in boys' work, was responsible for creating one of the first Protestant God and Country Awards in 1945.[16] Although the church's Boy Scout program grew slowly at first, with fifty troops registered in 1954, between 1956 and 1958, the General Conference reported a 34% increase from sixty-seven units to ninety-two units, including 1,014 Boy Scouts enrolled in the RLDS God and Country program.[17]

Zion's League

Mesle describes the state of the Zion's League program in 1947 at the Stone Church in this anecdote from his 1975 Oral History. "[T]here were 24 Zion's Leaguers attending meetings at the Stone Church. They were all girls! The boys hung out, waiting for the girls to finish so they could go on dates." He continued, "Well, you can't build the kingdom without men, so we focused on programs that ministered [to] and attracted boys..."[18]

By 1954, under Mesle's leadership, there were estimated to be 420 organized Zion's Leagues church-wide.[19] An increase in youth conferences, retreats, and youth leaders' training institutes no doubt accounted for the increase to 439 Zion's Leagues with 5,800 young people involved by 1958.[20]

Junior Zion's League

The success of the Zion's League program led the Church Youth Director in 1954 to report to the First Presidency, "A church-centered, coed Zion's League-type program for junior high boys and girls eleven through fourteen is now under

---

14. Mesle Oral History, 16-18.
15. Charter #2686, Original in P63, W. O. Hands Papers, Community of Christ Archives, Independence, MO. The troop number was later changed to 223 following a fire that destroyed original records.
16. Mesle Oral History, 17.
17. *Conference Bulletin*, October 5, 1958, 55.
18. Mesle Oral History, 4-5.
19. *Conference Daily Edition*, October 5, 1954, 12.
20. *Conference Bulletin*, October 5, 1958, 55.

development."[21] The challenge was to develop materials specifically for this group that would correlate with the other boys' and girls' programs and the regular Zion's League materials. By 1958, success in this effort resulted in 110 branches reporting that they had junior high Zion's Leagues.[22]

Camping

The church's camping program began in 1928 at Nauvoo with some thirty campers. By 1953, there were nearly 4,000 junior and senior high campers attending thirty-nine camps, which grew to fifty-seven camps in 1955.[23]

Mesle's approach to camp leadership was to spend time in camps across the country, return home to develop leadership materials, and then go back to the field for face-to-face volunteer training to augment the materials. He began the next year's camp helps while in the midst of the current camp season to document successes and problems in order to make the next year's season go better. He also had an established relationship with the American Camping Association for camp standard accreditation.[24]

Mesle's philosophy about camping was unique among Christian church camping programs. "Most churches were conducting preaching in the woods, Sunday School in the outdoors...where the kids got stuffed up to their ears with Paul's travels and came home and didn't want to go to church for six months."[25] He continued, "Camping is a great Christian experience where you have some teaching, worship and fellowship." He felt it connected the kids to the church because "they see that the church is really interested in having fun, having great fun...that helps young people identify with the church." He added elements to reach the boys like skeet shooting, horsemanship, paddle boarding and water skiing where available, as well as the usual swimming, boating, canoeing, and archery, with experienced instructors for each activity. These were interspersed with a religious class or two and some short devotionals. The day always closed with a campfire that included songs, skits, sometimes testimonies by the campers, and always a meaningful devotional.

By 1958, 4,550 campers were served by 1,338 staff members. Nonmember campers totaled 572, suggesting the church camp experience was an effective missionary

---

21. *Conference Daily Edition of The Saints' Herald*, No. 1. Independence, MO April 4, 1954, 12.
22. *Conference Bulletin*, October 5, 1958, 55.
23. *Conference Daily Edition*, 1956: 91.
24. Mesle Oral History: 13. Mesle served on the ACA National Board and reported that "others were interested in how we ran our camps."
25. Mesle Oral History, 12-13.

tool as well as providing members a powerful connection to the church and to one another.[26]

Older Youth Programs

Recognizing a disparity of interests in the older young people (ages 19 to 24) compared to high school students, and observing that this was the age group of greatest loss to the church, the church Youth Director pushed for at least a half-time appointee to meet this need.[27] This development came about in an unexpected way that will be discovered later in this paper.

Carl Mesle's Leadership Style

In 1950, Mesle's assignment expanded to General Church Youth Director, responsible for all the church's youth programs, including camping.[28] He had a vision, too, and was a natural successor to F. M. Smith, Closson, and McDowell.

Lee Hart, a new employee hired to care for church grounds called The Campus, worked for six months with Mesle before assuming the role of Center Stake Youth Director.[29] During that time, the two men laid the groundwork for Hart to develop some very creative youth activities in the "Center Place."

The church owned nineteen acres just east of the Auditorium in Independence on which sat the Swope Mansion, formerly the home of a wealthy family, many of whom died under suspicious circumstances in the mansion.[30] It seemed appropriate, then, that for several years the Swope Mansion was turned into a haunted house at Halloween by industrious Zion's Leaguers. The Campus, as the nineteen acres were called, became a prime community recreation area in the summer with volleyball, basketball and softball fields for Zion's Leaguers and all their friends and family,[31] serving also the nearby high school's gym classes in spring and fall.

The area set into the slight hill on the south side became an amphitheater where summer Sunday evening church services were held. But, more exciting to the young people, were the operettas that were performed there every summer. One year it was

---

26. Conference Bulletin, October 5, 1958, 56.
27. Carl Mesle to First Presidency, January 8, 1954.
28. Mesle Oral History: 5. See also *Conference Daily Edition of The Saints' Herald*, April 6, 1952, 114.
29. Ibid, 6.
30. "Headlines Were Made at Campus in Distant Past," *Conference Daily Edition of The Saints' Herald*, No. 6. April 9, 1954, 96.
31. F. Carl Mesle memorandum to Apostle W.E. Timms, "Youth Loss in Center Stake." September 26, 1967. In the author's possession.

Gilbert and Sullivan's *The Mikado*,[32] another year it was Talbott and Reubens' *The Blue Moon*. And another year it was George and Ira Gershwin's *Of Thee I Sing*, then Lerner and Loewe's *Brigadoon*. The young people—high school and older youth—were the performers, but everyone and their parents got involved with sets, costumes, orchestra, staging, and promotion.

Opportunity for drama extended through the school year when local congregations produced their own one-act plays, an activity which culminated in a competition for the best play in the stake.

The RLDS Auditorium at that time was still in pretty rough shape, meaning the hallways and ramps (not staircases) were concrete. The lowest level, with its own covered entryway, served as a gymnasium. Saturday nights were dedicated to recreation activities for Zion's Leaguers—and their friends. They had a trampoline and volleyball net, a wrestling mat, and lots of board games. The evening always ended with a short, campfire-style vespers.[33]

Carl Mesle believed in communication. He made clear to the First Presidency, since they were his direct supervisor, the purpose of youth programs as he envisioned them:[34]

a. To have fun
b. To build skills
c. To provide creative and positive activities like art, drama, music, camping, service
d. To avoid negative activities like dancing, sex, drugs and alcohol
e. To build connections to the church
f. All for the purpose of experiencing fellowship

These represented the four official activities of Zion's League: Service, Study, Worship and Recreation.

Repeat: Mesle believed in communication. As early as 1950, Mesle began to push for a magazine that would speak directly to the interests and needs of teenagers.[35] *STRIDE*, a monthly magazine edited by Roger Yarrington, was launched in October of 1956.

---

32. Mark S. Scherer, *The Journey of a People: The Era of Worldwide Community, 1946 to 2015* (Independence: Community of Christ Seminary Press, 2016), 29.

33. Carl Mesle memorandum to Apostle W.E. Timms, September 26, 1967. In the author's possession.

34. Mesle memo to First Presidency, January 8, 1954. In the author's possession.

35. Ed Brown, Carl Mesle, exchange of letters, June 10 and June 16, 1950. In the author's possession.

In January of 1954, Mesle wrote an expansive two-part memorandum to the First Presidency (Israel A. Smith, W. Wallace Smith, and F. Henry Edwards) to express his vision for the future of the church's youth programs.[36]

Using his standard style, he enumerated six separate areas of youth work, each accompanied by three to five dense and detailed paragraphs on the personnel needs of each program, why they were needed, and suggestions for men—it was always men—who could do the jobs well. The program positions were:

1. Editor for a Youth Paper
2. A Director of Young Adult Work
3. Executive Secretary for Ministry to College People and to Servicemen
4. A Director of Junior High Programs
5. A Camping Guidance Man
6. Chaplain at Graceland

He concluded this lengthy memo:

At first glance this might seem extravagant of manpower, but we are constantly reminded that up to one-half of our membership falls within the age group listed above and that it is within these ages that our greatest losses occur. This has been due largely to our past inability to supply the specialized ministry to meet their needs. With adequate tools and training, our volunteers can provide that ministry under the general supervision of our appointees in the field.

The shorter memo addresses the organizational relationship of all youth programs to the Department of Religious Education. The perception at that time was that the primary responsibility of the department was for the Sunday Church School materials with all the other youth programs being subordinate. Mesle was pushing for each of the six areas he discussed above to have its own line of reporting to the department director, including a separate reporting line of the Sunday Church School. Such a relationship in the department would be reflected at the congregational level where the church school director, which is a full-time volunteer position, would be responsible for Sunday Church School only. The other youth programs, referred to as activity programs, would have their respective volunteer leaders, making these programs much stronger. Although the need to coordinate the development of program materials should prevail, the activity programs require separate planning, materials, and training of volunteers to meet the needs of the age groups.

The amount of detail Mesle included in these two persuasive memos intended to reorganize the entire Department of Religious Education must have left the members of the First Presidency exhausted and overwhelmed. What must it have been

---

36. Carl Mesle to First Presidency, January 8, 1954. In the author's possession.

like to supervise Carl Mesle? Their response, however, showed that they paid attention. The April 4, 1954, *Conference Daily Edition of The Saints' Herald*,[37] the official recorder of General Conference business, made the recommendation for this division of assignments. The 1956 *Daily Edition* showed Mesle's new assignment: "Mesle, F. Carl. Young People's Camps, Ministry to College Students, Ministry to Armed Forces Personnel."[38]

This change in assignment for Mesle felt like a rebuke. Responsibility for the youth activity programs that he loved was taken from him. Now he would be responsible for the older youth programs—college students and military personnel. He and Lee Hart in their respective oral histories mention Mesle's getting crosswise with the First Presidency. Dick Lancaster reported the same in an email and in conversation.[39] Perhaps this was why Mesle's youth work assignment was ended altogether when, at the 1958 General Conference, Lyle Woodstock was appointed the first full-time Camping Director.[40]

Nonetheless, in the 1960s Carl Mesle's vision of how youth work should be led began to come to life. But as Newton described in his Third Law of Motion, for every action there is an equal and opposite reaction. That describes precisely the church's youth programs in the 1960s.

The Blossoming of Programs in the 1960s

Richard Lancaster, the Director of Youth Division from 1956-1960, echoing Mesle, wrote a lengthy memo to the First Presidency describing modern young people and their needs. He noted the loss of youth leaders like Dr. McDowell, Charles Neff, Carl Mesle, and Roy Cheville to age or other assignments. He reiterated that youth needed leadership for the many activities and programs they craved. Their local leaders depended on assistance from General Church leaders, but there were almost none. He impressed upon them the necessity of youth leaders being out in the field, sharing the experience of youth work, and training volunteer leaders instead of being rooted to the office at headquarters, churning out materials blindly.[41] As Carl Mesle described it, "They were turning youth ministers into editors."[42]

---

37. *Conference Daily Edition*, 13.

38. Ibid, 118.

39. Lancaster phone conversation, September 8, 2019.

40. *Conference Daily Edition of The Saints' Herald*, October 5, 1958:,107.

41. Richard B. Lancaster memorandum to The First Presidency, "Needs of Youth Work," April 15, 1959.

42. Mesle Oral History, 24

1. In 1960, Lee Hart, who had so ably and creatively followed Carl Mesle as Center Stake Youth Director, was called back from a four-year assignment in Los Angeles Stake to assume the role of General Church Youth Director.[43]
2. The demand for materials for junior high youth resulted in Hart's establishing Zioneers in 1962, replacing the Junior High Zion's Leagues.[44]
3. In 1962, Joe David Donald was appointed full-time director of Zioneers and Zion's League.[45]
4. In 1964, Hart produced the first World Church Camp and Youth Leaders' Training Camp at Camp Doniphan, the same year he began the Older Youth Service Corps.
5. In 1966, Church leadership appointed Larry Cavin followed by Robert Taylor as full-time boys' director, they renamed the Youth Division as Youth Ministries Division, and they appointed William Outhouse as the first full-time Youth Ministries editor.[46]
6. Edna Easter continued her strong leadership of Girls' Work—Skylarks, Orioles, and in 1969, O'Teens for older Orioles. An abundance of materials and training were provided for both congregational Skylark Bands and Oriole Circles and for girls' camping.

The church seemed to be doing it all: increasing programs, appointing full-time appointees for each program, and providing dynamic training for volunteer leaders.

The Demise of Programs in the 1960s

But the world and the church shifted in orbit and the reaction began even as the explosion in leadership and programming took place.

1. Of significance was that Carl Mesle, the face of the church's youth programs,[47] was gone from youth work altogether. In the 1960s, Lee Hart carried the torch skillfully and with passion.

---

43. Hart Oral History: 26. Hart reported that F. Henry Edwards was surprised that Lee wanted to continue to do youth work. He (Edwards) saw it as a steppingstone to something more important. Handwritten manuscript, September 11, attached to p. 26.

44. Hart Oral History, 11.

45. *Time Line: Organized Youth Ministry in the Restoration*, 1969. Community of Christ Archives, Independence, MO.

46. Ibid.

47. Mark Scherer, email communication to author, July 9, 2018, "... let me do say that I am probably archetypical of world church youth fully engaged in such programs during the 1950s, 1960s, and 1970s. Any young person who was actively involved became a product of Carl Mesle's influence, whether it be while attending Sunday School or at youth camps. Carl's voice no doubt was heard through his ministry. We all have him to thank for our spiritual nurturing, denominational grounding, and deep church roots."

2. The world changed in the wake of the Civil Rights Movement, which inadvertently gave equal rights to women as well as the intended minority: African-Americans; the Women's Movement, which found women entering the workforce in greater numbers; the Vietnam War, which created political division; and the Student Movement.
3. In 1962, the World Conference Report of the First Presidency included the following: "While due concern should be given to the interests of the several age groups, we would point out that in some areas the division between these groups has been so strongly defined as to disrupt the unity which we seek and has tended to the development of activity programs rather than the pursuit of Saintliness with its requirement of high endeavor and fervent testimony."[48]

   When this report was written, W. W. Smith's two counselors were F. Henry Edwards, who had been there through the development of all these youth activity programs, and Maurice Draper, who had served as an apostle for nine years, four of which were in Australia, and whose children had the advantage of all these programs.
4. The gymnasium in the Auditorium was closed to youth recreation in order to provide meeting rooms.[49]
5. The church was moving, like the trembling of tectonic plates, from the one-and-only true church to a church with a mission, committed to taking its story to the world.

   As Charmaine Chvala-Smith commented when learning about this thesis, "The church couldn't create materials because they didn't know what message to give young people. They couldn't tell them any longer that we were the one-and-only true church, and the church leadership had not yet developed the nature of the church's mission, as in 'we are a church of mission.'"[50]

   The shift of the church's image created tension and dissension among the church membership, such that a substantial contingent separated from the main body and founded other groups, taking with them significant revenue.
6. The federal government created two service programs that proved to be popular with young people, the Peace Corps for service abroad and VISTA–Volunteers in Service to America, referred to as the domestic Peace Corps.
7. In 1968 Joe Donald noted in his "Case for Christian Service"[51] his rationale for engaging the church young people in serving human needs in their Christian capacity, much as the Peace Corps and VISTA did in their secular capacity.

---

48. World Conference Bulletin, No. 4, 87.

49. Hart Oral History, 5.

50. Charmaine Chvala-Smith, personal conversation at Community of Christ Library, July 30, 1919.

51. Joe D. Donald, "Case for Christian Service: A preliminary statement of rationale for the new Zion's League program," Department of Religious Education, April 1968. Community of Christ Archives (RG22 F233).

The Zion's League Handbook, which he released in 1969 in his role as Director of Youth Division, reflected the shift from broad activity programs to service programs.[52]

8. In 1968, *STRIDE* magazine ceased publication and was folded into six pages of the *Saints Herald*.

9. No new materials for girls' programs were created until the mid-1980s, and those were the last.

What Followed

Of interest is that the World Conference Bulletin of 1972 included no mention of a Youth Division, unlike every other Conference Bulletin since the 1940s. In 1973, the church did support the creation of Sports Spectacular by a group of concerned church members including Tom Cochran who served as Director.[53] Over 1,000 high school students and their leaders from across the country and Canada spent a week on the Graceland University (then Graceland College) campus in Lamoni, Iowa, participating in multiple sports, art, music and leadership activities as well as worship.

Throughout the 1970s, reporting of the youth programs at World Conference was merely perfunctory. The church allowed its activity programs to fade.

Similar changes were happening within churches nationally. Churches were recognizing the competition for funds from their myriad youth programs and so began pulling back support, declaring youth should be more involved in their local congregations.

In lieu of creating their own materials, an expensive product when done right, youth ministers of all faiths began looking outside their institutions for resources. An organization called Youth Specialties was started by two part-time youth ministers in 1968, Wayne Rice and Mike Yaconelli, and by Group Magazine and Publishing, started by Thom Schultz in 1974. "By 1970 Rice and Yaconelli took a risk by sponsoring an event which became known as the National Youth Workers Conventions…Through high quality resources, communications, and training events, these youth ministry trendsetters would begin a process that would lead to the recognition of youth ministries as a profession."[54]

In the 1980s, society changed. The church changed. Reaching out to an international membership, the church redirected its finite resources to building a Peace Temple,[55] and resources are finite.

---

52. *Zion's League Handbook*, 1969. Community of Christ Archives, 6.

53. David Goehner, *The Graceland College Book of Knowledge* (Lamoni, Iowa: Graceland University, 1997), 286.

54. Hoffman, 23.

55. Wallace B. Smith, April 6, 2019, as cited in *The Forum* (Nauvoo, Illinois), Community of Christ Historic Sites Foundation: 2. (It was a time of unrest and upheaval, an unpopular war, changing women's roles, and a

In 1990 Jerry Ashby, World Church Youth Minister serving under President Wallace B. Smith, created Forefront Ministries,[56] an umbrella for all children's and youth programs.

In 1994, Michael Hoffman began his service as the last full-time Director of Youth. He was serving in this capacity when, in June 1997, President W. Grant McMurray announced the church leadership's new initiative, Transformation 2000. It provided funds for the church's Youth Minister to hire dozens of youth ministers in order to reach out to 20,000 children, youth, and young adults.[57] Those funds were no longer available the next year, so new ways had to be devised to reach young people. Forefront Ministries leadership discussed publishing RLDS curriculum on CDs or the Internet.[58]

Hoffman noted in 1998, "It will be important to financially support youth ministry, regardless of economic conditions, to reach the current generation of children and youth and each new generation with the old, old story."[59] He was reassigned to Phoenix, Arizona, in 2004.

Within two years the First Presidency, under the leadership of Stephen Veazey, quietly closed the Office of Youth Ministries.

Today, Spectacular is going strong on the Graceland campus every summer. There are full-time youth ministers assigned to some but not all Mission Centers, a wide geographical area that may include up to twenty congregations.

The Heartland Mission Center, which includes Des Moines and Lamoni, Iowa, is one of the few mission centers that can afford to have a full-time youth minister in its employ. The youth, boys and girls together, are divided into three age groups for the purposes of activities and focus: Juniors, grades 1–5; Junior High, grades 6–8; Senior High, grades 9–12. They participate in myriad activities offered by a variety of organizations, so assembling them at least once a month for recreation and service activities is a challenge. Their gatherings generally include all the youth from the mission center and occasionally are joined by another mission center. Once a month, they plan and direct the worship service for one of the mission center congregations. Youth camps are offered in the summer as they have been since 1928, always bringing together teenagers from two or more mission centers. Even weekend winter retreats are held at local campgrounds.

---

changing understanding of the church's mission. As president and prophet I was much distressed. But the Spirit impressed on me more and more that a Temple dedicated to teaching, healing, and reconciling was needed."

56. Ibid, 25.

57. Ibid, 29.

58. Ibid, 32.

59. Ibid, 33.

The world church provides no program guidance or training materials for its youth ministers except required safety rules; rather, they learn their ministry through experience and from the youth leaders who preceded them. Youth ministers depend on parent volunteers whose time is already consumed with ferrying their youngsters to ball games, Scouts, and school activities. Adults who do wish to register as regular volunteers are interviewed by the youth minister and then undergo a background check arranged for by church headquarters. This screening process, the first instituted by a Christian denomination, was begun in 1995 by then full-time youth minister Mike Hoffman.[60]

It is the rare congregation that still calls its teenage program Zion's League. Small congregations struggle to offer any of these activities if, indeed, there are any children to engage. As Peter Jackel, full-time Youth Minister for the Heartland Mission Center, observed:

> Kids are different from what they used to be. They are guarded by their parents and the adults in their lives. Also, they have so many demands on their time and attention that they fit their church youth activities into their schedules as they can, rather than as the priority.[61]

The good news is that this group of full-time youth ministers are driven by their desire to spend time with the young people, expose them to activities both fun and somber, and share with them their dedication to church values and beliefs.

Why did the church's youth programs disappear after a half-century of success? Hoffman describes one lesson from his research: "An examination of major agencies of youth ministries over the past two centuries supports the idea that effective ministry peaks and begins to decline around either a fifty-year cycle or the death of the ministry's founder."[62]

Whether inevitable or not, many share the feeling of loss expressed by Mark Scherer: "I cannot conclude this without reflecting on the sinking feeling I had as our entire youth division at headquarters disappeared now more than a decade ago. I watched from my office in the Temple and was so saddened as today's youth program disappeared into the institutional quicksand along with the Zion's League and Zioneer programs that were so influential upon me."[63]

---

60. Hoffman, 19.
61. Peter Jackel in conversation with author, Lamoni, Iowa, November 26, 2019.
62. Hoffman, 6.
63. Mark A. Scherer, personal email communication to author, July 9, 2018.

Before and after raising two children, SHERRY MESLE-MORAIN spent most of her professional life in higher education, most recently as Director of Financial Aid Services at Graceland University in Lamoni, Iowa, her city of residence. She has a BA degree from Tufts University and an MSW from Smith College School for Social Work. She served as the JWHA Executive Director for three years and as President in 2017-2018.

Forerunner or Revisionist? The Puzzle of Solomon Chamberlin

Johnny Stephenson

Prelude: Summer, 1989

Rick Grunder is a rare document/book collector and dealer, and wrote that on:

2:22 on the afternoon of Friday, August 11, 1989, I received, by Federal Express, a packet of ten small pamphlets from my friend and colleague Susan Heller…The pamphlets were primarily Shaker…I checked each one off her typed inventory list routinely, including [the third item]:

SKETCH OF THE EXPERIENCE OF SOLOMON CHAMBERLIN TO WHICH IS ADDED A REMARKABLE REVELATION OR TRANCE OF HIS FATHER-IN-LAW PHILIP HASKINS; HOW HIS SOUL ACTUALLY LEFT HIS BODY AND WAS GUIDED TO THE HOLY ANGEL…Lyons, N.Y., 1829.[1]

This pamphlet was bound in "contemporary plain blue wrappers; rather crudely stitched," and Rick observed that "the printing quality [was] fairly primitive." He began to do some research on this Solomon Chamberlin and noticed that the historians who had written about him, quoted from an autobiography whose title didn't match the one listed by Susan Heller. The historians were quoting from an autobiography called "A short sketch of the Life of Solomon Chamberlin."[2]

---

1. Rick Grunder, Discovery of the Solomon Chamberlin/Chamberlain Pamphlet, unpublished manuscript in possession of the author. I wish to thank H. Michael Marquardt, Rick Grunder and William Morian for their invaluable help with my presentation and this article.

2. Solomon Chamberlin, *A Short Sketch of the Life of Solomon Chamberlin*, holograph, 1858, MS 5886, (LDS) Church History Library. Hereafter, *A Short Sketch, 1858*.

Rick subsequently sold the pamphlet to Brigham Young University where Larry C. Porter, Professor of Church History and Doctrine, published its contents in 1997.[3]

Until the discovery of that 1829 *Sketch*, there were only two known autobiographies of Solomon, one that he gave to John Taylor in Nauvoo in 1845[4] and the other (a holograph) written in Utah in 1858.[5]

The reason why this pamphlet is so important to Mormon historians is because, in those two later accounts, Solomon Chamberlin claimed to have had a vision of an angel who told him about the coming restoration (which would include a companion book to the Bible) more than a decade before the experiences told by Joseph Smith Jr. Because of this, he is sometimes referred to as some kind of forerunner to Smith.[6] These are remarkable claims that this newly found pamphlet might possibly verify.[7] Here is Solomon's story, before and after his encounter with the Book of Mormon and the reason (perhaps) he felt the need to revise it.

"I rolled sin under my tongue…"

Solomon Chamberlin was born on July 30, 1788, at "old Canaan" in the northwest corner of the state of Connecticut, just five years after the Treaty of Paris was signed, ending the Revolutionary War. In his later 1858 *Sketch*, he described his father Joel as a hard-working, successful farmer who had "accumulated considerable property."[8] Solomon wrote that his father was originally from Tolland, Connecticut, in the northeastern part of the state, and that his mother Sarah Dean was also "born in the same state."[9]

---

3. Larry C. Porter, "Solomon Chamberlin's Missing Pamphlet: Dreams, Visions, and Angelic Ministrants," *B.Y.U. Studies Quarterly*, Vol. 37, Issue 2, 4-1-1997.

4. John Taylor journal 1844 December-1845 September, handwriting of George Q. Cannon, Church History Library, MS 7277, 52. Hereafter, *John Taylor Journal 1844-45*.

5. See note 2.

6. For example, see Val D. Rust, "Mormonism and the Radical Religious Movement in Early Colonial New England," *Dialogue, A Journal of Mormon Thought*, Vol. 33, No. 1, Spring 2000, 25-55; Mark D. Thomas, *Digging in Cumorah, Reclaiming Book of Mormon Narratives*, Signature Books, 1999, 61; Dieter F. Uchtdorf, "A Great Work of God," First Presidency Message, April 2010, 1.

7. Larry Porter wrote, "Obviously, the content of that [1829] pamphlet might prove to be a valuable resource in identifying the circumstances that brought this earnest seeker after truth to Smith's door. It might also give a more inclusive narration of his personal associations with angelic visitors." (Porter, op. cited, 115).

8. *A Short Sketch 1858*, 2.

9. Ibid. Joel Chamberlin was born on 4 October 1747, d. circa 1800. Joel was first married to Hannah Palmer, b. 21 May 1749, d. 18 March 1769, born in Coventry, Windham County, Conn. Daughter of John Palmer & Abigail Boynton, Married Joel c. 1768 in Tolland, died at age 19, 10 days after giving birth to a daughter named Hannah, b. 8 March, 1769. Hannah later married Joseph Chamberlin, b. 1765 who was perhaps a cousin. (See Chamberlain GEDCOM File, compiled by David Conrad Chamberlin Sr., Salt Lake City, Utah, File imported 11 September 2005).

By 1756, the last of the Indian tribes had been pushed out of Connecticut except for about a thousand who were (for the most part) friendly to the settlers. They had gathered around the town of Kent, a temporary refuge for those who struggled to maintain their traditional way of life. As the natives were pushed out, more and more settlers flocked to what was then deemed the far west.[10]

By November 1774 Joel had settled in the town of Canaan, where he married his second wife Sarah Dean.[11] According to available birth and genealogy records, all of Joel and Sarah's children were born in Canaan, Litchfield County, Connecticut, where Joel lived with his family until just shortly before his death in c.1800.[12] Solomon recalled in his 1829 account that when he was in his ninth year, his father "moved to Hillsdale, in [New] York State, and a few years after departed this life, leaving no evidence behind that he had closed his eyes in peace."[13]

Solomon would later write in 1858, "what little property I received from my father's estate did me little or no good,"[14] indicating that he may have received a small inheritance of land when he reached adulthood.

Since his father had given him no indication of being a religious man, his death "made a solemn impression on my mind," but this "soon wore off."[15]

These would have been trying times for a widow raising a handful of children under the age of 15, including a two-year-old toddler. About six months after his father's death, Solomon also lost a younger brother and began to "feel awful on account of my sins" and "thought I should die and go to hell."[16]

At that time, Solomon would have been no stranger to religion; when his mother Sarah moved to Green River, Columbia County, New York, she joined the Congregational Church, pastored by the Reverend John Morse, a teacher of the New Divinity.[17]

---

10. History of Litchfield county, Connecticut, J.W. Lewis & Company, Philadelphia, Pa., 1881, 264ff

11. Sarah Dean was born on 7 Jan. 1757, married Joel Chamberlin in 1774 and died c. 1811. (Conrad, op. cited).

12. Children of Sarah Dean and Joel Chamberlin: Son Chamberlin b. c 1775, d. c 1775, John Chamberlin b. c 1780, Joseph Chamberlin b. c 1782, Sarah Chamberlin b. c 1785, Solomon Chamberlin b. 31 Jul 1788, d. 20 Mar 1862, Son Chamberlin b. c 1792, d. c 1799, Lewis Chamberlin b. c 1794, Electa Chamberlin b. 25 Apr. 1796, Polly Chamberlin b. c 1798.

13. Solomon Chamberlin, *A Sketch of the Experience of Solomon Chamberlin, to which is added a remarkable revelation, or trance of his father in law Phillip Haskins How his soul actually left his body and was guided by a holy angel to Eternal Day*, Solomon, Lyons, NY, self-pub, 1829, 1. Hereafter, *Sketch, 1829*.

14. *A Short Sketch*, 1858, 2.

15. *Sketch, 1829*, 1-2.

16. Ibid., 2.

17. John Morse, son of Dea[con] James and Hannah (Daniels) Morse, was born March 24, 1763, in East Medway. He became a Christian in early life and was very active in the revivals of 1785, holding meetings in Holliston, Medway, and other towns. Having determined to enter the ministry, he prepared himself for college, graduating in 1791 from Brown University, Providence, RI. He studied theology with the Rev. Dr. Emmons and the Rev. David Sanford. Having completed his professional studies, he began preaching in the then "far west" and became, in

Church records show that Sarah was received as a member on January 11, 1801 and that Solomon, Lewis, Electra, and Polly were baptized a month later on February 11, 1801.[18] Solomon was fearful that he too might be struck down like father and brother, leading to his remorse and pledge to "lead a better life." But those promises were soon broken during his troubled youth.[19]

Solomon's pastor, the Reverend John Morse, came from a long line of New Divinity teachers—men who gave birth to the Second Great Awakening in America.[20] Growing up in Green River, New York, Solomon could not have had a more competent teacher than the Reverend John Morse, "whose meetings" Solomon would claim in his 1829 *Sketch*, "I had attended from a child."[21]

Yet, as the young man said of himself, he, "...became noted for wickedness" and "rolled sin under my tongue, and turned a deaf ear to all the tender whispers of Christ..."[22]

In 1807, at age nineteen, he dreamed about being pulled "down to the regions of the damned and while standing in the door or gates of the prison...[he] saw them blowing up the flames and preparing red hot irons to lay their faces on to all eternity..." Suddenly, "a stranger appeared in the dream and told him that he could return to earth and take a year to prepare for his death."[23] Such episodes drew him back to Reverend Morse for guidance.[24]

But his pastor left him in a dilemma. In his 1829 *Sketch*, Solomon wrote that he thought Morse could tell him "what to do in order to be saved" since he was

---

1793, pastor of the Congregational Church in Green River, N. Y., remaining for twenty-three years before moving in 1816 to Otego, N. Y. He was installed over the Presbyterian Church in Otego, and served some twelve years. His last sermon, at age 78, was on the occasion of President Harrison's death. He died Jan. 3, 1844, in Otego, having spent over fifty years in the Free Grace ministry, a widely praised legacy. The Rev. Mr. Morse married, Feb. 4, 1793, Clarissa Sanford, daughter of the Rev. David and Bathsheba (Ingersol) Sanford. She was born Nov. 20, 1763, in Medway. (*The History of Medway, Massachusetts 1713-1885*, 417). Solomon claims that John Morse was a "Presbyterian Priest" in his 1829 *Sketch*. Chamberlin was well traveled and possibly knew that Morse had gone to Otego, New York, where he pastored a Presbyterian church.

18. Records of the Congregational Church of Green River (New York), 1792-1845, 26, 48, 75, LDS Family History Department, Salt Lake City, in Larry C. Porter, (1997) "Solomon Chamberlin's Missing Pamphlet: Dreams, Visions and Angelic Ministrants," *B.Y.U. Studies Quarterly*, Vol. 37: Iss. 2, Article 7, 126.

19. *Sketch*, 1829, 2.

20. See note 18.

21. Ibid., 3.

22. Ibid. For Chamberlin's verbiage here, see Matthew Henry's Exposition of the Old and New Testaments, New York, 1850, *Funk & Wagnalls*, Volume 3, 285. (Psalm 66) Henry writes: "If I regard iniquity in my heart, that is, If I have favourable thoughts of it, if I love it, indulge it, and allow myself in it, if I treat it as a friend and bid it welcome, make provision for it and am loth to part with it, *if I roll it under my tongue* as a sweet morsel, *though it be but a heart sin* that is thus countenanced and made much of, if I delight in it after the inward man, God will not hear my prayer, will not accept it, nor be pleased with it, nor can I expect an answer of peace to it." (added emphasis)

23. Ibid.

24. Ibid.

tormented by the thought that if he died in his present state he would be "eternally miserable."[25] But Morse told him not to be "too forward" but to "wait for the Lords time, and in his own due time he will bring you in."[26] Solomon, however, claimed that Morse had instead darkened his mind, causing him to believe he "was one of the reprobates," so that he would "die and go to hell," thereby forcing him to live under this "dreadful load."[27]

But Solomon wanted immediate forgiveness. Waiting on Jesus, as Morse had advised, was so unbearable to Chamberlin that he rejected his Calvinistic teachings altogether.[28]

"My burthern fell off"

Solomon joined the Methodists in 1805 after attending a meeting at Greenbush, New York (near Albany). He wrote of praying aloud so that his "burthern [burden] fell off" and he "felt a peace of mind." He remained with them for a time, and next with the Quakers, but felt that both were not in keeping with the Bible. His "greatest desire was to find those that lived the nearest to God."[29]

Over the next decade, according to the 1829 account, Chamberlin married[30] and began a successful career as a cooper but remained troubled by dreams about his own salvation.

He wrote of an 1816 dream in which he was travelling a very straight road in search of a righteous community, soon finding himself looking down a valley at a house where he encountered a solemn-faced man with a woman and others who he deemed were "children of God."[31]

Solomon's next step on his spiritual odyssey was to the Reformed Methodists, whom he encountered in Readsborough, Connecticut. The group was led by the very man Chamberlin was sure he had seen in his dream—William Lake—along with another reformer, Elijah Bailey.[32] Lake had been a preacher for the Methodist

---

25. Ibid.
26. Ibid.
27. Ibid., 3-4.
28. Ibid., 4.
29. Ibid.
30. Solomon Chamberlain married Hopestill (Hopee) Haskins on 23 October 1809 at Pownal, Bennington County, Vermont, America.
31. *Sketch*,1829, 4.
32. According to Elijah Bailey's son Wesley: "The Reformed Methodists took their origin from a feeble secession from the Methodist Episcopal Church, in the towns of Whitingham and Readsborough, Vermont, January 16th, 1814. We say feeble secession, because their entire number did not exceed fourteen persons...on the 16th of January, 1814, met in convention at Readsborough ; Elijah Bailey was called to the chair...At this convention they formed themselves into a church under the above name, and appointed a conference to be held on the following 5th of February, at which they adopted articles of religion and rules of church government. At this conference

Episcopal Church but had broken with them to return to what was called "primitive Methodism" that, like Solomon himself, had renounced the episcopal mode of church government.[33]

The Reformed Methodists subsequently bought a farmhouse in the middle of several hundred acres resting on the Vermont-New York state line. Members were encouraged to move there into a community of joint ownership, ostensibly to resemble that of the Book of Acts. Solomon joined "the Combination," as he called it, in Shaftsbury.[34]

Solomon's 1829 *Sketch* states that he in 1816 he experienced a vision at a camp meeting of the "Reformers." This including seeing his "supposed Saviour," who was really "Satan, who had transformed into an Angel of light," followed by the "blessed son of God," who stood close "and said, give your case to me."[35] He sprang up and cried out: "Lord Jesus, live or die, dam'd or saved, all I have and am is thine—I give it thee!"[36] Solomon wrote that it felt as though a pail of water was being poured over his body,[37] giving him humility and a great peace which "became as a river."[38]

But that peace was to be short lived, thanks to some bad luck and weather (1816 was the year without a summer). The Combination failed and the Reformers scat-

---

their number was somewhat increased. Wm. Lake, a local preacher of the Methodist Episcopal Church, united with them at this time...The Reformed Methodists hold the fundamental doctrines of the Methodist Episcopal Church. On the Trinity and the Sonship of Christ, they are with John Wesley, Fletcher, Benson, and Watson, and opposed to the views of Dr. Adam Clarke...Elijah Bailey...[was] bred a Congregationalist...until the Methodist preachers came into Vermont. He was among the first fruits of their labours; was awakened, convicted, and received into their society. (I. Daniel Rupp, *An Original History of Religious Denominations Present Existing in the United States*, (Philadelphia: J.Y. Humphreys, 1844), 456-73).

33. "William Lake...was a native of White Creek, N. Y., of Low Dutch descent, and inherited all the roughness of character peculiar to that class of our citizens in this state. Previous to his conversion he was a gambler, a horse-jockey, boxer, &c., a rare specimen of a man to look up, of an ardent temperament, hasty and undaunted in any thing [sic] he undertook. After his conversion, his ardour, zeal, and physical energies, were all turned into a new channel. He was as zealous for God and the salvation of souls, as he had before been the devoted of all unrighteousness. Having much of the 'good things of this life,' he brought not only his own personal services to the aid of the cause, but by his money did much to sustain his poorer brethren." (Rupp, *An Original History*, 473-74).

34. They may have called it "the combination" based on a basic principle of doing good. As the Reverend John N. Atlerod taught: "American Reformed Presbyterians approve of the great principle of combination for good under the oath of God"...and hold themselves in readiness, when the exigencies of the times may demand, to exemplify it themselves as the age, country, and special circumstances of their condition require." Rupp, *An Original History*, 535. For a short history of the State Line House before and after the Reformed Methodists, see *Mystery, Myth and Memoirs Surrounding the Life of Captain David Matthews, The Man who built the State Line House*, by Corinne Eldred, PDF online, https://www.hoosickhistory.com/pdf/capt_david_mathews.pdf, accessed September 22, 2019.

35. *Sketch, 1829*, 6.

36. Ibid.

37. Ibid.

38. Ibid.

tered.³⁹ Chamberlin returned to Adams, Massachusetts, and joined the Episcopal Methodists.⁴⁰

"I saw my Savior..."

According to his 1829 account, Solomon had the most striking of his dreams in 1819, writing of his "great concern" for fellow church members in Adams.⁴¹ While working in his shop, he described feeling sudden weakness despite being "well in body."⁴² The weakness increased until he was "in awful awe and glory of the presence of Christ [which] filled the room" and his mind "was wonderfully drawn up into heaven." Solomon noted that his appetite for food was "wholly taken away" such that he ate very little for the next week. It was then that he "cried with a vocal voice and said Holy Ghost teach me from the eternal world" and prayed. At that moment, Solomon wrote, he observed "a departed spirit" entering the room.⁴³

This spirit was described as "a woman that formerly had belonged to the society and died happy in the Lord; she was the wife of Daniel Arnold." She saluted him in the apparition with the words: "don[']t you remember the exhortation that I gave you while on my dying bed?" Solomon then, "knew her in a moment" and remembered her comments.⁴⁴

This "sister spirit" was evidently Welthian Holden Arnold, who had died in 1813 at the age of 32. She had informed Solomon he must not live "so light and trifling" and to be more "sober and watchful," and that her husband and others were backsliding from the church in Adams, so that he must give them a message at the next Sunday service.⁴⁵

---

39. Wesley Bailey spoke of "the combination" as follows: "Of the progress of the cause in Vermont, I need not farther speak. The year of the close of the war, with a view to thrust labourers into the field, a sort of community was formed, Wm. Lake, K Bailey, E. Davis, E. Amadon, and [1812] several others being members of it. They bought a farm on the state line in the town of Bennington, Vt, and Hosack, N. Y. This farm [The State Line House] consisted of several hundred acres, and the community, of near a dozen farmers. Providence did not seem to smile on the undertaking, though conceived in the purest benevolence. The cold season's coming on, the want of funds to pay in advance for the farm, rendered it impossible for them to pay for the place, and after remaining near two years on the premises, they were compelled to scatter; not scattered to abandon their principles, but to promulgate them in other regions, where Providence might open the way. (Rupp, *An Original History*, 474).

40. *Sketch*,1829, 6.

41. Solomon claims that what led him to have this vision was being rebuked by the class leader for teaching "sanctification" to unbelievers. But Chamberlin felt that he had simply recognized "the fallen state that the church was now in, and the power of Antichrist." (*Sketch, 1829*, 6-7).

42. *Sketch, 1829*, 7.

43. Ibid., 8. Chamberlin does not refer to these departed spirits in his 1829 account as angels.

44. Ibid.

45. Ibid. Welthian Holden was born in Warwick, Kent, Rhode Island, United States on 1781 to Philip Wightman and Freelove Barton. Welthian Holden had 4 children. She passed away on 05 Jul 1813 in Adams, Berkshire, Massachusetts, United States. (ancestry.com GEDCOM file). Adams appears as a circuit in 1802, with Samuel

Solomon described that he had felt a "spirit of discernment" indicating that the church was on a "sandy foundation."[46] Feeling humbled, he "saw my Saviour stand before me with the bible in his hand, and said to me this is the book—live in the spirit that this was wrote and you shall shine in the eternal world on high."[47] The denouement of this experience gave rise to a reliance on the Bible as the penultimate message of his 1829 pamphlet.

"Many refreshing seasons"

The final and most important message of Solomon Chamberlin's 1829 *Sketch* was an assurance that he was on a righteous track at the time because of his reliance on the Bible. And this is also perhaps the greatest puzzle that he leaves for historians because he does not write about any dissatisfaction he may have experienced subsequent to his 1819 experience but instead lauds the "many refreshing seasons" he had enjoyed.

Solomon ended his 1829 *Sketch* with a mention of the death of his sister Mary in 1818, and that he would "follow the lamb of God withersoever he shall be pleased to lead..."[48]

"Peace be to this house"

But, as a man ever amenable to new ideas, when the reports about a "gold bible" began to circulate in upstate New York soon after publication of his *Sketch*, he felt the need to investigate them.

Sometime between 1820 and 1827, Solomon Chamberlin moved his family from Adams, Massachusetts, to Lyons, New York, about twenty miles east of Palmyra. There, he bought a house which was also known as the "Pilgrimsport Tavern."[49]

In the fall of 1829, Solomon was sailing to Canada by way of the Erie Canal and felt compelled to get off at Palmyra,[50] allegedly because "some genii [sic] or good spirit" directed him to disembark and spend the night in a nearby farmhouse. His later 1858 *Short Sketch* described his learning about a "Gold Bible" being published in Palmyra for which he had been "led in this singular manner."[51]

Solomon sought local directions and traveled "across lots" until he arrived at Hyrum Smith's cabin to be met by Hyrum himself at the door. When he learned that Joseph was not there, he asked Hyrum if anyone in the house believed in visions

---

Merwin as preacher. There were several preaching places within the bounds of the circuit besides that established at Jacob Jenks' and several miles apart. One of these appointments was at this time made in the "Notch," chiefly through the agency of the brothers Harris and Daniel Arnold, and the first meetings were held in Daniel Arnold's barn.

51. Ibid.

and revelations, and Hyrum answered in the affirmative. Solomon then gave Hyrum his newly published *Sketch* to read, which was reportedly well received.[52]

He stayed at Hyrum's cabin for two days learning all about this "gold bible", the Book of Mormon. When he was ready to leave, Hyrum was evidently so impressed by Solomon that he took him to Grandin's print shop where he was given sixty-four unbound pages of the manuscript. Solomon took them with him to Canada, as he "preached along the way." He would write that the people with whom he shared them "knew not what to think of it."[53]

Soon after this, in the spring of 1830, Solomon was baptized by Joseph Smith in Seneca Lake and ordained a priest.[54] He then embarked on a mission to bring this "great work of God" to whoever would listen.[55] Solomon returned to Canada with some newly printed copies of the Book of Mormon, managing to sell but a single copy.[56] He returned to Lyons and in the summer of 1830 was visited by Phineas and Joseph Young, also Reformed Methodists on their way to Canada to preach. According to Phineas:

> ...he [Solomon Chamberlin] began to preach Mormonism to us; he told us there was a church organized, and ten or more were baptized, and every body [sic] must believe the Book of Mormon or be lost.
>
> I told him to hold on, when be had talked about two hours, setting forth the wonders of Mormonism—that it was not good to give a colt a bushel of oats at a time. I knew that my brother had but little idea of what he was talking and I wanted he be should have time to reflect, but it made little difference to him, he still talked of Mormonism.[57]

Chamberlin was not aware that Samuel H. Smith had already given a copy of the Book of Mormon to Phineas, who had read it and believed it.[58] Solomon then

---

52. Ibid., 8-9. He writes that "Father Smith was one and some of the Whitmer's."

53. *John Taylor Journal 1844-45*, 52.

54. Ibid., 52-53. I could find no record which gives the exact date of Solomon's baptism although he claims it was in the Spring of 1830 in Seneca Lake. Solomon later recalled that, "In the spring of 1830, I was ordained a Priest, under the hands of Hyrum Smith. I remained in that office about 10 years. I magnified it to the best of my ability. I then was ordained an Elder, and remained in that office until the first conference after the death of Joseph, by the council of Brother Brigham [Young] and under the hands of George Miller, I was ordained a High Priest and still remain in that quorum and the faith and confidence in the doctrine and principles of the Church are as good as ever they were, and in all the authorities of God's Kingdom, and am perfectly satisfied with all things as they roll along." (*A Short Sketch*, 1858, 18).

55. *A Short Sketch*, 1858, 18.

56. Ibid., 11.

57. *Deseret News*, "History of Brigham Young," February 3, 1858. Joseph Young later recalled: "It was at this place I first had sight of the Book of Mormon. It was shown to us by Solomon Chamberlain. Nothing could have been more acceptable to my famishing soul. I hailed it as my Spiritual Jubilee, a deliverance from a long night of darkness and bondage." (*Joseph Young Autobiographical Sketch Circa 1872*, MS5993, Church History Library, 6).

58. Ibid.

left for Massachusetts with eight or ten copies of the Book of Mormon "to sell and to preach" because, he wrote, it was very difficult to sell one without a great deal of preaching. He "worked hard for eight days and sold one book."[59]

Solomon next made his way to the Reformed Methodist Conference in Manlius Center, Onondaga County, New York, with the Book of Mormon. There he found "Phineas and Brigham Young," who were attending the conference.[60] Chamberlin believed that he "could soon convince the whole conference of the truth of the Book of Mormon," but was instead roundly rejected.[61] Solomon added that he was badly abused by "[o]ne of their greatest preachers so called, by the name of Buckly, (if I mistake not)."[62]

After leaving Manlius Center, Solomon attended another Reformed Methodist camp meeting and once again tried to persuade them to believe in the Book of Mormon. He was met with stiff resistance, especially by his old friend William Lake, who asked him, "if it was of God, do you think He would send such a little upstart as you are around with it?"[63]

Failing to convert any of his former church members did not deter Chamberlin. On his way back to Lyons, he stopped and preached to a congregation in Spafford, New York, at "the Free Will Baptist Church, and they received it, and soon after the Church was established a number of them were baptized."[64]

---

59. *John Taylor Journal 1844-45*, 52.

60. Ibid.

61. Ibid.

62. *A Short Sketch, 1858*. More than likely this was Elijah Bailey who lived in Manlius. Solomon adds that Bailey was "soon taken crazy, and died a miserable death." Elijah Bailey's obituary reads: "Elder Elijah Bailey, formerly of Readsboro in this county, died in Brewster, Mass., on the 23d ult., in the 80th year of his age. Most assuredly a good and upright man has gone to his reward. His labors as a Methodist preacher for more than sixty years have been abundant, and our earliest recollections are associated with his memory, as the earnest apostle of Jesus, He was a true Jeffersonian Democrat, and for sixteen years represented Readsboro' in the Legislature—for sixteen years he was a Justice of the Peace, but never issued an execution, as all his his [sic] courts were those of conciliation." (*Vermont Gazette*, Bennington, Vermont, 26 May 1847, Page 2). Chamberlin may have consulted with Phineas H. Young, who wrote: "One man whose name was Buckley, and an elder in the Methodist Reformed Church, railed on brother Chamberlin and abused him shamefully. He immediately went crazy, and was carried home to the town of Smyrnia, [Smyrna] a distance of 20 or 30 miles, and died in a few days raving mad." (*Deseret News*, "History of Brigham Young," February 3, 1858). Chamberlin sent his 1858 Sketch along with a cover letter dated July 11, 1858 to Albert Carrington.

63. Solomon also felt the need to add that Lake "soon after died a poor drunken sot," but Lake died on October 27, 1840 in Granby, New York, and is buried in Bowens Corners Cemetery, Oswego County, New York.

64. Silas (son of Mayhew and Sarah Hillman) lived in Spafford, New York, and later wrote: "In the year 1831, a man by the name of Chamberlain came there bringing the Book of Mormon. He gave history of its origin, how it was obtained, and its translation." (See, Rhean Lenora M. Beck, *A Short History of the Life, Ancestry, and Descendants of Mayhew Hillman and His Wife, Sarah (King) Hillman* (independently published,) 1968). Chamberlin preached at the Freewill Baptist Church, of which Zerah Pulsipher, Shadrach Roundy and the Hillmans were members. Zerah Pulsipher would later recall that, "In the fall of 1831 there was a Book of Mormon brought into town I succeeded in getting it I directly read it through twice gave it a thorough investigation and believed it was true." (Zerah Pu[l]sipher, "History," 12, CHL, MS 753). John Pulsipher remembered how they discussed

Soon after returning from his missionary journey to Massachusetts, Solomon accompanied the church to Ohio, but didn't stay long. In the fall of 1831, he left Kirtland with William W. Phelps, Algernon Sidney Gilbert, and others for Missouri.[65]

There is no mention whatever in his 1829 *Sketch*, any other contemporary writings, or any later reminiscences of early church events that Solomon Chamberlin ever claimed to have foreknowledge of Joseph Smith's activities. That would come only later in retrospect, after Solomon settled in Nauvoo.

Solomon the Revisionist

In his two later autobiographies, Chamberlin revised and omitted many events as recorded in his self-published 1829 *Sketch* to make it appear that God had given him some kind of foreknowledge of the restoration.

In his 1858 reminiscence, he affirmed that he had led a wicked life early on and that he had a vision of hell. He then added that he had "reformed" and had another vision of "three heavens, and their glories, and the third one, far exceeded the others."[66] He also mentioned joining the Methodists and the Reformed Methodists and living in the "Combination."[67]

In his 1845 recollection to John Taylor, Solomon gave few details of his early life and visions as published in the 1829 *Sketch* but began by claiming that when he was nineteen (1807) he had joined the Methodists. He claimed that he had studied the Bible and found the Methodists mistaken, so he joined the Reformed Methodists with whom he stayed until sometime after 1816. He spoke of living in what he later called "the combination," but that "we were wrong in many things, we had no prophet nor priesthood."[68]

He told Taylor that in 1816, "we found we were mistaken in many things" and then in a channeling of Joseph Smith's words, he averred that if they "lacked wisdom

---

the book "with the neighbors Elijah Cheney, Roundy and others would sit and read and talk day and night 'till they read it through and through. They believed it was brought forth by the power of God, to prepare the way for the second coming of the Son of Man—it was just what they were looking for." (John Pulsipher's History, in Pulsipher Family Book, ed. Thomas S. Terry, Terry Lund, N. H. Lund, and I. L. Holt (1953), 47, also A Short History of John Pulsipher, CHL M270). About twenty members of that congregation were baptized about a year later by Jared Carter. A year after his baptism Zerah would baptize Wilford Woodruff in Richland, New York.

65. The Chamberlins traveled to Missouri by water. Solomon later claimed that he brought over a ton and a half of furniture with him. (Missouri Redress Petition) This company was under the direction of William W. Phelps and Algernon Sidney Gilbert. Phelps was accompanied by his wife Sally and their six children. Gilbert traveled with his wife Elizabeth and her sister, Keziah Rollins, and her three orphaned children, James Henry, Mary Elizabeth and Carolyn Amelia Rollins. Also numbered in the group were the wives and children of Edward Partridge, John Corrill, Isaac Morley, and many others. Corrill and Morley were ordained counselors to Bishop Partridge on June 3, 1831. (Minute Book 2, 3 June 1831.)

66. *John Taylor Journal 1844-45*, 50-54. This is an anachronism taken from Joseph Smith's teachings in Kirtland.

67. Ibid.

68. Ibid. Again, anachronistic language added to the 1829 material.

and humbled ourselves before God in mighty prayer, and asked in sincerity" they would be answered. Solomon claimed he used this formula and that God "answered my prayer."[69] He described "a vision of the night" in which a male angel appeared to him and that he asked the angel "if we were right." The angel told him that "not one of us were right, and that there were no people on earth that were right; but that the Lord would in his own due time raise up a church, different from all others, and he would give power and authority as in the days of Christ; and he would carry it through, and it should never be confounded."[70] Solomon would "live to see the day, and know the work when it came forth; and that great persecution should follow."[71] Solomon also told Taylor that he "proclaimed it to the world and all people what I had seen and heard; and that all the denominations on earth were as John said constituted the great whore of all the earth."[72] In his 1858 *Sketch* he added that "there would a book come forth, like unto the Bible and the people would [be] guided by it, as well as the Bible."[73]

These later revisions by Chamberlin in 1845 and 1858 have mistakenly characterized him as a "forerunner" to Joseph Smith, who had been providentially led to the Smith's house after the Book of Mormon manuscript was finished (but as yet unprinted), to show him that "this was the work" he had been looking for.

Even though Solomon Chamberlin, in fact, had no foreknowledge of Joseph Smith or the restoration he heralded, he remained a believing Latter-day Saint until his death. This story, beginning at his disembarkation at Palmyra, is the true story of Solomon Chamberlin and does not need those apologetic revisions.

What is puzzling about Solomon Chamberlin is that his loyal faith did not seem to be enough for him, as a comparison between his later reminiscences and his 1829 *Sketch* reveal. Because of his revisions, he has been touted by some as a prophetic figure who foresaw Joseph Smith's actions. For example, Larry Porter in an article published in the *Ensign* from 1988 wrote:

> In 1816, an angelic visitor had informed him that "there would be a book come forth, like unto the Bible and the people would be guided by it, as well as the Bible." Solomon Chamberlain had since maintained a constant vigil for that book. The angel, furthermore, had instructed him that the gospel of Jesus Christ had been taken from the earth and that the true church would soon be fully restored.[74]

---

69. Ibid. See *Joseph Smith--History*, 1:8-17.

70. Ibid, 50-51.

71. Ibid.

72. Ibid. For example, 1 Nephi 14:10 (3:220-224a CofC).

73. Ibid.

74. Larry C. Porter, "From a Book Coming Forth," *Ensign*, July, 1988.

In an article featuring the then newly discovered 1829 pamphlet, Porter reaffirmed that in 1816 Chamberlin was told by an angel about the Book of Mormon.[75] In the article, Porter tried to incorporate Chamberlin's later anachronistic revisions into the narrative in the 1829 *Sketch*.[76]

Further, as recently as 2010, a member of the LDS First Presidency wrote:

> Sometime around 1816, Solomon was promised in a vision that he would live to see the day when the Church of Christ would be organized after the apostolic order was established once again on the earth.[77]

Why did Solomon feel that he needed to revise his history with elements of Joseph Smith's story? One reason may be William Lake's comments to him at the camp meeting where they sparred in 1830. Lake had dismissed him as an unimportant upstart, and perhaps Chamberlin did not want to be perceived as someone who sprang up suddenly with this new message. I believe he tried to accomplish this by claiming he had been given foreknowledge long before Smith published the Book of Mormon. And yet, he was an influential player in spreading the new religion during its birth pangs. His story has no need for the embellishments. Even the last few months of his life were a harrowing experience for "Old Buckskin."

Epilogue

On July 11, 1858, Solomon penned a short letter to Apostle Albert Carrington, explaining that he was sending him "a short sketch of my life" for publication in the *Deseret News*. Near the end of this *Sketch*, Solomon wrote that he felt "as tho [sic] my years are not many more in this life," and that he longed to return to Jackson County, Missouri.[78]

In January 1862, Solomon was living in Santa Clara, Washington County, Utah Territory, as he had been asked to settle there by Brigham Young. Chamberlin had built a small one-room log cabin near the Santa Clara river and Jacob Hamblin's mill where he lived with his 12-year-old daughter Louisa.[79] According to news reports, on the nights of January 17 and 18, 1862, it rained "tolerably heavy" in the Santa Clara area, and on the following night, the Virgin and Santa Clara rivers overflowed and

---

75. Porter 1997, 120.

76. Porter mentioned the 1819 vision in Solomon's 1829 *Sketch*, but did not explain why Jesus told him "the Bible is the book" he must adhere to as having the correct principles to live by or why Solomon didn't mention another book.

77. Dieter F. Uchtdorf, "A Great Work of God," *Visiting Teaching Message*, April 2010.

78. *A Short Sketch*, 1858, 18.

79. Sarah Louisa Chamberlin was born to Solomon and Terressa Morse on October 8, 1849. She was the plural wife of Lemuel Hardison Redd. They lived in Colonia Juárez, Mexico where she died in 1908.

swept away the fort, Hamblin's mill, and many of the homes, orchards, and crops in the area.[80]

That night, it was raining heavily while Solomon and Louisa were asleep in their cabin when she was awakened by a strange sound. Stepping outside, she was horrified to find the nearby river swelling so rapidly that the rushing waters and debris would surely engulf their cabin to sweep them away, galvanizing her to attempt to wake her malaria-stricken father. But, as she struggled to get her father out, he resisted, arguing that she should leave him, for he was too sick to go anywhere. He assured her that he was ready to die, and she must save herself.

This was unacceptable to this pioneer daughter and she refused to leave him. She dragged Solomon from the cabin and spied the only place she felt they would be safe from the encroaching water—the branches of a stout tree. Leaving him for the moment, Louisa pulled one of her father's heavy workbenches over to the tree and helped him climb into the lower branches. As Solomon clung to the branches, he watched Louisa run back to the cabin and emerge with a small wooden box that she had filled with important papers. Louisa joined her father in the tree to spend an uncomfortable night in their precarious perch. The next day, they watched from the tree as the cabin and its possessions were swept away by the floodwaters.[81]

Solomon, his head cradled in his daughter's lap, may have thought back about how another daughter had almost drowned when she had slipped and plunged into the Missouri River as the family sailed to Independence, Missouri.[82] Or, perhaps, he was thinking of his time hunting in Adam-Ondi-Ahman and farming in Daviess County, or of selling his goods in Far West where his encounters with angry neighbors had left him homeless.[83] Maybe he recalled that time he wore a full buckskin suit with a wolfskin cap that still had the ears.[84] "Old Buckskin" was ready then to wreak vengeance on the Missourians with his rifle, dirks, pistols and broadsword, but chose instead to trek with others of his faith to a new place called Nauvoo.[85]

---

80. *Deseret News.* February 14, 1862.

81. See Todd M. Compton, "The Big Washout-the 1862 Flood in Santa Clara", *Utah Historical Quarterly*, Vol. 77, No. 2, 114, 119.

82. Emily Partridge remembered: "We went down the Ohio River to Cincinnati in a keel boat. Then we took a steamboat and went up the Missouri River...Once when the boat landed, one of our company, a young woman, Electa C[h]amberlin, slipped from the plank into the water, but was soon rescued again. When we were within about one hundred miles of our destination we met the ice coming down the river so thick that the boat could not proceed and we were forced to land at a place called 'Arrow Rock'." (Emily Partridge, "What I Remember," 1884).

83. In his redress petition Solomon wrote: "I was one of the first that setled at farwest I owned a house and lot in far west and 5 miles north of there I owned a timber lot and had a deed of it and had it under fence and a good large hewed house and other buildings about 40 miles north west of far west I had another place and was living on it at the time the troubles Commenced..." (Solomon Chamberlin, Bill of damages, Jackson, Clay Daviess, Caldwell Hancock, Illinois, January 6, 1840, Utah State University, Merrill-Cazier Library, MSS 19).

84. Andrew Jenson, *Latter Day Saint Biographical Encyclopedia*, Vol. 2, 1914, 605.

85. Ibid.

"Old Buckskin at Adam-Ondi-Ahman"
Painting by Johnny Stephenson

He might have remembered his first plural wife, Emiline Waterman,[86] the dinners at his Nauvoo home with his friend Brigham Young,[87] or the tragic death of his first wife Hopee at Winter Quarters.[88] Perhaps he remembered his first trip across the plains with his fellow Latter-day Saints.[89] Or maybe it was his deathly sick trip back to Winter Quarters with Brigham Young.[90]

Did that ordeal in the tree conjure up images his mind of how he had survived so many brushes with death before, like the cholera episode near the Green River in Wyoming,[91] or perhaps of his return to Salt Lake from the California gold fields through Indian-infested territory with only a mule and a pocket knife?[92]

Perhaps he thought of that time after his return to the Salt Lake Valley when had settled in the south at Brigham Young's direction—or when he had helped settle Parowan and Cedar City and from there went to Beaver and finally Santa Clara.[93] Did thoughts of his life of adventures give him the strength to make it through another brush with death in that tree? Indeed so, for Louisa and Solomon held on through that storm and were soon rescued, then to watch as the tree that had saved them was swept away just after they made it to higher ground.[94]

But the malaria and the storm had taken its toll. Less than two months later, Solomon breathed his last,[95] still loyal to his faith. Despite the lack of any remaining personal effects, a portrait has yet emerged from the accounts that he and others left behind.

---

86. Solomon's first wife Hopewill (Electa) Haskins left him sometime before 1842, but they never divorced. Solomon married John O. Waterman's wife Emeline Shepard Waterman. Concerning the Watermans, a notice appeared in the Nauvoo Neighbor by John O. (who was baptized by Joseph in 1836) that his wife had left his "bed and board", and that he would no longer be financially responsible for her (July 23, 1845). On 18 Dec. 1845, Emeline and Solomon Chamberlin both received their endowments together in the Nauvoo Temple. They were married 15 Jan. of 1846. Waterman was said to have gone crazy and died in 1876 at Moline, Rock Island County, Illinois. Emeline later returned to her first husband John. In his 1858 *Sketch*, Solomon laments the loss of "the wife of his youth" and said he was "alone" (his daughter Polly who also died at Winter Quarters) and was a plural wife of Emer Harris. The 1842 Nauvoo Census lists Solomon and Polly with the Emer Harris family. (2nd Ward) Chamberlin never mentions Emeline Waterman. Terressa Morse also left him and became a plural wife of John D. Lee. I am grateful for the help of H. Michael Marquardt for the information on the temple sealings. For more information on Lee and Morse see, Some Descendants of John Doyle Lee, Compiled by Lorraine (Richardson) Manderscheid, Chapter 19, self-pub., 2000.

87. For example, see *History of the Church*, ed. by Dan Vogel, Vol. 6, 219.

88. *Sketch*, 1829, 16.

89. Ibid.

90. Ibid., 15-16.

91. Ibid. 14-15.

92. Ibid., 16-17.

93. Jenson, op. cited.

94. Compton, op. cited.

95. *Deseret News*, April 16, 336.

With the 1989 discovery of Chamberlin's 1829 *Sketch*, his later claims to foreknowledge of the restoration must be set aside. But the more complete picture emerging of his early life is just as compelling as his years as a Latter-day Saint. Although there are still gaps in the history of the life of Solomon Chamberlin, what can be pieced together gives us a fascinating view of one man's experiences decades both before and after the advent of Mormonism.

JOHNNY STEPHENSON (mormonitemusings.com) is an independent historian and researcher of Mormon History. In 2012, he discovered and was the first to publish about an unknown photo (taken by Jacob Hicks) of the Book of Mormon "Caractors" sometimes misidentified as the "Anthon Transcript" (and once possessed by John and David Whitmer). His four-part series on the Joseph Smith "Caractors" is being expanded for publication as a book, which will include new material on the Kinderhook Plates.

The Temple Lot in Jackson County, Missouri, and How Early Church Members Worshipped

H. Michael Marquardt

Background

THE PURITANS WHO SETTLED in America believed they were God's chosen people who had found a land of promise. The idea of a western New Jerusalem had been mentioned in the seventeenth century by Samuel Sewall when he asked, "why the Heart of America may not be the seat of the New Jerusalem." Cotton Mather considered the New Jerusalem would be west beyond the confines of New England.[1]

While some looked for a New Jerusalem in the state of New York, others spiritualized the idea and saw the cause of Zion in the revivals of the 1820s. Such expressions as "growing zeal for the prosperity of Zion," "enquiring the way to Zion," and "wishes well to the cause of Zion" were expressions of the revival movement and referred to the building up of the church.[2]

Out of this background came the Book of Mormon. According to this record, Jesus Christ had given instructions to the forefathers of the Native Americans concerning the New Jerusalem to be built in the Americas. The Gentiles who believe "shall assist my people, the rem[n]ant of Jacob; and also, as many of the house of Israel as shall come, that they may build a city, which shall be called the New Jerusalem."[3] This article explores events relating to the Temple Lot in Jackson County, Missouri. It includes the 1831 visit of William E. McLellin who, years later, would demonstrate to visitors the location of the Temple Lot. From correspondence, it has become clear that Latter Day Saints prayed, worshipped, confessed their sins, and spoke in tongues during their early meetings. Some members who originally believed would in time reassess their relationship with the movement. Their various stories were written in letters and published in newspapers that are now available to historians.

Upbuilding of Zion and Mission to the Lamanites

In September 1830, five months after Joseph Smith Jr. organized the restoration-themed Church of Christ, one of the eight witnesses to the Book of Mormon, a man named Hiram Page, claimed to have received revelations through the medium of a seer stone, "concerning the upbuilding of Zion" and other matters.[4] "Finding however that many (especially the Whitmer family and Oliver Cowdery) were believing much in the things set forth by this stone," Joseph Smith soon proclaimed that divine guidance had determined Page's revelations to be invalid.[5]

Shortly thereafter, Oliver Cowdery, the second elder to Smith, was directed to "go unto the Lamanites [Native Americans] & Preach my Gospel unto them & cause my Church to be established among them."[6] Concerning the city called New Jerusalem, Oliver was told that "it is not Revealed & no man knoweth where the City shall be built But it shall be given hereafter Behold I say unto you that it shall be among the Lamanites."

Later, three others—Ziba Peterson, Parley P. Pratt, and Peter Whitmer Jr.—were instructed to accompany Cowdery on the mission. Cowdery himself stated that he was going "to rear up a pillar as a witness where the Temple of God shall be built, in the glorious New-Jerusalem."[7] Following a church conference at Kirtland, Ohio, in June 1831, certain men were instructed to convene the next conference in Missouri where those missionaries to the Indians had gone. Missouri was:

> the land which I will consecrate unto my people, which are a remnant of Jacob, and them who are heirs according to the covenant…if ye are faithfull [sic] ye shall assemble yourselves together to rejoice upon the land of Missorie [sic] which is the Land of your inheritance, which is now the land of your enemies but behold I the Lord will hasten the City in its time.[8]

---

4. Manuscript History of the Church, Book A-1 [written in 1839], Church History Library, The Church of Jesus Christ of Latter-day Saints, Salt Lake City, (hereafter cited as CHL), A-1:54; Brigham H. Roberts, ed., 7 vols., *History of the Church of Jesus Christ of Latter-day Saints* (Salt Lake City: Deseret Book, 1959), 1:109-110; Karen Lynn Davidson, David J. Whittaker, Mark Ashurst-McGee and Richard L. Jensen, eds., *Histories, Volume 1: Joseph Smith Histories, 1832-1844* (Salt Lake City: Church Historian's Press, 2012), 436, 438.

5. "A Book of Commandments & Revelations," cited hereafter as BCR, MS 22505, Church History Library in Robin Scott Jensen, Robert J. Woodford and Steven C. Harper, eds., *Revelations and Translations: Manuscript Revelation Books, Facsimile Edition* (Salt Lake City: Church Historian's Press, 2009), 41. See also Book of Commandments (Zion [Independence, MO]: Published by W. W. Phelps and Co., 1833) [in press], chapter 30, verse 11; in LDS Doctrine and Covenants, section 28:11 and CofC Doctrine and Covenants, section 27:4.

6. BCR, 41, September 1830; Book of Commandments 30:7; LDS D&C 28:8; CofC D&C 27:3.

7. Statement signed by Oliver Cowdery and dated October 17, 1830, cited in a letter of Ezra Booth to Rev. Ira Eddy, November 24, 1831 and published in *Ohio Star* 2 (December 8, 1831):3, Ravenna, OH. Also cited in Michael Hubbard MacKay, Gerrit J. Dirkmaat, Grant Underwood, Robert J. Woodford and William G. Hartley, eds., *Documents, Volume 1: July 1828-June 1831* (Salt Lake City: Church Historian's Press, 2013), 204.

8. BCR, 89, June 6, 1831; Book of Commandments 54:1, 43-44; LDS D&C 52:2, 42-43; CofC D&C 52:1, 9.

By the time Smith arrived at Independence, arrangements probably would have been made with Jones H. Flournoy to survey the land where the New Jerusalem temple could be built. As Jean Addams explained, Flournoy had squatters' rights to a large acreage such that discussing the option of purchasing land from him would be something that most likely had been done.[9]

On July 20, 1831, at a meeting of church leaders in Independence, Joseph Smith proclaimed a revelation concerning the location for the city of Zion. The document declared:

> the land of Missorie [sic] which is the Land which I, have appointed & consecrated for the gathering of the Saints. Wherefore, this is the land of promise & the place for the City of Zion. yea and thus saith the Lord your God, if ye will receive wisdom here is wisdom. Behold the place which is now called Independence is the centre [sic] place.

The American New Jerusalem would be located south of the Santa Fe Trail just outside the Independence city boundary: "the spot for the Temple is lying westward upon a lot which is not far from the court-house."[10]

Lands were to be purchased for what Smith would term an "everlasting inheritance." Bishop Partridge would divide the land on behalf of the church members. Sidney Gilbert, a merchant from Ohio, was given three responsibilities: first, to be an agent to purchase property; second, to establish a store to obtain money for buying land; and third, to take the gospel to the Lamanites. This last instruction was, "let my servent [sic] Sidney obtain license (behold here is wisdom & whoso readeth let him understand) that he may send goods also unto the lamanites even by whom he will as clerks employed in his service & thus the gospel may be preached unto them." The same revelation established William W. Phelps to be a printer for the church and for Oliver Cowdery to assist him.

Dedication of the Spot for the Temple

The land and site for the temple was outside the Independence city boundary. Sidney Rigdon had been instructed on August 1 to "consecrate & dedicate this land & the spot of the temple."[11] On Wednesday, August 3, 1831, two weeks after Smith's

---

9. R. Jean Addams, "The History and Acquisition of the Original Temple Lot Property in Independence, Jackson County, Missouri," *Mormon Historical Studies* 20 (Spring 2019): 1-76. See also Addams, *Upon the Temple Lot: The Church of Christ's Quest to Build the House of the Lord* (Independence, MO: John Whitmer Books, 2010).

10. BCR, 93, July 20, 1831; LDS D&C 57:1-5; CofC D&C 57:1. The revelation was not published in the Book of Commandments. On the courthouse see Max H Parkin, "The Courthouse mentioned in the Revelation on Zion," *Brigham Young University Studies* 14 (Summer 1974):451-57. On additional background see Pearl Wilcox, *The Latter Day Saints on the Missouri Frontier* (Independence: author, 1972), 15-42.

11. BCR, 97; Book of Commandments 59:70; LDS D&C 58:57; CofC D&C 58:13.

July 20 revelation, church leaders met "where the temple is to be erected." According to Oliver Cowdery:

> Sidney Rigdon dedicated the ground where the city is to Stand: and Joseph Smith Jr. laid a stone at the North east corner of the contemplated <u>Temple</u> in the name of the Lord Jesus of Nazareth. After all present had rendered thanks to the great ruler of the universe. Sidney Rigdon pronounced this Spot of ground whol[l]y dedicated unto the Lord forever: Amen.[12]

Ezra Booth, a former Church of Christ member, explained in a November 1831 letter to his friend Rev. Ira Eddy why he withdrew from the church. He explained that the temple site was "one half of a mile out of Town, to a rise of ground, a short distance south of the road." In the wooded area, he described a sapling, debarked on the north and west sides:

> On the south side of the sappling [sapling] will be found the letter, T. which stands for Temple; and on the east side ZOM for Zomar; which Smith says is the original word for Zion.[13] Near the foot of the sappling [sic], they will find a small stone, covered over with bushes, which were cut for that purpose. This is the cornerstone for the Temple.[14]

Two days after the dedication of the temple site, bishop Edward Partridge wrote to his wife Lydia in Kirtland, Ohio, that he needed to stay through December because either he or Sidney Gilbert "must be here to attend the sales in December," since it was known when the land would be available to purchase. He half-apologized, writing, "You know I stand in an important station, and as I am occasionally chastened I sometimes fear my station is above what I can perform to the acceptance of my Heavenly Father."[15]

---

12. As copied into "The Book of John Whitmer Kept by Commandment," chapter 9, page 32, Community of Christ Library-Archives, Independence; in *Journal of History* 1 (January 1908):59-60 and Bruce N. Westergren, ed., *From Historian to Dissident: The Book of John Whitmer* (Salt Lake City: Signature Books, 1995), 86-87; also in Karen Lynn Davidson, Richard L. Jensen, and David J. Whittaker, eds., *Histories, Volume 2: Assigned Histories, 1831-1847* (Salt Lake City: Church Historian's Press, 2012), 45.

13. That Joseph Smith considered "Zomar" to be Zion see "Grammar & A[l]phabet of the Egyptian Language," 23, MS 1295, Folder 1, Church History Library, Salt Lake City; 1835 manuscript in H. Michael Marquardt, comp., *The Joseph Smith Egyptian Papers* (Cullman, AL: Printing Service, 1981), 49-50; also in Robin Scott Jensen and Brian M. Hauglid, eds., *Revelations and Translations, Volume 4: Book of Abraham and Related Manuscripts, Facsimile Edition* (Salt Lake City: Church Historian's Press, 2018), 160-61.

14. Ezra Booth, letter to "Rev. & Dear Sir" [sixth letter to Rev. Ira Eddy], November 14, 1831, *Ohio Star* 2 (November 17, 1831):3, Ravenna, OH. For additional information on Booth see H. Michael Marquardt, "Ezra Booth on Early Mormonism: A Look at His 1831 Letters," *John Whitmer Historical Association Journal* 28 (2008):65-87.

15. Edward Partridge to "My Dear wife" [Lydia Partridge], August 5-6, 1831, MS 23154, Edward Partridge letters, 1831-1835, Church History Library. Also quoted in D. Brent Collette, "In Search of Zion: A Description of Early Mormon Millennial Utopianism as Revealed through the Life of Edward Partridge" (M.A. thesis, Brigham Young University, 1977), 148-49.

On December 19, 1831, following Joseph Smith's return to Kirtland, Partridge delivered $130 to Jones H. Flournoy and Clara Flournoy to obtain the 63-acre site where the New Jerusalem temple was to be erected.[16]

Shortly after Smith laid the cornerstone and Rigdon dedicated the temple site, non-member William McLellin arrived in Jackson County. Having heard about the new religion, McLellin acted on his interest by traveling from Paris, Illinois, to Independence, where he was shown the location where the dedication had taken place. Shortly thereafter, McLellin was baptized into the Church of Christ on August 20, 1831, by Hyrum Smith. Four days later, he was ordained an elder and, on the following day, joined Hyrum Smith on a mission.[17]

The Saints Reproved and Solemn Assemblies Held

David Pettigrew was a recent convert who had joined the Church of Christ in 1832. In December that year, he moved to his 159-acre farm six miles west of Independence. Having purchased the farm at an earlier date, he now relocated to Jackson County. A short time later, his family was baptized. He wrote in an autobiography:

> [u]pon my arrival at Jackson County we were reproved by the Lord, through revelation, for treating lightly the book of Mormon and the former revelations, and were to remain under condemnation if we did not repent, and remember the Book of Mormon and the revelations.

The September 1832 revelation that mentioned "the whole church under condemnation" was recorded in the manuscript volume Book of Commandments and Revelations kept by John Whitmer.[18] Pettigrew continued:

> Soon after this, Bishop Partr[i]dge, appointed a Solemn asembley [sic] in all the branches, which is to be held as a day of confession, and repentance, he went from branch to branch ex[h]orting, until he had gone through them all, and in a few months, we were informed that we had repented, and the Angel's [sic] were rejoiceing [sic] over us, but there yet remained a Scourge and a Judgement to be poured out upon the children of Zion, these things Sunk deep in my mind.[19]

In a council of high priests that met on February 26, 1833, Partridge "laid before the council the effect of the proceedings of the Solemn Assemblies as held throughout Zion."[20] During the same month a succeeding church member, Salmon Sherwood, wrote:

---

19. "A History of David Pettigrew," MS 22278, p. 15, writing started in 1840, Church History Library.
20. Conference Minutes, and Record Book, of Christ's Church of Latter Day Saints, copy of minutes, LR 7874 21, p. 34, Church History Library; also in Donald Q. Cannon and Lyndon W. Cook, *Far West Record: Minutes of The Church of Jesus Christ of Latter-day Saints, 1830-1844* (Salt Lake City: Deseret Book, 1983), 60.

I have visited the Mormon meetings, one of which was called the solemn assembly, where the Bishop declared by vision from Joshua [sic; Joseph] Smith, that they were all under condemnation for not reading the book of Mormon, and that they must repent or they would be cut off and Zion would be removed somewhere else. He also declared that the seer, Joseph Smith, had the keys of the kingdom of heaven, and could see the multitudes of the angels.[21]

Receiving the Gift of Tongues in Zion

John Whitmer wrote:

Zion is prospering at pres[e]nt and high priests are stationed to watch over the several branches. Decmbr [sic] 1, 1832, there are now 538 individuals in this land b[e]longing to th[e] church. And it came to pass that in the fall of th[e] year 1832, th[e] disciples at Ohio rec[e]ived th[e] gift of tongues and in June 1833 we received th[e] gift of tongues in Zion.[22]

A further insight into church activities comes from letters written by a church member around December 1833 "to his aged father" that were later combined into a single letter-to-the-editor that was published in Boston, Massachusetts:

One half a mile to the west there is a beautiful cultivated spot of one hundred and fifty acres. Notwithstanding the dark cloud which appears to hang over our heads at this time, on this spot of land will shortly be built the temple, and the city of the New Jerusalem, into which our Lord and Saviour [sic] will descend in a cloud from heaven with power and great glory. We have a plan given by revelation of the city and the temple. The temple is to be like Solomon's, only far more splendid. Many of our dear brethren, who have been driven from this land by our enemies, will shortly return in the Lord's due time, and help to accomplish this great and glorious work. I have sufficient authority for saying this, for the Lord hath spoken it.

Besides living near where the temple was going to be located, the Latter Day Saints held services on the Sabbath (Sunday):

You wished to know how we spend the Sabbath. We mean to spend it as the Lord has commanded us by revelation. We are strictly forbidden to do any other work on the Lord's day but to prepare our food, and to assemble ourselves together to worship the Lord.

---

21. "The Mormons," Independence, Missouri, February 25, 1833, *Sangamo Journal* 2 (April 6, 1833):2, Springfield, Illinois. The letter was reprinted in the *Missouri Intelligencer and Boon's Lick Advertiser* 17 (April 20, 1833):1, Columbia, MO.

22. "The Book of John Whitmer Kept by Commandments," in Karen Lynn Davidson et al, *Histories, Volume 2: Assigned Histories*, 51.

Next was explained the duties of church members:

> We commence our service with prayer. Then it is the duty of every member, both old and young, to arise, one at a time, and speak of the goodness of God, and to confess our sins, if we have committed any the past week, to one another and before the Lord. This is frequently done in an unknown tongue, and then interpreted by one who may have the spirit for this work. Here is the wisdom of the Lord to search out all iniquity; for many of us have been moved by the Spirit and spoke in another tongue that which, when interpreted, would prove to be the secrets of the heart and sinful deeds that we should not confess in our own tongues. Many a one has risen with tears in his eyes, and confessed the truth of the interpretation.

It was further told how the sacrament was observed:

> Furthermore, in obedience to the commands of the Lord, we on every Sabbath commemorate the death and sufferings of our Lord and Saviour [sic], by partaking of the bread and wine, yea, pure wine, the clear juice of the grape. Our branch made one barrel this fall.

Explaining the struggles through which members had gone, the writer wrote:

> We have had many trying scenes to pass through since we arrived here one year ago. The Lord spake by revelation that he was not well pleased with his children in Zion, and that we all had great need of repentance, pointing out our greatest sins, which were, breaking the law of the celestial kingdom, and not reading the book of Mormon. Again[,] we received the word of the Lord in June by revelation through the prophet in Kirtland, that we had much iniquity amongst us, that he would not have his holy land polluted, and that there was a scourge and a judgment awaiting the inhabitants of Zion. Accordingly[,] our chastisements were very severe. Many were cut off from the church from that time. For several weeks we received great blessings from the Lord. The most of the church that stood received the gift of tongues, to speak in the language of the Lemanites [sic] as well as in those of the isles of the sea and the nations of Ur. It was given to some in each branch of the church to interpret all that was spoken; and also it was given to many of us to prophesy of things shortly to take place.[23]

William McLellin Shows Visitors the Location of the Temple Lot

The location of the spot where the latter-day temple would be built is based in part on what William McLellin had told visitors of his experience when he had been there in 1831. After Joseph and Hyrum's murders, and having joined various

---

23. "Extracts of Letters from a Mormonite," *The Unitarian* 1 (May 1, 1834):251-53, Boston, Massachusetts. Quotation marks in the article are omitted.

William E. McLellin (left) and Mark Forscutt (right).

Restoration churches through the years, McLellin settled in Independence in 1869.[24] In 1879, when Mark Forscutt visited the temple area, McLellin indicated to him that he "knows it is within ten feet of it, w[h]ere the dedication of it was made for a Temple."[25]

John L. Traughber Jr., who collected material on early Latter Day Saintism, also wrote about William McLellin showing him the location for the temple:

> I visited Dr. McLellan in April, 1881, and walked with him over the "Temple Lot" lying west of the court house in Independence...He said that the laying of the cornerstone of the temple, which is spoken of in Mormon works as something great, consisted of a ceremony over a rock which Martin Harris picked up in a little hollow which is on the temple lot.[26]

In a January 1882 letter, Reorganized Church apostle William H. Kelley told of visiting McLellin five months later in September 1881:

> The doctor was able to point out the identical spot where Joseph [Smith] stood when he first visited it, and which is the place of the corner stone. He visited it soon after

---

24. See William Shepard and H. Michael Marquardt, *Lost Apostles: Forgotten Members of Mormonism's Original Quorum of Twelve* (Salt Lake City: Signature Books, 2014), 316-21.

25. Mark Hill Forscutt journal, February 17, 1879, Mark Hill Forscutt Collection, Vault MSS 811, Box 8, Folder 9, L. Tom Perry Special Collections, Harold B. Lee Library, Brigham Young University, Provo, UT.

26. John L. Traughber, "Some Statements by Dr. W. E. McLellan," May 23, 1884, John L. Traughber Collection, MS 666, Manuscripts Division, Marriott Library, University of Utah, Salt Lake City.

himself, when it was all covered with young poplars thickly standing. Joseph cut his way in through this thick growth of trees, brush and saplings, and marked the spot by blazing a tree near by [sic], cutting away the under brush [sic] for a few feet around and setting up a small stone that had been picked up in the ravine below. This was all the corner stone that was ever laid upon it, and it only to mark the place of the corner.[27]

Summary

The spot for the temple was established and dedicated in August 1831. The land is considered sacred by the majority of Restoration churches and groups who envision that a temple will be erected there in the near future.

The accounts and letters cited above illuminate the lives of the early pioneers of the Restoration, confirming what was taught and practiced by the early Latter Day Saints. Testimonies, confessions of sins, and the gift of tongues prevailed among these members in Jackson County. Though the Lamanite mission was not a success, church leaders did accomplish the task of locating the spot for their temple. Ezra Booth's recollection of the area where the temple would be built is a connection to the events in the life of the early church. Much later, William E. McLellin would add his insight into the location of the latter-day temple of the New Jerusalem, based on his own visit to the site in 1831.

Located on the original 63-acre site are buildings of three Restoration churches: The site for the temple owned by the Church of Christ (the Temple Lot church); the visitor center of the Church of Jesus Christ of Latter-day Saints; and a temple constructed for worship by Community of Christ.

H. MICHAEL MARQUARDT (research@xmission.com) is an independent historian and research consultant. He is on the editorial board of the *John Whitmer Historical Association Journal*. He is the compiler of *Early Patriarchal Blessings of The Church of Jesus Christ of Latter-day Saints* (Smith Pettit Foundation, 2007); *Later Patriarchal Blessings of The Church of Jesus Christ of Latter-day Saints* (Smith Pettit Foundation, 2012); author of *Joseph Smith's 1828–1843 Revelations* (Xulon Press, 2013) and co-author with William Shepard of *Lost Apostles: Forgotten Members of Mormonism's Original Quorum of Twelve* (Signature Books, 2014).

---

27. "Letter From Elder W. H. Kelley," January 16, 1882, *Saints' Herald* 29 (March 1, 1882): 67. Orson Pratt, who also visited the spot in 1831, remembered, "The ground, then was covered with the common trees of the forest." Orson Pratt Sr., to "My Dear Marian," September 18, 1878 as cited in Kate B. Carter, comp., *Heart Throbs of the West* (Salt Lake City: Daughters of Utah Pioneers, 1944), 5:417.

Book Reviews

Scott Esplin. *Return to the City of Joseph: Modern Mormonism's Contest for the Soul of Nauvoo.* University of Illinois Press, 2018. 199 pages. illus, $99.00 (cloth), ISBN 978-0-252-04210-2, $24.95 (paperback) ISBN 978-0-252-08381-5, $14.95 (e-book) ISBN 978-0-252-05085-5.

Reviewed by David J. Howlett

In *Return to the City of Joseph*, historian Scott Esplin explains how the small riverside town of Nauvoo, Illinois, once the Mormon capital in the 1840s, became a Mormon sacred site in the 20th century, visited annually by hundreds of thousands of contemporary members of the Church of Jesus Christ of Latter-day Saints (LDS). Esplin focuses on the reconstruction and restoration of the historic Mormon sites by the two largest denominations descended from Joseph Smith's early church, the LDS and the Reorganized Church of Jesus Christ of Latter Day Saints (RLDS)/Community of Christ, and how these reconstruction programs stoked religious rivalry, promoted inter-denominational cooperation, and breathed new economic life into a small town in rural Illinois.

Before detailing Esplin's interventions and contributions, I need to make a full disclosure about my relationship to this work. I was one of the manuscript reviewers for Esplin's book at the University of Illinois Press. I read the first draft of his manuscript, made substantial comments on it, and, when I received his revised manuscript, found that he had addressed all of my substantive criticisms. These disclosures necessarily orient my comments to a different task in this review. Here, I will summarize the contributions of Esplin's work and point out the larger scholarly questions and literature that it addresses.

In his book, Esplin makes two important interventions. First, the history of the early Mormon Nauvoo period has been covered in minute detail since the publication of Robert Bruce Flanders' groundbreaking *Nauvoo: Kingdom on the Mississippi* (1965) to Benjamin Park's *Kingdom of Nauvoo: The Rise and Fall of a Religious Empire on the American Frontier* (2020). However, scholars have largely neglected the twentieth-century story of Nauvoo, and here Esplin fills this lacuna. Second, all of the works on the restoration of Nauvoo, such as Benjamin Pykles's 2011 book, *Excavating Nauvoo*, focus almost exclusively on the LDS Church's restorations. Esplin convincingly demonstrates how the RLDS/Community of Christ's story and the LDS Church's story in Nauvoo are intertwined. By doing so, Esplin shows how Nauvoo served as a platform for inter-denominational contestation and cooperation.

In 150 engrossing pages, Esplin charts the sometimes parallel, sometimes intersecting stories of the two churches that restored Nauvoo. He shows how the RLDS Church in the early twentieth century used inherited Smith properties to construct an RLDS proselytizing site, only to move in the late twentieth century toward a largely desacralized and de-polemicized interpretation of Nauvoo that focused upon academically-shaped public history narratives. Then, Esplin tracks the LDS Church's entry into Nauvoo in the middle of the twentieth century, one that shifted from creating a "Williamsburg of the Midwest" to using the site as a venue for proselytizing outsiders and a pilgrimage-like destination for the faithful. Thus, Esplin shows how the story of the century-long restoration of Mormon Nauvoo reveals the divergent trajectories taken by Mormonism's largest denominations: the RLDS/CofC moved away from their sectarian tendencies and attempted to create themselves as an ecumenical denomination, while the LDS undertook a period of ecclesiastical retrenchment and standardization, a process that created the current global LDS Church.

Beyond the story of "Mountain Saints" (LDS) and "Prairie Saints" (RLDS) in Nauvoo, Esplin addresses a third narrative—the story of how non-Mormon residents of Nauvoo reacted to and shaped the restoration of Nauvoo. Much of the latter story occupies the final chapters of Esplin's book, as Nauvoo residents looked on while the LDS Church in the late 1990s and early 2000s proposed, built, and dedicated a new Nauvoo Temple. Here, Esplin highlights the tensions that this transformation wrought as hundreds of thousands of LDS revisited the small river town. In particular, Esplin gestures toward what Hal Rotham called the "devil's bargain of tourism," in which small towns find that tourism pumps needed dollars into their economies but also gives outside investors and outside interests far more control over local affairs than residents at first have anticipated. Rotham, who applied his "devil's bargain" framework to tourism in the American West, called the resulting relationships a second colonization of the West. Esplin does not go so far as to call the restoration of Nauvoo a second colonization. However, his sensitive contextualization of local anxieties about Mormon tourism shows that contemporary Nauvoo participates within a much larger story beyond Hancock County, Illinois.

This last thought points toward the broader academic questions that frame Esplin's study: the creation and uses of heritage, the cultural phenomenon of nostalgia, and the cultural significance of memorialization. In four pages in Esplin's first chapter, we glimpse a world of scholarship that wonders about the reasons that Americans, at different times and places, have sought to memorialize a selective historical past. Esplin forthrightly shows how these questions apply to Nauvoo's restoration. In doing so, he does not weigh down the reader with scholarly jargon, making his work imminently readable without sacrificing academic insight.

While Esplin details conflicts between various stakeholder communities in Nauvoo, he writes with an irenic sensibility in which all actors should be able to see themselves sympathetically portrayed. This is no mean accomplishment, given the varied contested interests of contemporary and past communities in Nauvoo. Beyond this, Esplin has crafted an insightful book that should appeal to professional historians of Mormonism and history buffs alike. As such, Esplin's *Return to the City of Joseph* will undoubtedly be the standard history of modern Nauvoo for years to come.

DAVID J. HOWLETT is the Mellon Visiting Assistant Professor of Religion at Smith College in Northampton, Massachusetts. He is the author of *Kirtland Temple: The Biography of a Shared Mormon Sacred Space* (University of Illinois Press, 2014) and the co-author of *Mormonism: The Basics* (Routledge, 2017). He serves on the editorial board for the *John Whitmer Historical Association Journal*, the advisory board for the *Mormon Studies Review*, and the steering committee for the Global Mormon Studies network.

Scott Esplin, *Return to the City of Joseph: Modern Mormonism's Contest for the Soul of Nauvoo*. University of Illinois Press, 2018. 199 pp., illus., paperback, $24.95. ISBN 9780252083815

Reviewed by Christin Mackay

IN THE FALL OF 2018, I climbed into the bucket of our lift that would take me to the top of the Nauvoo House roof that had been leaking. As I rose through the sky, I looked towards the Homestead as it became tinier and tinier in the distance below. The Homestead feels larger when you're inside. Tourists have a difficult time imagining just the two-room log structure it was when the Mormons arrived, but the view from the roof of the Nauvoo House made it easy to see how small it really was, and I could visualize the Smiths going in and out, people camping on the lawn facing the river, and steamboats arriving with new converts and the curious.

The Nauvoo House needed a new roof. We tarped the roof in October, began the process of hiring a contractor, and waited for the weather to clear. The snow arrived in November and didn't abate until mid-March, and then the rains came. With the rain came the third-highest crest on the Mississippi River in Nauvoo's history. We turned our attention from the roof to the levee that protects the House, and our LDS neighbors to the south asked what they could do to help. By May we needed to raise the levee about three feet, so we called the LDS Mission and asked if a few people might be available to help the next morning. They sent a frontend loader to aid our own tractor in building up the sand piles along the length of the levee. The next day, 25 young sister missionaries, who had just arrived the night before, were on the levee to help us spread the visqueen and secure it in place with sand bags. Their first taste of Red Brick Store root beer completed the morning. In *Return to Nauvoo: Modern Mormonism's Contest for the Soul of Nauvoo*, Scott Esplin interprets the relationship between the Community of Christ and the Church of Jesus Christ of Latter Day Saints in Nauvoo over the past 150 years or so—a relationship that I live out every day in my work at the Joseph Smith Historic Site.

An observation I've made over the last few years is that members of the Church of Jesus Christ of Latter-day Saints always look for the temple upon arriving in town, an act that will continue to grow with the addition of the "Temple District" among the Historic Nauvoo properties that will interpret the temple and its construction, scheduled to open in the fall of 2020 (144). For Community of Christ, we look for the river, in large part because the Smith properties all overlook the mighty *Mississippi* and the church's campground (which also features a river view). Over the years we've found our peace in Nauvoo looking out at the river. Emma Burton, as caretaker in the 1920's, summed up her view as, "Many come to drink of the icy cold water from the old oaken bucket that hangs in the well of the Old Homestead . . .

How pleasant it is to sit on the green, sloping bank, in front of the Homestead, in the friendly shade of one of those trees, and watch the steamer coming to the landing, and the gasoline boats darting about, causing little wavelets to lap the shore almost at our feet." (43)

Esplin explains how the Reorganized Church, now Community of Christ, came to acquire the Nauvoo properties from the Smith family and other locals. He includes a wonderful, yet sad, account of Joseph Smith III's last visit to Nauvoo and his encounter with stepbrother Charlie Bidamon, who was selling off family heirlooms. Mary Dean Haycock, a cousin to Joseph III, said that while they were visiting Emma's bedroom in the Nauvoo House, Joseph III, "[M]oved on to a small square table and murmured as tho to himself. . . 'Ah this is my father's favorite old checkboard table. See! The top is inlaid with two different sorts of wood for the checkers'. . . then, reaching under the table he pressed a spring that popped out the drawer which I still believed contained the checkers." (40) Joseph III asked how much Charlie would like for the table, but the price was too high, so it was left behind with a drunk Charlie.

The relationship between Community of Christ and the Church of Jesus Christ of Latter-day Saints was contentious throughout the nineteenth and first half of the twentieth century. Esplin explains that this led to a competitive building boom in Nauvoo for a time. As Nauvoo Restoration Incorporated (NRI) came to fruition, so too did the Community of Christ's expansion efforts in Nauvoo. Archeology projects began, reconstruction of the Homestead Summer Kitchen and Red Brick Store were completed, and treasure troves like the Mansion House privy were discovered. All the while the LDS church was excavating the temple lot and other building sites on the flats.

Esplin goes into great detail about the construction and town sentiments surrounding the Nauvoo Temple in the lead-up to its dedication in 2002. While the construction of the temple surely changed the town forever and the way in which LDS folks visited it, I would argue that the greatest impact on the town has been the spectacle of the "Nauvoo Pageant" and its prequel, the "British Pageant."

If there was one area overlooked in Esplin's work, it would be the effect that the "Nauvoo Pageant" has had on Nauvoo tourism and residents. The pageant's predecessor "The City of Joseph" ran from the late 70's to 2004. "The City of Joseph, was designed for the nonmember," as the author of the play, R. Don Oscarson states, "It is low key; it doesn't preach . . . yet it shows Joseph going into the grove to pray and presents all the principles of the gospel." (p. 100) When the "Nauvoo Pageant" and the "British Pageant" replaced "The City of Joseph," it was clear that the LDS church had decided to take a different tack with the summer evening's entertainment. Gone were the celebrations of singing, dancing, and fireworks of "The City of Joseph." In came the faith-promoting "Nauvoo Pageant," where King Follett is a major character, and LDS temple theology is on display. While great for building up the faithful, those not familiar with temple marriages, sealings, and baptisms for the dead were left wondering where the happy pioneer people of Nauvoo had gone as they watched the citizens struggle to "build" the temple for two hours.

In an effort, perhaps, to bring more people to town, the pageant's duration has had the unintended effect of compressing the summer into four weeks instead of ten to twelve because everyone wanted to visit during the "pageants" and, as a result, hotel space is limited, restaurants are booked up and visitors queue in long lines to visit homes that were meant for a dozen people to visit rather than hundreds at a time. The compression problem has also resulted in most tourist dollars being spent in Iowa rather than Nauvoo, as the larger towns are better equipped with eating establishments and hotel rooms.

After the river crested in early June 2019, we turned our attention back to the Nauvoo House roof. In late June a work crew ascended the roof, working through the heat with music playing in the background. I marveled at their ability to work on such a high, steep roof for long periods in the sun. The foreman said the roofers were immigrants, mainly from Honduras. I wondered if they, too, thought the Homestead looked small and if they could imagine boats arriving on the river so long ago. During the week they worked, the only time I heard the music turned off was on June 27 when visitors and those with LDS connections gathered in the Smith Family Cemetery at noon for a service of remembrance for Joseph and Hyrum Smith on the 175th anniversary of their deaths. Though the service was organized by Community of Christ, speakers and musicians from three Restoration faith movements took part in the service. We came together with our neighbors once again to worship in Nauvoo. I stopped by the jobsite on the last day to see a handful of the workers looking up at the glowing new roof on the Nauvoo House. Many of them were taking pictures with their phones, and some were taking selfies. It was abundantly clear that they were proud of their work, and while they may not know the story of Nauvoo, they could marvel at the buildings constructed so long ago. The relationship between Community of Christ and the Church of Jesus Christ of Latter-day Saints continues today in a spirit of exploration and dedication to the remembrance of our shared past on this bend in the river.

CHRISTIN MACKAY is the Director of the Joseph Smith Historic Site in Nauvoo, Illinois. Christin has served as a Board Member and Treasurer for JWHA. She is currently the Journal Book Review Editor and President-Elect for JWHA. Most recently she was published in *Ancient Order of Things: Essays on the Mormon Temple* (Signature Books 2019).

Will Bagley, *River Fever: Adventures on the Mississippi, 1969-1972*. Signature Books, 2019. 269 pp., paperback, $18.95, ISBN 978-1560852780.

Reviewed by Michael Allen

IN THE AFTERWORD to *River Fever: Adventures on the Mississippi, 1969-1972*, Will Bagley writes, "My romantic attachment to the nineteenth century was the driving force behind my youthful adventures as I sought to experience what life was like long before I was born." (235) Perhaps the most compelling of Bagley's "youthful adventures" involved two trips down the Mississippi River, from the upper river to New Orleans. He made the first voyage in 1969 with his girlfriend Suzy and four friends (all but Suzy eventually jumped ship) on a twenty-eight-foot raft, buoyed by eighteen empty fifty-five-gallon oil drums and powered by an 18-horsepower Johnson outboard motor. On a second 1972 voyage, he descended solo in a twelve-foot rowboat.

Fifty years later, Bagley, a noted Mormon historian and author of *Blood of the Prophets*,[1] began to rework his 1975 "non-fiction novel" about the trip. That manuscript had gone through several "variations," including a version that was a "straight history." He calls the published version of *River Fever* "a young man's memoir." (235, ix) The result is a fascinating look at the Mississippi Valley heartland during a pivotal time in American history.

"[We] left California and re-entered America," (52) Bagley recalls of his 1969 cadre's departure from the Santa Cruz environs, headed east for Rock Island, Illinois. They built their raft and headed downstream that fall, warned by locals that the Mississippi was as dangerous as it is grand. "I was going into America's heart of darkness where I could find a vanished past," (40-41) he rhapsodizes.

As the trip unfolds, the reader meets scores of Mississippi Valley folk and learns their ways; the reader also learns about the history, climate, environment, politics, and sociology of seven young men and women living together in cramped quarters. Their route—from the Quad Cities of Illinois and Iowa to New Orleans via St. Louis, Memphis, Greenville, Natchez, and Baton Rouge—sounds familiar, but readers also visit places like Cairo, Metropolis, and Nauvoo, Illinois; Columbus, Kentucky; New Madrid, Caruthersville, and Cape Girardeau, Missouri; Helena, Arkansas; and Greenville and Vicksburg, Mississippi. Bagley's solo trip comprises a second, smaller section of the book, dramatically culminating with his "near-death encounter with the *Olinda Chotin*," (235) a towboat that accidentally ran over and capsized his craft on April 14, 1972.

---

1. Will Bagley, *Blood of the Prophets: Brigham Young and the Massacre at Mountain Meadows*. (Norman, OK: University of Oklahoma Press, 2002)

Bagley's account reflects the social and political tumult of America in the late 1960s and speaks of drugs, anti-war sentiments, racism, and the civil-rights struggles in various locales dotting the great valley. Stopping over in St. Louis, the rafters sought out a movie theater to view the iconic 1969 "hippie" movie, *Easy Rider*. While they find a land that fits some of that movie's negative stereotypes, Bagley and Suzy nevertheless "fell in love with the south," and their "fear melted slowly but completely away" (96-97) as they floated down the great river.

River Fever's afterword is a detailed (36 pp.) overview of Bagley's subsequent life working in the Mormon history field, a story filled with experiences that sometimes bordered the precariousness of his river adventures.

Will Bagley's lively narrative is peppered with his liberal political views, accounts of his recreational drug use, and celebration of the Age of Aquarius. Bagley candidly refers early on to the "arrogance of youth" (ix) and that too can be found in *River Fever*. There are a few factual errors. Lincoln was a corporal, not captain, in the Illinois militia during the Black Hawk War. (60) Some historians might agree with Bagley that Joseph Smith was a "charming scoundrel…and confidence man," but none would support his assertion that Smith "got rich speculating in real estate." (77) Henry Miller Shreve's *Enterprise* was not "the first steamboat to travel down the Ohio River to New Orleans" in 1814; (106) Nicholas Roosevelt's *New Orleans* made that first journey during the winter of 1811-12. And it was New Orleans, not New Madrid, that served as the "one-time capital of Spanish Louisiana." (168)

This is an engaging and, at times, delightful book. Complete in its own right, *River Fever* and its afterword nevertheless leave the reader wanting to hear more of Bagley's subsequent life in the Mormon history field. This reviewer hopes to one day read such a book.

Will Bagley, an inactive Latter-day Saint, is obviously proud of his reputation as, in Dale Roberts' words, "the sharpest thorn in the side of the Mormon historical establishment." (264) Readers of *River Fever* get a good dose of the makings of "this Mormon boy gone bad." (59) Yet, in his seven-page telling of his 1969 visit to Nauvoo and his recounting of other adventures, we hear the ambivalence of a man who "never found any social aspect of Mormonism attractive but still considers its history among the greatest stories ever told." (244) "At the time I considered myself an ex-Mormon," Bagley reflects, "but I've since come to believe that being a Mormon is a lot like being Jewish. Once you are one, you are one. That's how it worked out for me, anyway." (78)

A final important aspect of Bagley's ambivalence is his view of the nature of history and the work of historians. He echoes the mantra of his fellow UC Santa Cruz graduate Richard White (who wrote the lead blurb on the book's back cover) that "memory" is the enemy of historians. Like many contemporary historians, Bagley derides "…that willful trickster, memory. Messing with this manuscript has demonstrated that if the mind can't remember some ancient event, it will make it up to fill in the details." (ix) Repeatedly, Bagley warns of "...the deceptive nature of memory and how, when the mind forgets something, it often creates recollections to fill the void." (233)

Yet having at last finished the writing of *River Fever: Adventures on the Mississippi, 1969-1972*, Bagley simultaneously arrives at a different conclusion: "Reading the manuscript indicates I recall more than I thought. (ix) Like many primary sources, Will Bagley's memories and voice are a source historians can trust.

From 1977-1981, MICHAEL ALLEN, Professor Emeritus of History at the University of Washington, Tacoma, worked as a towboat deckhand, oil tankerman, and cook on the Upper and Lower Mississippi, Illinois, St. Croix, Ouachita, and Arkansas rivers and the Gulf of Mexico. He has authored *Western Rivermen, 1763-1861: Ohio and Mississippi Boatmen and the Myth of the Alligator Horse* (Baton Rouge: Louisiana State University Press, 1990), the #1 *New York Times* best seller *A Patriot's History of the United States: From Columbus' Great Discovery to the War on Terror* (co-authored with Larry Schweikart, New York, Penguin Group, 2004, 2014, & 2019), and "Zion's Landing: Riverboating in Old Nauvoo, 1839-1860," *John Whitmer Historical Association Journal* 39 (Spring/Summer 2019), 58-71. He lives in Ellensburg, Washington and each fall leads tours at the Joseph Smith Historic Site.

Ron Romig, *Behind the Scenes Tour of the Kirtland Temple: From Basement to Bell Tower.* (Independence, MO: John Whitmer Books, 2019), 72 pp., illus., paperback, $9.95 ISBN:9781934901205

Reviewed by Christin Mackay

Having lived in Kirtland for many years, I was excited to read Ron Romig's latest book, *Behind the Scenes Tour of the Kirtland Temple: From Basement to Bell Tower*. The text is the actual behind-the-scenes tour given at the temple today, even asking you to grab a hard hat and flashlight as you investigate areas of the temple not included on the standard temple tour. In the introduction, Barbara Walden, a former Temple Site Director, gives a brief explanation of the tour:

> Behind the Scenes tours have gone on informally since the temple's construction, it wasn't until 2006 when a formal public tour was offered. A typical tour of the temple takes about an hour, the behind-the-scenes tour lasts anywhere from two to three hours, exploring the building from basement to bell tower.

There are over 100 interior images of the temple included in the book, from the stone pillars that bear the load of the building to slates from the roof that were removed because they were too heavy. Photos of modern sprinkler heads are included as well as the molds used in making sconces for the lower court by handyman and ceramicist Earl Curry.

The Kirtland Temple has had many caretakers and guides throughout its history. Romig includes an account of Rebecca Dayton who lived across the street from the temple in the 1870s. She occasionally gave tours of the temple and became dismayed that Joseph Smith III had asked that the first level of the Melchisedec pulpits be removed in order for worshippers to have a better view of the floor and seating area of the elders' pulpit. She wrote to him requesting permission to restore the pulpit and hired a carpenter to reinstall the front of the Elders' pulpit.[1]

The "tour" focuses on the construction of the temple and those who built and maintained the building over the past 178 years. Another interesting historical moment in the book mentions the temple's cornerstone: "In 1933 the RLDS Church commemorated the laying of the cornerstone…history reports that commemoration leaders opened the cornerstone and found and removed a penny. Today, we do not know where either the cornerstone or penny is located."[2]

---

1. Ron Romig, *Behind the Scenes Tour of the Kirtland Temple: From Basement to Bell Tower* (Independence, MO: John Whitmer Books, 2019), 15.

2. Romig, 23.

The Kirtland Temple bell has rung in the bell tower since 1890. On the "tour," we learn that the bell was not originally cast for the temple. RLDS Apostle Gomer Griffith helped to raise funds for a temple bell, and $300 was collected in all:

> As Griffith was traveling in southern Ohio, he stopped at a Cincinnati foundry. The owners told him that a new bell would cost much more than three hundred dollars. They showed him a bell that another church had ordered, then decided not to install. Griffith bought that bell for $300.[3]

The bell was transported to Kirtland to be installed in the temple bell tower.

Sprinkled throughout *Behind the Scenes Tour of the Kirtland Temple: From Basement to Bell Tower* are historical tidbits about the years of maintaining and preserving the temple from construction to present day. It is a wonderful resource for those interested in the minutia of the materials used to build the temple.

CHRISTIN MACKAY is the Director of the Joseph Smith Historic Site in Nauvoo, Illinois. She has served as a Board Member and Treasurer for JWHA. She is currently the Journal Book Review Editor and President Elect for JWHA. Most recently, she was published in *Ancient Order of Things: Essays on the Mormon Temple*, Signature Books, 2019.

Jana Riess. *The Next Mormons: How Millennials Are Changing the LDS Church.*
Oxford University Press, 2019. 328 pp. Hardcover, $29.95. ISBN 978-01908-8520-5.

Reviewed by Katherine R. Pollock

THE NEXT MORMONS: *How Millennials Are Changing the LDS Church* is a mixed-method sociological work detailing the results of the Next Mormons Survey (NMS), a new nationally representative study of members of the Church of Jesus Christ of Latter-day Saints in the United States, combined with interviews of American Millennial Mormons and several younger members of Gen X. This work has several important but complex goals: to understand who Mormons are and what they believe, to define the generational differences between them, and to recognize what can be said about the attitudes and beliefs of Mormons who stay versus Mormons who leave.(7) Latter Day Saints (of all kinds) make up less than 2% of the United States population, and while some nationally representative data is collected by the Pew Research Center and other think tanks, NMS is revolutionary for its depth of questions and answers in understanding Latter-day Saints of the "mountain" variety.

This book is a modern success story of independent research funding and academic collaboration. Gen X author Jana Riess has a PhD in American Religious History from Columbia University with a successful career in journalism and the publishing industry, currently serving as a Senior Columnist for Religion News Service. She teamed up with another Gen Xer, Benjamin Knoll, a political scientist at Centre College, specializing in American public opinion and voting behavior as well as statistical analysis. Using the crowdfunding platform Kickstarter, the two raised almost $20,000 plus a subsequent $6,000 to fund this specialized study using 130 questions on a variety of topics. They contracted with the firm Qualtrics, which found them 1,156 Mormons and 540 former Mormons from four generations (Silent, Boomer, Gen X, and Millennial) as their research pool. At the time the survey was fielded from September 8, 2016, to November 1, 2016, Millennials (born 1981-1996) would have been between ages 20-35. It should be noted that former Mormons included only "those who were raised LDS or converted as children/adolescents (not adults) and later stopped attending."(240) This was out of the researchers' desire to understand long-term trends and retention of Mormon-raised youth. A detailed explanation of methodology can be found in the book's appendix.

The Next Mormons weaves together different survey results and oral histories with similar themes. The book is divided into three parts—Foundations, Changing Definitions of Family and Culture, and Passages of Faith and Doubt.

In Part I, Foundations, elements of being a person of faith were surveyed. General Christian and Restoration doctrines were measured on a six-point scale of certainty: the strength of connection to God, the top three aspects of being Mormon, and the factors (locational, educational, economic) that are associated with greater belief. History of missionary service was also explored by generation and gender, including growth in the number of young female missionaries and those things that were valued most about the experience. Topics about early-returned missionaries, correlations with mission service and church activity, and interviews about faith and doubt on missions were also explored. Millennials have, in fact, taken more LDS missions than any preceding generation. Participants were also asked if their first experience with the Endowment was positive or negative, how often they are now returning to the temple, the experience of women in the temple, how much temple preparation was received, and variation in garment-wearing practices.

Part II, Changing Definitions of Family and Culture, shares findings on how Latter-day Saints are experiencing changes in American culture and the special experiences of minority identities in the faith. The study looks at the challenges singles have in a family-orientated church, the average age of marriage, whether Mormons prefer "traditional" or "egalitarian" marriage, the variability in the level of belief between single and married members, questions about sexual behavior, and what Millennials see as the positives and negatives of "singles wards." Later in part II, information is sought concerning women's experiences with the church, comparison of belief between women and men, concern over women's roles by generation, the changing size of the Mormon family, educational comparisons between women and men, and the increasing number of working mothers. The racial makeup of the American LDS population, comparison of belief and political differences between white and non-white Mormons, prevailing views of racial folklore and the priesthood/temple ban, and questions around increasing racial diversity, immigration, and globalization in the US are also included in the survey. Issues around LGBT Mormons and former Mormons, the sexual-orientation demographics of the American Mormon population, religious beliefs of LGBT Mormons, and levels of support for the divisive November 5, 2015 policy complete Part II.

Part III, Passages of Faith and Doubt, explores findings about religious practice, social and political views, views on sources of authority, and disaffiliation. Participants were asked about their prayer life, beliefs in scripture, home and visiting teaching, sharing faith with others, Word of Wisdom adherence, consumption of popular culture (media and pornography), and tithing. Also probed were potentially divisive topics such as political affiliation, voting patterns in the 2012 and 2016 presidential elections, level of agreement with American exceptionalism, military service by generation, and ranking of top social and moral issues. They were asked about which types of authority are most important (institutional, local, and personal), whether they watch General Conference, subjects preferred for leaders' guidance, appropriateness of rejecting a calling (i. e., volunteer church position), and how Millennials view and interpret their patriarchal blessings. In Chapter 11, titled "Exodus: Millennial Former Mormons," demographics were explored, including which group is more likely to leave the church, current religious affiliations of former Mormons and their beliefs about God, Christian, and LDS teachings. Riess notes that most people who leave the LDS Church don't seem to come back. She believes that in a culture of religious disaffiliation, the LDS Church would need some "special ability" to be outside that trend.

Riess concludes *The Next Mormons* with a short epilogue titled "A Mormonism for the Twenty-First Century?" While sociologists have skill in tracking current social trends, Riess notes that their record of failure in long-term predictions makes her thereby cautious to make her own. As a self-identified progressive, she is worried that the church body will continue to polarize until it turns into an echo chamber. She worries that young adults may be "collateral damage" in the church's resistance to change. She turns to Armand Mauss' classic sociological study *The Angel and the Beehive* (1994) for answers to the future possibilities: "The LDS church has accommodated change before, and it can do so again. The issue is whether it will choose to."(135)

This is a groundbreaking work about the contemporary LDS Church. As a midwesterner with convert parents and a working mom, I was pleased to find some of my experiences reflected in these pages. I can now see my experiences in the context of larger trends. While updates will need to be explained amidst President Russel M. Nelson's administrative changes, this is a notable work for explaining Mormon "lived religion" with full and nuanced explanations in all three parts. I would recommend this, as appropriate, for classroom work.

Other branches of the Restoration will most likely never get this level of sociological coverage, although a comparable intergenerational study of Community of Christ members would indeed be interesting. Otherwise, I think that members of an ecumenical historical association like the John Whitmer Historical Association might use *The Next Mormons* to better understand the religious life of Latter-day Saints and perhaps overcome any lingering stereotypes that may exist. Despite what some LDS members assume, many nonmembers don't understand the nature of LDS religious life. People from the broader Restoration tradition might also think about how young adults from their own churches would answer these questions and why.

Readers will find the book's subtitle *How Millennials are Changing the LDS Church* lingering in their minds after they finish. How will the Church of Jesus Christ of Latter-day Saints change in the future? What directions will the next generation take the church? Will more traditional members like those changes? The world's future feels so uncertain in 2020 that anxiety is rising. *The Next Mormons:*

How Millennials Are Changing the LDS Church is a wonderful gift to the sociology of American religion, but the next "so what?" question is for the church itself.

I would personally like to thank Jana Reiss, Benjamin Knoll, and the countless acknowledgements listed in the back of *The Next Mormons* for their time and effort in learning about my own generation. I highly recommend this book.

KATHERINE POLLOCK is a Millennial finishing a B. S. in Religious Studies at Missouri State University. She doesn't know everything the future holds, but she's planning to go to graduate school anyway. She has done several internships with Community of Christ Historic Sites and completed a sociology project at the Kirtland Temple Historic Site in 2019.

www.ingramcontent.com/pod-product-compliance
Lightning Source LLC
Chambersburg PA
CBHW081132170426
43197CB00017B/2835